Thomas Starr King, Richard Frothingham, Andrew Dickson White

Patriotism

And other Papers

Thomas Starr King, Richard Frothingham, Andrew Dickson White

Patriotism
And other Papers

ISBN/EAN: 9783337306977

Printed in Europe, USA, Canada, Australia, Japan

Cover: Foto ©Suzi / pixelio.de

More available books at **www.hansebooks.com**

Patriotism,

AND

OTHER PAPERS.

BY

THOS. STARR KING.

With a Biographical Sketch,

BY

HON. RICHARD FROTHINGHAM.

BOSTON:
TOMPKINS AND COMPANY,
25 CORNHILL.
1864.

CAC

GEO. C. RAND & AVERY,

STEREOTYPERS AND PRINTERS.

THE great work laid upon his two-score years
Is done, and well done.   If we drop our tears
Who loved him as few men were ever loved,
We mourn no blighted hope nor broken plan
With him whose life stands rounded and approved
In the full growth and stature of a man.
Mingle, O bells, along the western slope,
With your deep toll a sound of faith and hope!
Wave cheerily still, O banner, half-way down,
From thousand-masted bay and steepled town!
Let the strong organ with its loftiest swell
Lift the proud sorrow of the land, and tell
That the brave sower saw his ripened grain.
O East and West, O morn and sunset, twain
No more forever!—has he lived in vain
Who, priest of Freedom, made ye one, and told
Your bridal service from his lips of gold?

JOHN G. WHITTIER.

CONTENTS.

V

INTRODUCTION.

THE following pages are presented to the friends and admirers of the late Rev. THOMAS STARR KING, under circumstances of more than ordinary interest, and by the promptings of a more than ordinary motive.

The event of the death of Mr. KING has so recently transpired, that the first gush of grief which swayed the public mind, throughout the land, and welled in the hearts of those who knew and loved him best, — on reception of the sudden, and unlooked-for tidings of his decease, — has scarcely subsided, and left the mind sufficiently calm for reflection. The heavy tide of sorrow which has rolled over so many hearts, has not ebbed back its mighty and oppressive waves; and, of course, the time is not yet for that fitting tribute to his memory, his genius, and his worth, which the pen of affection and respect will ere long delight to bestow. But even in advance of this, it has been thought that a monument of enduring fame might be reared to his memory, by gathering from the various quarters where they had been strown, the scattered stones which his own hand had so exquisitely polished, and using them in the rearing of a structure which may not only speak of him, but by him, in the ages to come.

It is well known to many that the rare scholarship, and .

the rich literary taste of Mr. KING had often been employed in the production of articles which, at the time, found but a limited and transient medium in various periodicals which have temporarily stored their wealth. The publications in which they have appeared, too, it is equally well known, have been sustained and read, principally, by the supporters of a particular religious sect, and have not found their way to the public generally; while, from their nature and character, and the truly catholic spirit which they have always breathed, they have been well calculated to enrich the minds of all classes.

Nothing, seeing the light, has ever emanated from the pen of Mr. KING which has not been well adapted to add to the treasures of human thought; nothing which might not be profitably pondered by the votary of any creed, or the adherent to any party. While oftentimes gems of thought, brilliant with the flashes of a powerful and fervid mind, have been strown abroad with a lavish hand. From a soul charmed with the profound lore of metaphysics, and the deep mysteries of the world of thought, they have been thrown out; yet not crude, and dull, and uninviting. For his sentences are not read as though the mind were compelled to toil amidst the ruins of a cast-iron edifice to find them; but they come lucid, simple, and transparent in thought, while they are profound in wisdom, woven in a richness of imagery and a wealth of diction which inspires an interest and admiration wherever they are read.

While the recollection is deeply saddening to the soul, that one so large in power, so gifted and versatile in talent, and still so rich in promise, while so preëminently useful, should be removed from the field of his labors and his love, at so early a day, ere the meridian of life's sun had shed its effulgence upon his course, and when the past and present com-

bined to inspire bright hopes of even greater good to come, —
it is nevertheless profoundly gratifying that so large a labor
had been accomplished by him, and so much has been left
as the fruitage of his toil, which may so fully enrich the
minds of those who shall make a study of his efforts.

Each article found in this volume, we trust, will be acknowledged worthy of a more enduring position, and a wider
circulation than it has hitherto attained, and to effectuate this
has been the main purpose of the compilation.

The articles have been drawn from the pages of the "Rose
of Sharon," from the "Universalist Quarterly," and some
of them from publications even far less enduring, — all of
which were necessarily limited in their circulation. They
are now placed in a position, and we hope in form, which
will gain for the volume a place in many a library, and for
its treasures a place in many a mind which, otherwise, might
not even have been cognizant of their existence.

It might have been true of the writings of Mr. KING, as
it doubtless has been of many an author, that very much, of
great and permanent worth, should be lost to the general
mind, merely from the early attendant circumstances of their
production. For in this regard, sometimes, as well as from
considerations of a wider range, the poet's words are true, —

> " Full many a gem, of purest ray serene,
>   The dark, unfathomed caves of ocean bear;
>   Full many a flower is born to blush unseen,
>   And waste its sweetness on the desert air ! "

So uncertain is FAME amid the world of letters, that
doubtless many of the treasures of literature now lie
buried in remediless obscurity ; while, on the other hand,
many of the golden thought-gleams, which now illumine the
pages of literature, in both prose and poetry, have come
to us only through the fissures which the throes of time have

rent in the incrustations of the past; while the *names* of those from whose minds they have emanated, are entirely forgotten to the world. And this simply through the neglect of those whose privilege it might have been to confer a benefit upon the race, and upon the authors' names a lasting gratitude, by gathering them from their straying, into a connected and enduring form.

The thoughts and words of the good and gifted among men often live, after their authors are no more, only through the thoughtful care of those who appreciate their value, and are faithful to the duties which circumstances devolve.

We attempt no criticism, nor comment on the various articles here presented, from the pen of Mr. KING. They will speak for themselves in a power more convincing than any sentences which we might frame; and we are confident that they will commend themselves to the favorable regard of the intelligent of all classes, without the effort of extrinsic aid.

We offer no apology for the insertion in this volume of the excellent article on the life, character, and death of Mr. KING. It was written by one who knew his subject intimately; the young man passing from early youth to that rich maturity which he attained in manhood's morning, under his immediate eye; the observation of his course being prompted by a solicitude born of respect for the honored father of Mr. KING, which could not but create both anxiety and pride, as his young friend, wrestling with the difficulties and dangers of youth, passed rapidly the period of adolescence to an early, a rich, and vigorous mental and moral manhood. The tribute is just, and worthy of its able and discriminating author. It will stand henceforth among the noblest tributes paid to a mind which, in the midst of an environment of difficulties, and embarrassments of no ordinary character, rose suddenly and securely to an eminence and celebrity which few indeed are permitted to attain.

And here we would stop; but we cannot lay down our pen without the added remark, with reference to Mr. KING, cognizant now, of those who knew him the most intimately, that when his powers shall be analyzed it will be found that not the bright promise of his manhood in youth; not the quick, leaping vigor of his intellect as it moved amidst coruscations of emitted light; not the rich and stately flow of his eloquence, which charmed to admiration wherever it was poured out; not the power and purity, or even the sublimity of his thoughts, alone or combined, constituted the chief grace and glory of his character; but that, beneath all these, and many other qualities which, singly, might have made the wealth of an ordinary mind, lay, as a base, that rich and affluent mine of FILIAL AFFECTION AND DEVOTION, whose treasures flowed from his young heart at the instant touch of necessity, and, under Christian influence and guidance, poured blessings upon a widowed and bereaved household, deprived early of their ordinary support, — which, besides leaving a bright and endearing example to the young, could not fail to draw down the approving benediction of Heaven!

This single trait in the character of THOMAS STARR KING leaves an example not only for youth to imitate, but for the world to admire and honor.

Might we be permitted, we would fain dedicate this volume to the *bereaved mother and her children*, as a self-wrought monument of a worthy son and brother, whose memory can live in their hearts only as a constant incentive to gratitude for the gift and life of one whose untiring devotion to their good ceased only with the latest pulsation of his large and loving heart.

Invoking the blessing of Heaven upon this compilation of

a portion of the works of one who has ascended to a higher
and more radiant sphere, we commend it to the patronage
and study of the many brethren and friends in whose hearts
his memory is evermore enshrined, and to the general public,
who have received a benediction in the life of the author.

T. J. G.

A BRIEF SKETCH OF THE LIFE OF

THOMAS STARR KING,*

By HON. RICHARD FROTHINGHAM.

THE expression of sorrow at the death of Thomas Starr King, both in this region where his days of preparation and early service were passed, in places where his varied labors made him known, and on the Pacific shore, indicate a general sense of a public loss ; and the feeling that one of uncommon gifts has gone to his reward. He was ready to meet the Master, to whose service, even as youth was budding, he consecrated the powers with which the Almighty had endowed him.

This morning consecration — this inner spring of motive working in every outward phase — developed itself very early ; it lingered like a guardian angel ; it was ever triumphant, and it is the key of this remarkable and beautiful life.

Thomas Starr King was born in the city of New York (1824), passed his early boyhood in Hudson and Portsmouth, and at ten years of age, when a good

* From *Boston Post*, March 10, 1864.

Latin and French scholar, was taken to Charlestown (1835), when his father became the pastor of the Universalist Society of that place. Thomas Farrington King was a genial, generous, noble-hearted man, of a sympathetic nature, full of humor, and of theological views which, much as he loved the order to which he belonged, could not be narrowed to the lines of creed or sect. Starr, as he was familiarly called, was the oldest child; and his father saw, with all a father's pride, the unfolding powers and bent of his gifted son, who took his place as a pupil in the public schools and was constant at the Sunday school. It was soon plain enough that Charlestown had no institution that met the wants of this bright youth; and that the preparation for a collegiate course, . which his father designed, must be found elsewhere. His bent was seen in a sermon which at the age of thirteen while his father was absent at the West,⁻ he wrote, and sent to a newspaper; and it appeared in type.

In a year or two after this settlement, a long and deep-seated disease sapped the vitality of the good pastor, and at the age of forty-two (September, 1839), death closed his labors. An impressive funeral service in the church, a great procession of the people, a gathering of thousands on the ancient burial-ground of Charlestown, a spontaneous closing of places of business, testified to the affection and respect that bore the sacred remains to their resting-place. On the evening of this funeral there was preaching in the vacant pulpit by a young man and

a stranger in the place. The theme selected was
Faith ; and, with the emblems of the recent mortality hanging about the church, the lesson was enforced
with uncommon effect. The manuscript was mostly
followed until near the close, when the preacher,
summoning the lesson of the passing hour for illustration, left his notes, and abandoned himself to his
subject, his deep, rich voice, full of emotion, rising
and swelling organ-like into a pathos, and a power
which thrilled the great and breathless assembly. It
was eloquence, for it was an inspiration of soul.
The preacher was Edwin H. Chapin, who was the
successor of the deceased pastor, and the close, life-
long friend of Thomas Starr King.

The sickness and straitened circumstances of the
father defeated the plans for a collegiate course for
Starr ; and, instead, a place temporarily had been
found for him in a dry goods store in Charlestown,
where he was the book-keeper. Now began that
filial and fraternal piety that gilds a purest ray serene
the whole of this extraordinary life ; for the lad of
fifteen was the main stay of his mother, and as a father
to the five younger children. Labor for such objects
was sacred. His genuine life, however, was not in
the accounts which he pored over ; for then he was
ministered to by his noble aspirations, his commun-
ings were with the great masters of thought, and as
he mused the fire burned. His efforts were never
turned from self-culture, nor his thought from his
mission.

. It happened that the members of the school com-

mittee of the town knew these circumstances, and a
place was made for Starr as an assistant teacher in
the public school which he first entered as a pupil,
— the principal of which was Mr. Benjamin F.
Tweed, now a professor of Tufts College, and another
early and life-long friend of Starr. The young teacher
entered with a light heart on his new vocation,
brought to its tasks abundant resources, and soon
lived down whatever doubts were felt as to the judgment of the selection. The calling, as well as the
pursuits of his leisure hours, now helped on his
work of discipline. His hope for the future bright-
ened and strengthened as he grew in years. Only
those who heard him talk can tell, what a ministry
to his spirit were the affluence of utterance and the
companionship of his beloved pastor.

At length a vacancy in a Medford grammar school
(1842) made an opening for a higher position, because independent, and the young teacher applied
for the place. It seemed at the time to him and to
his friends, but the simple question of a wider field
of duty and a larger means of support for him and
his ; but, in the light of after events, it looks more
like Providence shaping his ends. This town then
enjoyed the blessing of the influence of Rev. Hosea
Ballou 2d, who became subsequently the president
of Tufts College, who was of child-like simplicity of
character, of varied and profound learning, wise and
good and great. He was a member of the school com-
mittee, interested himself successfully for the appli-
cant whose youth suggested doubts as to the expedi-

ency of the appointment; and a few weeks after the transfer, he said, that while Medford had gained a competent and faithful teacher, he had found a rare and precious friend. What love and confidence between these gifted and kindred souls! The one of silver locks, rich in ancient and modern lore, the other thirsty for knowledge, and scaling the heights with a scholar's enthusiasm; and both of wit that was quick, easy, of constant natural flow, elicited by the commonest things, but diamond-like, sharp, and sparkling. Nothing could exceed the admiration which Dr. Ballou habitually expressed for the intellectual gifts of his young friend, and no one ever heard from the lips of Thomas Starr King aught but love and gratitude for his Theological Father. The correspondence between them, rich in the play of the fancy and in the soundings of the depths, will be a feature in the memorials of their lives.

While discharging the duties of teacher, there went on a systematic course of study with a view to the ministry, under the direction of Dr. Ballou. It was labor he delighted in. He was familiar with the utterances of Channing, and had imbibed their spirit; indeed, he was ever quick to know things of note in theology; and no sooner did they appear than he would have them in hand, either from the choice storehouse of his pastor, or from elsewhere; for neither, if he could help it, would sleep without knowing the last word from a real teacher. At this period Professor Walker, of Harvard College, delivered his Lectures on Natural Religion before the

2

Lowell Institute in Boston, which were of absorbing
interest to the young student, who came regularly
from Medford, not merely to listen to them, but to
bear them away in copious notes from which he wrote
out the lectures in full. He did more. He made the
great theme his study. He revolved over in his mind
the tough problems which they dealt with. He consulted the authors to which reference was made in
them. His capacity for the subtleties of metaphysics was wonderful. He threaded easily, as by intuition, through intricacies of thought where others
had to rough-hew it to find their way. The capacity grew by what it fed on. He ascribed much
fixedness of opinion on important points to the study
and direction which these lectures gave him ; not
improbably they saved him from that experience of
doubt and unbelief which so many gifted minds
pass through.

While thus engaged, his friends were enabled to
tender him a desk (1843) in the naval storekeeper's
office in the Charlestown navy yard, which promised to double his means of living and to multiply
his choice selection of books, — the silent never-com-
plaining companions which he was lovingly gathering
in. It was accepted. This was a crisis period of his
life. Young as he was, he had experienced the ministry of suffering in most of the forms that rive the
human heart. The struggle at times had been severe ;
but his high aim, his inner motive — just the simple
truth — enabled him to bear up and to press on ;
now the prospect ahead began to be a clear sea and

halcyon sky ; and seldom is seen a happier soul than for two years was Thomas Starr King, as he still kept steadily in the road of progress, that he might make himself worthy to enter upon his father's vocation ; for none could look with greater disfavor than he certainly did upon unpreparedness, either in heart or mind, for the ministerial work. He now paid close attention to the German ; often he left the communion of his pastor to listen to discourses in this language ; and far into midnight he would talk of Gœthe Schiller, and the divines of the school of Tholuck and DeWétte. He had long been familiar with Plato, and so closely studied the father of the progressive school of philosophy that he seemed to live with him. On one occasion returning, from a season of communion with his mentor, Dr. Ballou, his bright eye had an uncommon sparkle and his countenance was aglow with joy, at the judgment of this ripe scholar on a manuscript essay which he had prepared on knotty points of the Platonic works. This was not flattery in one of the truest and sincerest of men ; it was not vanity in a devoted explorer in the realms of truth ; it was recognition by one having authority of an intellectual triumph ; and joy in the young enthusiast at another mark of progress up heights which he felt necessary to attain, even though he might have the crowning qualification of the Christian gifts ere he could be a worthy minister of the Gospel.

His circle of friends was now widening. His genial, generous, sympathetic nature, like magnetism, drew all hearts to him wherever he went; for the natural gentleman was behind those brilliant conversational powers that made him the delight of society. He had much communion with ingenuous young men of Harvard, who knew of "Starr King," sought his acquaintance, and with some of whom,—now standing high in their callings,—who might be named, he compared notes of progress. Of friends who passed on before him, were John and Sarah Edgarton, both of whom, with rare spiritual natures, believed with the young student, that they had an appointed work to do. Nothing but good influences grew out of such communions, which were as free from anything like cant as they were ennobling.

The temptation is strong to linger on the simple "Starr King,"—as his friends call him,—when he was about to step on manhood's threshold and responsibilties, and before the public eye was fixed on him. He did not dwell apart, a solitary, in severe contemplation, affecting ways of greatness; but lived as a true man of the world, interesting in what was going on around him, a close observer of common life, seizing with zest passing incidents having touches of humor in them and telling them with a right merry, ringing laugh; and there was so much and such heartiness in this, that a casual acquaintance might suppose that, to tell stories, was his great ambition. This would have been unjust. His real life continued to be the high spiritual communion that strengthened his character and carried him nearer to his goal. Of his literary friends of his own age, perhaps there were none dearer to him than John Edgarton, already named, — a pure, quiet, undemonstrative soul, but deeply religious, who died just as he completed his collegiate course at Harvard. Both had a like philosophical turn ; both aimed for the clerical office and both were of singular promise. His death, in the high hope of manly youth, was a great bereavement ; another ministry of suffering, quickening and deepening the wells of sympathy in with him.

As he approached his majority, wise advisers in the ministry judged him qualified to assume its duties. Still it was with unaffected diffidence that he delivered at Woburn (September, 1845), his first sermon ; and he preferred that none of his intimate friends should hear him. His services were acceptable. His calls to supply pulpits were numerous, perhaps more than he cared to answer ; for he looked on study for a long time yet as a duty. It now happened that Rev. E. H. Chapin felt it a duty to accept (January, 1846) a call for a wider field of labor in Boston ; his society sought to have the young preacher for their pastor ; and a year after Mr. King preached his first sermon, he was installed over this society. The services were impressive. Rev. Hosea Ballou 2d made the charge to the pastor, and the sermon was by Rev. Edwin H. Chapin.

The young minister brought to his work a rare combination of experience. He had mingled much with the world. He had not, it is true, threaded the dark paths, to study human nature ; he never had an

eye for the rotten side of life; but his warm and
sunny nature drew inspiration from the exhibitions
of duty in the humble Christian's walk and wherever
he met the good, the true, and the beautiful. He
had, too, free contact with men and things, and a
large common sense. And, joining the lessons of the
practical, with the fruits of steady study, for two
years he poured forth wise, mature, profound utterances that dropped like golden words from the desk.
Then in the round of pastoral duties, in the seasons
of joy and of sorrow, he drew from deep, inward
fountains of feeling, — his own experience, — and to
these he added unwonted outward grace and dignity.
He saw his labors prosper under his hand.

It was but natural, however, that he should meet
with obstacles; that many should not have recognized in his own land the prophet. No university
crowned him with its honors; the circle of fashion
could hardly comprehend his glorious merit; no
great patrons sounded his fame; and it seemed to
many not possible that Saul could step from the local
counting-room, the grammar-school or the navy-yard.
Though all might well know that as man thinketh
in his heart, so is he, but few could really know the
great thought and inner motive power that nerved and
moved his soul; and the index of it, his words whatever they might be, had to penetrate a thick crust of
prejudice, or of envy, or, harder than all, of conceit;
and to get through this requires time and outside
help. The wonder is that so many saw and bowed
before the extraordinary gift.

His frail frame reeled under the labors and anxiety of the charge ; but a voyage to Fayal (1848) brought to him renewed strength, and on his return, his spirit was buoyant and he seemed in pristine vigor. This year he accepted a call to fill the desk in Boston, in Hollis Street, once occupied by a Holley. It cost him a severe struggle to part with old friends and the friends of his father ; and it grieved them to part with him. He announced his purpose in a characteristic note to his society, frank, warm, and beautiful. It was just in his way — his modesty of manner and his under-estimate of himself — to write (September) as to the course he felt compelled to take : "It is but just to say what is sufficiently obvious, that no cause of dissatisfaction has been furnished by the society, neither has any grown out of its circumstances or condition. Its prosperity is evident ; and I have ever been treated by its members with kindness and forbearance. They have been more faithful to their duties than I to mine."

And here this tribute to this remarkable life may appropriately stop. It is but a sketch of its preparatory work and may be pronounced presumption to have attempted to do this. There succeeded sixteen years of labor, of service — in Boston, over half the land, in California — by the pen, in the desk, in the lecture room, in the home. It hardly left the required time for the quiet progress of self-culture. The demand was incessant for service, and this in a certain sense is growth. The fruitage is too well known to need enumeration. His new fields

of labor won ever for him hosts of friends ; and
the ripe in years and the profound in learning, as
well as the unlettered and the young, bore ready
testimony to the charm of his varied gifts both in
public and private. When the time came for him
to part with his Hollis Street circle, there was
another struggle ; and the ministering brother whom
he invited to be with him in the last service in this
church, was a kindred spirit — Rev. C. H. Leonard,
of Chelsea. · "I know not how I can go through with
it," he said, as he was about to enter the desk. "You
cannot go through with it ; you will be carried
through," was the reply.

The work done in California — the strengthening and even building up of a society — the erection
of a noble church — the gift of a magnificent organ
from the proceeds of lectures — to say nothing
of a personation of the patriotism and loyalty of the
people in this crisis of country, — rounded off this
remarkable life. The crowning of glory is the complement of the morning consecration. His private
letters, for months, show how near the pastor's heart
was this whole field of labor. He wrote of the beautiful Temple of Worship as his monument. He longed
to have it completed. He wished to see it free from
debt. At length it was finished ; but as his friends
were anticipating rest from labors that taxed heavily
his body and mind, he received the mysteriously
ordered summons hence. He was conscious to the
last. He said he was " HAPPY TO GO. " And while
the society who buried the father and welcomed the

son, were listening in silence and in tears to touching words by his brethren in the ministry, in a Union commemorative service, — when lines of creed and sect were forgotten, — the noble society on the Pacific shore were placing beneath the monument raised by his own divine energies all that was mortal of Thomas Starr King.

God tempers the wind to the shorn lambs off there! But let the sacred sorrow under the roof that filial piety so long provided, light up with joy for a son and a brother whose life was without a stain, and whose name is among the immortals.

PATRIOTISM, AND OTHER PAPERS.

I.

PATRIOTISM.[1]

It has been questioned by some, whether there is any such distinct virtue as Patriotism. Not a few moralists have indulged suspicions as to the harmony of such a passion with the soul's integrity. Many Christians have openly denied its consistency with the moral temper which the New Testament would inspire; while others have strenuously urged that it is the very royal grace of character, and oversweeps all virtues. There is a sliding scale of judgments as to its legitimacy and worthiness, from the declaration of Dr. Johnson, that "Patriotism is the last refuge of a scoundrel," to that of Cicero, that it is a duty more sacred than the filial tie.

In abstract controversy we may dispute with some plausibility the moral healthiness of the sentiment, and may not be able to free it from all haze, and discern its disc; but the living world braces the mind and refutes its skepticism. History refuses to countenance the analytic ethics of spiritual dreamers. It thrusts upon our notice, Leonidas, Tell, Camillus,

[1] The substance of this article is from a discourse, delivered in Boston, before the Ancient and Honorable Artillery Company, on the occasion of their two hundred and thirteenth Anniversary, June 2d, 1851.

Hampden, Winkelried, Scipio, Lafayette, Adams, Bolivar, and Washington, in whom the sentiment has become flesh, and gathered to itself the world's affection and honors. An honest heart cannot help feeling, when it reads their biographies, that their line of greatness is as legitimate as that of poets, philosophers, philanthropists, and priests. We cannot be so sure that the principles which would expunge their names from the world's honorable regard, or throw suspicion upon their virtue, are right, as we ought to be that the result is wrong and base, and therefore, that the principles must be false.

The virtue of Patriotism has been provided for, and is expected of us, by nature. Some moralists, as we have already intimated, have condemned all private and restricted affections, as inconsistent with the law of universal love. They argue that our love must be for *being* in general, and must be proportioned by the moral worth of the object, without regard to relationships, ties, and personal associations. But they only argue against nature. The method of Providence in invoking our spiritual sentiments is always from particulars to generals. God " hath set the solitary in families," and bound the families into communities, and organized communities into nations ; and he has ordained special duties for each of these relationships, and inspired affections to prompt those duties and to ennoble the character.

The law of love is the principle of the spiritual universe, just as the force of gravity is the governing law of space. It binds each particle of matter every other particle, but it attracts inversely according to the square of the distance, and thus becomes practically a series of special and local forces, binding our feet constantly and irresistibly to one globe, and allowing only a general unity, which the mind appropriates through science and meditation, with the far off and kindred spheres. The soul that has most of the universal Christian sentiment of love, will have the most intense special affections. We cannot love the whole world and nobody in particular. However deep the baptism of the spirit in general good-will, a man must look with a thrill of love that nothing else can awaken, into the face of the mother that bore him ; he cannot resolve the ties that bind him to filial responsibilities and a brother's devotion ; and so Providence has ordained that, out of identity of race, a common history, the same scenery, literature, and laws, though in perfect harmony with a sense of good-will to all men, the wider family feeling, the distinctive virtue, Patriotism, should spring. If the ancient Roman could believe that the yellow Tiber was the river dearest to heaven ; if the Englishman can see a grandeur in the Thames which its size will not suggest; if the Alpine storm-wind is a familiar home-song to the Swiss mountaineer ; if the Laplander believes that his country is the best the sun shines upon ; if the sight of our nation's flag in other lands awakens sentiments that speed the blood, and melt the eyes ; if the poorest man feels a proud consciousness of property in the great deeds that glow upon his country's annals, and the monuments of its

power and glory ; let us confess that the heart of
man was made to contract a special friendship for its
native soil, its kindred stock, and its ancestral traditions, and that where the sentiment of Patriotism is
not deep, a sacred affection is absent, an essential
element of virtue is wanting, and religion barren of
one great witness of its sway.

I know it has been said that the Bible does not
justify and commend Patriotism, in any of its precepts. No, but it sanctions and illustrates it by
splendid examples. The prime instructions of the
Old Testament are Patriotism and the fear of God.
They blended in the heart of Moses. In the wilderness he bore the Hebrew people in his heart. Religious patriotism stimulated his genius, supported him
in perplexities, and made the desert green. When
at last he stood upon Mount Pisgah, and looked upon
that rich landscape of Palestine, which his sand-
stained feet must not press, its loveliness wore a tinge
of beauty, which the sunbeams could not shed, from
the thought that there the ignorant people for whom
he had toiled should have a home, and begin their
mysterious mission among the nations of the earth.

The story of Samuel, whose heart, will, prayers,
wisdom, and virtue were for his countrymen, is a
lesson of Patriotism. Pointing to that name, the
Jew may now dispute with us, against the career of
Washington, for the honor of giving to the race the
model patriot. When we pronounce the name of
David, we think of the enthusiasm that wielded the
hero's sword, and touched the poet's harp, for the

glory of his nation. Nobler than his military valor, was the ambition that urged him to rouse the dormant genius of his land, and to enshrine and celebrate its hallowed memories in odes and jubilant hymns. From his heart, burst the gush of feeling which the Christian Church now uses as the expression of a spiritual Patriotism, — "Pray for the peace of Jerusalem, they shall prosper that love thee. Peace be within thy walls, and prosperity within thy palaces. For my brethren and companions' sakes, I will now say peace be within thee." And it is in the Psalms that we read the touching lament, as from the heart of Patriotism itself, — "How shall we sing the Lord's song in a strange land? If I forget thee, O Jerusalem, let my right hand forget her cunning . . . let my tongue cleave to the roof of my mouth; if I prefer not Jerusalem above my chief joy."

In the prophecies, too, the authority of God and the evil of sin are blended inseparably with aspirations for the glory of Israel. A prophet could not brace his breast to denounce an impending woe, without casting his eye farther on, and hailing the light of future national eminence, which made his heart swell with reverent pride, and in which the darkness of the threatened judgment melted away. Although the highest office of Revelation is to point to, and prepare us for, the "better country, even the heavenly," no one can rightly read the pages of the Bible, without catching enthusiasm for his earthly

3

country, the land of his fathers, the shelter of his
infancy, the hope of his children.   .
 Do we not read that even He whose love embraced
the whole race in its scope, the eternal and impartial
Love made flesh, who pronounced the parable of the
good Samaritan, and shed the warmth of that spirit,
through his life, into the frosty air of human sentiment, felt more keenly the alienation of his countrymen according to the flesh, than he felt the spear-point
and the nails, and paused over the beautiful city of
David to utter a lament whose burden swept away
the prospect of his own lowering destiny, — " O
Jerusalem, Jerusalem, . . . how often would I
have gathered your children together, even as a hen
gathereth her chickens under her wings, and ye would
not! Behold your house is left unto you desolate."
 When we say that the Bible justifies and encourages patriotism, we virtually say that it is a sentiment subject to the sway of the moral law, requir-
ing, like all our natural instincts, guidance, Christian
light, and training. There are base theories about the
superiority of this sentiment to any Christian limita-
tions. There are base counterfeits of the sentiment
itself. It is not the pugilistic passion that estimates
glory solely by battle-fields, weighs national worth by
vigor of muscle, and culls the anthology of its bloody
traditions in a sort of " Pirate's Own Book," by which
its brutal appetite is nourished. It is not the sense-
less sentimentalism that so often with us, on public
occasions, finds literary expression in tawdry rhetoric,
flaccid apostrophes, and sophomoric gasconade, and

which has sometimes raised the problem before sensitive minds, whether on the whole, the service of our
national holiday to liberty compensates for its de-
bauching influence on literary taste.

The patriotism that is a virtue, and that ennobles
character, is a spirit of devotion to one's couñtry,
from a purified instinct and for purposes of enlightened benefit. It is nursed and hallowed by Christian principle and draws to its aid all the resources
of genius. It is a *constructive* quality, quickening
the intellect by its love of country to zealous ambition
to improve it and raise it higher. It is an imaginative
sentiment. Imagination is essential to its vigor. It
comprehends hills, streams, plains, and valleys in a
broad conception, and from traditions and institutions
— from all the life of the past and the vigor and
noble tendencies of the present, it individualizes the
destiny and personifies the spirit of its land, and then
vows its vow to that. So that it is of the very essence
of true patriotism to be earnest and truthful, to scorn
the flatterer's tongue, and strive to keep its native
land in harmony with the laws of national thrift and
power. It will tell a land of its faults, as a friend
will counsel a companion; it will speak as honestly
as the physician advises a patient; and if occasion
requires, an indignation will flame out of its love,
like that which burst from the lips of Moses when
he returned from the mountain, and found the people
to whom he had revealed the holy and austere
Jehovah, and for whom he would cheerfully have
sacrificed his life, worshipping a calf.

The distinctive feature of true patriotism is that it is pledged to *the idea* which one's native country represents. It does not accept and glory in its country merely for what it is at present, and has been in the past, but for what it may be. Each nation has a representative value. Each race that has appropriated a certain latitude which harmonizes with its blood, has the capacity to work out *special* good results, and reveal great truths in some *distinctive* forms. God designs that each country should wear a peculiar ideal physiognomy, and He has set its geographical characteristics as a bony skeleton, and breathed into it a free life-spirit which, if loyal to the divine intention, will keep the blood in health, infuse vigor into every limb, give symmetry to the form, and carry the flush of a pure and distinct expression to the countenance. It is the patriot's office to study the laws of public growth and energy, and strive with enthusiastic love to guard against every disease that would cripple the resources of the frame and thus prevent the lineaments of vice and brutality from degrading the face, which God would have radiant with truth, genius, and purity.

He was the best patriot of ancient Greece who had the widest and wisest conception of the capacities and genius of Greece, and labored to paint that ideal winningly before the national mind, and to direct the flame of national aspiration, fanned by its heroic memories, up to the noblest possibilities of Grecian endeavor. The truest patriot of England would be the man whose mind should see in the English genius

and geography, what it could do naturally and best
for humanity, and seizing on the traditional elements
that are in harmony with that possibility, use them
to enliven its own sympathies, and quicken the
nation's energy. A pure forward look is essential to
patriotism. The patriot must express the genius of
his land in miniature.

From this point we see the patriotism of Paul. His
countrymen denounced him. They said that he had
cut the ties which bound him to his race, because he
preached that Moses was not the highest and final
religious teacher. He slighted the temple-worship
and labored zealously for the new sect of Nazarenes,
and the Jews, wherever he travelled, echoed the cry
of the priestly party in Jerusalem, that he was a
traitor to the traditions of his fathers, and an enemy
of the Hebrews. But the noblest patriotic spirit was
in him. In that respect, he may be safely copied by
those who love their country in every age. He saw
what was the mission of the Hebrew race. He read
clearly God's hieroglyphic message to them, written
over the face of their providential past. He saw
that they were an organized hope, that they existed
to bear new religions from their bosom, and send
forth at last, the perfect faith that should sway and
mould the world. He saw that it was to be their
glory to lose themselves, in the benefit they carried
to the nations, as the snow upon the mountain-tops
melts into the rills that dispense fertility to many
meadows. Paul did not believe that he could improve God's design in raising the chosen nation, or

could permanently alter it. And in working for the
cause he adopted, in preferring the then despised
Messiah to the pomp of the ritual faith and the decrees of the Sanhedrim, he was in the line of sympathy with the patriotism of the past. The Apostle
to the Gentiles in taking a course so radical, which
diverged so widely from the popular path, was the
purest Hebrew, — in truth the very " Pharisee of
the Pharisees," for he was on the track which God
designed the whole nation to take, and was laboring
to perfect for his countrymen the promises and aspirations which, for ages, through prophets and poets,
had burst from the nation's heart. Paul was so
loyal to his people that he braved their ignorance and
bigotry in order to secure the fulfilment of the
national calling, and so attached to his blood and
race as to feel keenly his isolation from their sympathy, and to be willing to sacrifice himself, — everything but his country's mission, — even to be
" accursed from Christ for his brethren, his kinsmen
according to the flesh."

We may well lament that so many counterfeits of
this noble virtue have brought the reality into suspicion; that those who have arrogated it have so often
shown only the qualities of the demagogue, and
under its sanction thrown off allegiance to truth and
righteousness; for in our own land, in this juncture
of human history, and especially in this crisis of our
own national experience, we need the virtue of
patriotism. We need it as an offshoot from the spirit
of reverence to God and of Christian consecration.

We have everything in our position, our history, our advantages and calling, to justify, stimulate, and foster such a feeling. The old Jew could exclaim proudly, even in times of calamity, "he hath not dealt so with any nation," and could thank God more fervently than for all more private mercies, that he was born a Jew. If he travelled into any other country, he went trailing the glory of a miraculous past, that dwarfed the visible magnificence of the monuments amid which he stood, and with the thrill of cheering prophecies in his breast.

Were we to select the two lines of history that afford the most striking evidence of divine guidance in the affairs of men, they should be, first, the record of the Patriarchal, Jewish, and Christian religions in their successive developments; and, secondly, the history of America from its discovery, down through the persecution of the Puritans, the life of Washington, the war of Independence, the siege of Yorktown, and the treaty of Paris. The Jewish race were guided and guarded, that a universal religion might issue from their genius. Our land seems consecrated to the office of bearing a just and faultless polity that shall educate the world. Step by step, we may parallel the providential mercies of the one history by those of the other. The call of Araham to a new region, which God would reclaim from barbarism and make the centre of healthful and lasting influences upon humanity, has its echo in the call of Columbus, in whose brain the two hemispheres were welded into a globular idea.

The leading of the Israelites through the Red Sea
has a counterpart in the division of the waves, to let
the little Mayflower, with its precious freight of
principles and souls, sail safely through the winter
storms. And the line of Hebrew heroes who fought
for a great hope, and of prophets who towered at
intervals from the landscape of the nation's life, and
sent up into literature the flame of the nation's aspiration, are not dishonored, if we compare with them
the heroic men of our own history who labored for
a hope, and "builded better than they knew," and
the seers whose minds have glowed with the American idea.

Here we are, successors of noble men, heirs of a
providential past. Everything in our history incites
to patriotism. The winds would fan it into activity.
Every page of our annals preaches it. The man
who cannot thank God he was born an American, is
undeserving the blessing of such birth. That consciousness, enlivening the sensibilities, should equal-
ize fortunes. The poor man should not feel poor
when he thinks that his humble roof and circumstances are sheltered by a canopy of ideas and sentiments, such as never before arched over any palace
of the world. If the humblest Catholic feels pride
in being one member of a community that stretches
from Andes to the Indus, and which has Christ for
its founder and heaven for its goal, the lowest citizen
of this land should feel it an immense enlargement of
his being, — an enlargement which mere wealth
could never give, — that he has partnership in the

mission of a people, along whom God is pouring the
best life of the past, enriched with additional streams
of inspiration, solicited by our own genius, into the
future. For the tendrils of our blessings stretch far
out into the centuries, and twine around the most
precious elements of history to draw nourishment.
The human race is vitally one, and whatsoever is eminent or best, in any line of social manifestation, is
somehow connected with other and distant portions
of the common body ; as the topmast branch of a tree
bears life that is due, in part, to the health and fidelity of juices in the root, and as the wave that foams
upon the shore, discharges an undulation that began
far out upon the sea.

Our country is foremost in the line of public justice and orderly freedom, and therefore all the influences which, in distant lands and former centuries, supported and quickened those principles, are
somehow represented in the social blessings we enjoy. All that former thinkers have done to justify
the principle of freedom, and heroes have achieved
against the oppressions of despotism, and martyrs
have suffered for their perilous love of liberty ; all
the stimulus which religion, in the past, has given
to the heart's reverence for right, and the hand's
loyalty to truth ; all that eloquence has done to
make tyranny tremble, and fan the popular sense of
justice to a flame ; all that literature has preserved,
in treatise, song, or drama, of past devotion to
liberty, and longing for its triumph, are related, and
have contributed to our success in the structure of

a social polity. We may properly enjoy the pride, if we will be faithful to the privilege, of bearing in our institutions the best thought and life of the past, concerning public justice and social welfare.

Well did our eminent statesman say in a public address in Boston a few weeks since, "if a man is living here who has not an American heart in his bosom, let him tear it out." Surely if there is a man in this land who deliberately slights the sentiment of patriotism, and is conscious of no pride in his country, as a distinct affection, no devotion to his country, no feeling of deep interest in his country in unsettled times and shadowed hours, no impulse to sacrifice himself and all personal interest for his country's benefit, he has a heart that needs to be waked from paralysis and inspired with gratitude by religion itself.

And it is a striking glory of our land that the patriotism it asks for is of the highest stamp. The sentiment must here be stripped of every quality which has hitherto brought it into suspicion, or it cannot be American. If a person is afraid of narrowing his soul by cherishing any restricted affection, we offer him here a domain whose breadth is from Aroostook to San Francisco, and its depth from Minnesota to the reefs of Florida; and if this area is not large enough, and does not comprehend needs and interests enough, to satisfy his affectional hunger and exhaust the philanthropic resources of his heart, he has a genius for love that would justify the description once given by a countryman of ours of the boundless aspirations of the soul, "We wake in the morning with an appetite that could take in the solar system like a cake; we stretch out our hand to grasp the morning star, and wrestle with Orion." To a mind of ordinary capacity, the extent of our territory and the various needs of our population, furnish as fine a temptation, certainly, as can well be offered, for the exercise of the sentiment of *universal brotherhood.*

And when we define Patriotism as the sentiment of devotion to the *idea* which a nation is called to typify, we strip American patriotism of every element which makes it possible in a selfish demagogue, or repulsive to the most sensitive Christian mind. For *three* things are plainly indicated in the characteristics and posture of our country, as portion of the divine intention, and of the divine instructions to us. *First,* God has placed us on a fresh continent, separated by oceans from the ambition, plans, inteference, and diplomacy of the Old World, with no enemy near us, in order that we might read in our position the instruction to sheathe the sword and live in *peace.* The war-spirit and the patriotism that cherishes it, are denounced with sufficient intensity for their barbartiy and shamelessness in other lands, by the temper of the gospel; but with us *geography* also denounces them, and declares them to be the very idiocy of ruffianism. As though sick of blood, and the order and civilization it purchases, Heaven has colonized this land and whispered to us solemnly, — Let sundered Europe drench itself with gore, if it cannot learn the economy and beauty of friendship, but here the sword should be unknown. Offensive war cannot be justified here on any pretence. You are strong enough to be magnaminious in controversies, to appeal to arbitration in complicated diplomacy, to suffer wrong in cases of pecuniary and material interest, and exhibit the grace of endurance and forgiveness. History will adjudge you guilty of the last abomination, if you draw the sword — and thus contribute to debauch still further the code, of honor among nations — in any other crisis than the final necessity of self-defence against invasion, and the call thus to defend your commissioned ideas.

And *secondly*, the Almighty has given us a domain that may be the seed-field of the globe, mines that may enrich all nations, and streams that should fill the air with the hum of wheels, and thus has sought to redeem us from the appetite for territorial aggrandizement, and has consecrated us to every art and all varieties of industry. He has written upon every prairie, and enscrolled by the winds upon the surface of every lake and river, the command to beat swords into ploughshares, and spears into pruning-hooks, and to turn all the genius that is capable of being wasted in military art, to a scientific contest with the rocks that bar the free communion of traffic, and the mountains that interpose to make enemies of states.

And *thirdly*, God has entrusted to us the idea of political equality, and of the citizen as superior to

the state, for whose culture the state exists, and has
commanded us to unfold it, and exhaust its capacity of development in progressive institutions.
Peace, industry, and *cultured freedom* are the warp
of our country's mission, and there can be no patriotism on these shores that does not acknowledge
them, seek to deepen the passion of our people for
them, extend their blessings, and confirm their sway.
The temper of our public spirit should benefit, by
its calmness, breadth, justice, and comprehensiveness, the scale of the land we represent and rule.
"To men legislating for the area between two oceans,
betwixt the snows and the tropics, somewhat of the
gravity of nature will infuse itself into the code.
It seems so easy for America to inspire and express
the most expansive and humane spirit, — new-born,
fresh, healthful, strong, the land of the laborer, of
the democrat, of the philanthropist, of the believer,
of the saint, she should speak for the human race."

Patriotism is unselfish devotion to the idea of a
nation, its heaven-inspired soul, its representative
office and mission. And anything lower than this
form of it here, any interpretation of it equivalent
to a defence of every act of every administration,
even when that act does violence to the spirit of our
history and the providential pointings of our call, is
a disgrace to ourselves, an abuse of a noble word,
and an offence before God. If a country such as
ours is to raise no loftier, no more heroic type of
national virtue than that, our fertile zones will
indeed be barren of attractive fruit. Then we may

say, here is America, but where are the Americans?
Then, —

> " When we climb our mountain cliffs,
> Or see the wide shore from our skiffs,
> To us the horizon shall express
> Mere emptiness and emptiness.
> And to our eyes the vast skies fall,
> Dire and satirical,
> On clucking hens and prating fools,
> On thieves, on drudges, and on dolls;
> For Nature has miscarried wholly
> Into failure, into folly."

Moreover, a lower type of patriotism than that of
insight into, and devotion to the representative, or
ideal country of which our land is the projection,
with us is little else than suicide. Never was there
a people whom it so behooved to be patriotic in the
highest sense; for our patriotism is daily passing into
fact, and becoming part of the nation's substance.
We vote it, we speak it, we incarnate it in the men
we select to act for us. New States, almost while
we are reading these pages, are rising to have a
voice in the highest councils of the Republic, and
from their ideas of what this country is for, and from
the quality of their passion for it, the institutions
are springing which will mould, or powerfully control, the budding intellect that will soon be on the
stage. We are living for the future. It doth not
yet appear what we shall be. We can say only that
we are a mass of tendencies. And the sentiment
of patriotism that obtains is breathing year by year,
the life-element or the death-element into the structure of our land.

We have said that the form of patriotism which could harbor in the most Christian breast is called for, and is the only one that is justified by the situation and the *manifest destiny* of our country. We may also .say that such a form of patriotism is nourished and expected by the traditions upon which the lower forms of patriotism usually feed. It is a beautiful fact that the record and the memories of our revolutionary strife foster all grades of the patriotic sentiment. They stir the blood and the brain. They thrill the senses and satisfy the imagination. The plain of Concord, where "the embattled farmers stood," and the shaft that overlooks the metropolis from a neighboring city, tell a story that awakens a love of country in the plough-boy, while they quicken the faith of the Christian and the philosopher in the reality of principles, the influence of heroic self-sacrifice that counts no cost, and the power of ideas. The non-resistant peace-man, though his ear would throb with pain to hear the roar of musketry, that disturbed the air about us seventy-five years ago, loves the sweet, bodiless echoes it has brought, and still awakens in that depth of time. And while the passions of the caucus in Middlesex have, doubtless, been often stirred to the worst dregs, by appeals to what the fathers did when the country was in danger, no finer eloquence has vivified the air of the National Senate Hall, than the simple exclamation, "There is Lexington and Concord and Bunker Hill, and there they will remain forever." The unreflective man is thrilled with the contagious enthusiasm of our ancestors, who would not be trampled on by tyranny, and who put their lives in their hands to assert their rights. The great thinker sees the meaning of those three spots in the stormy history of the world, and how ideas were liberated from the shock of steel and the battle-smoke, which have since changed the destiny of the world. And while we may catch the physical enthusiasm from the determined spirit with which, on the bloody fields, our fathers resisted unto death, our patriotism must be inspired by the ideas which redeem those fields from the insignificance of skirmishes and the depravity of butchery, and must pledge itself to establish and unfold them in our country, according to the new needs and invitations of our age.

If the glory of the foundation of our land was in the establishment of a principle, the glory of its history must consist in the unfolding of that principle. True patriotism, therefore, which labors to keep a nation faithful to its mission, cannot be satisfied here unless the idea of human worth and privilege that awakened and supported our political struggle, ripen and produce their finest spiritual fruit. In this respect the growth of our country should be like that of an endogenous tree; the gradual development of the life-principle at the centre manifesting itself in the nourishment of new products, throwing the old results, year by year, farther out into history, till the political effects of the Revolution become the gnarled root, and tall, hardy stem,

which preserve and defend the active inward forces,
that now unfold in leaves and blossoms, and an-
nounce the harvest. In the peace movement, the
temperance reform, the judicious and practicable
schemes for the abolition of bondage, the attempts
to discover a more Christian organization of society;—in every association and all effort that seek
the highest welfare of man, and prepare the way
for his free culture and rightful enjoyment, as a
creature of God, the American idea justifies itself
and culminates; and by strengthening this tendency, and only thus, can Patriotism be faithful to its
law, and vindicate its nature.

Every mention of the ideas to which our land is
consecrated, and of the importance of its mission,
calls up the crisis which we have recently passed
through, and the danger with which, it is said, our
land was threatened. Patriotism has learned to
pronounce with emphasis the word Union. It is a
hallowed word to it. It does not like to hesitate in
uttering it. It has no desire that its tongue should
falter with it, or merely to lisp its utterance. But
there is danger in our reactionary eloquence that,
in eulogies of union and assertions that we must
have it, we overlook or too slightly estimate the
conditions of union. This country has an ideal
character, a representative value. Its mountains
were upheaved, its rivers were grooved, its prairies·
unrolled, its night-skies bent, for the home of an
idea. Its glory cannot spring from vast extent,
populousness, power, and wealth, but from the un-

4

questioned dominion of an idea. If we are to be one, we must have a great undying sentiment. "*Liberty* and Union, now and forever, one and inseparable;" that is the marriage-vow, that alone can be the marriage-bond. We cannot vote ourselves together, we cannot keep ourselves together merely by cultivating superficial, or commercial good feeling. The unity of our nation — the most marvellous and splendid organism of history — may stand forever unshaken by the diversities of climate which it includes, by the variety of material interests — commerce, agriculture, industry — which it enfolds; may indeed be all the stronger for the twisting of so many strands : but though nature made our vast landscape one; though it be interlocked by rivers, railways, and canals; though it be vascular with myriad arteries of human skill; though the geographer may find no place where he can split our country, the strife of hostile ideas will. rend it as the valley yawns by the wrench of the earthquake. It is the office of Patriotism to see this and to say it, — to say plainly and solemnly that no political unity, no charter however wisely concocted, or defended by the most stalwart mental muscles, can stand before the fierce and equal combat of two mutually destructive principles. There is no treason no lack of patriotism in saying this, unless it is unpatriotic to say that chemical wraths will not combine, and that powder and fire will not marry peaceably.

We need the feeling of brotherhood; we need to

be knit together in ties of cordial amity; but no
amity can be manufactured where the laws of spiritual affinity interpose a ban. Whatever peculiarities
of State institution, however wrong and heinous,
exist in the separate members of the confederacy,
let them keep, undisturbed by interference from
other States, till they choose to abolish them themselves. Whatever laws are demanded by a just and
strict construction of the central compact, let them
have, so long as we profess to have that charter, and
let them not be forcibly resisted. But, though the
sun now breaks through the recent cloudy screen, if
peace, harmony, and strength are to bless our nation,
there is one direction in which we must not go beyond the letter of the bond. The " pound of flesh,"
but not a tittle more must be asked, not another
fraction can be granted, not so much as will " turn
the scale even in the estimation of a hair." What
is local must be local. The inward, vivifying principle of our government must be sympathy with
liberty; its attitude must be respect for liberty; the
spread of its domain must be under the sanction
and for the ends of liberty, or the inspiring sentiment of union and the bond of unity, that which
filled the hearts and quickened the intellects of the
noble men who built our Constitution, that which
gives glory and renown to our charter, will wither
and die.

" Behold," said David, " how good and how
pleasant it is for brethren to dwell together in unity."
But if the time is to come when a large section of

our land insist that human bondage is to be sanctioned and extended wherever our banner and our eagles go; that the haggard genius of oppression must sit with equal privilege and honor with the spirit of freedom in the exalted seats of our confederacy, then — I utter only the simplest lesson of science — then there can be no unity, for we shall no more be *brethren;* the gulf of antagonistic ideas will divide us; the nerve of patriotism, in the best souls, will be shrivelled; for the ideal beauty of our nation will be expunged, its hovering genius will flee, and there will be no America to serve; and our glory, whose auroral promise tinges our first annals, and whose beams are now gilding the mountain-tops, will be stained with blood, and finally pale. Then, while he looks back and sees, as Paul saw in the past of his nation, that unto us pertaineth the adoption, and the glory, and the covenants, and the promise, and the fathers, and looks around to see the fatal faithlessness of the children to the divine idea and the providential intimations of the past, the only utterance of patriotism that will be possible, from the Christian breast, will be the sorrowful exclamation of Paul, " I could wish that I were accursed from Christ for my brethren, my kinsmen according to the flesh."

We conclude, then, by saying that patriotism is not only a legitimate sentiment, but a duty. There are countless reasons why, as Americans, we should love our native land. We may feel no scruples, as Christians, in welcoming and nourishing a peculiar affection for its winds and soil, its coasts and hills, its memories and its flag. We cannot more efficiently labor for the good of all men, than by pledging heart, brain, and hands to the service of keeping our country true to its mission, obedient to its idea. Our patriotism must draw its nutriment and derive its impulse from knowledge and love of the ideal America, as yet but partially reflected in our institutions, or in the general mind of the Republic. Thus quickened, it will be both pure and practical. The agency of an overruling and friendly power is suggested by the study of the critical seasons of our past history. But our patriarchal and heroic periods have passed. Having endowed us with the means of our own development, the divine agency retreats to leave the field for human responsibility. We cannot rely for our honors or safety upon the past; with the principle we must reject the privileges of primogeniture. We are here, by favor, to a vast and noble work. "To whom much is given, of him will much be required." We may feel, as we look upon our territory, which exhibits every zone, and represents lands that invite all varieties of industry, that God grooved our noble rivers, and stretched our prairies on their level base, and unrolled our rich savannahs, and reared the pomp of our forests, and washed the long line of our coasts with generous ocean waves, and wove all these diversities into one, to be the home of no mean people, and the theatre of no paltry destiny. The world waits to see the quality and energy of our patriotism. The book of our country's history, preserved by human heroism and providential care, is handed to us, that we may inscribe there the records of its glory, or its shame.

II.

WASHINGTON, OR GREATNESS.

Most people love to look on a great man. It is an epoch in the lives of persons, when they first behold some of the greatest natural sublimities or beauties of the material creation, such as the "White Mountains," "Niagara," a "Storm at Sea," the "Bay of Naples," or an "Italian Sunset;" but there is no landscape, or range of hills, that can afford so clear a manifestation of the divine wisdom, goodness, and glory, as is revealed to us through the faces and the works of the eminent men of the world. "The word made flesh" takes rank of all the forms of the word, as it is revealed in globe, or star, or sky. I should like to look up to Mont Blanc, from the valley of Chamouni, or stand under the shadow of the Pyramids, or see the panorama that stretches beneath the summits of the Andes, but should prefer of the two, to pass an hour with Plato, to study the beauty of Milton's countenance, to have seen the expression of Shakspeare just as Hamlet was completed, or to have stood among the circle that heard the apostle Paul at Lystra, or that listened to his defence before Agrippa in the city of Cesarea.

Next to the *sight* of great persons, the *ideal* knowledge of them is interesting and important, through
careful study of their careers. The way to keep up
our faith in virtue, if it flags, and to enlarge our conception of greatness, if it shrivels, is to turn from
the small proportions of the souls about us, and our
own easy defeats, and go into the society of the eminent servants of truth and right, whose devotion
cannot be questioned, and whose biographies are like
suns in the firmanent of history.

We need continually to be refreshed as to the relations of the moral element, of goodness, to human
greatness. Every man was made to be a subject.
There is law in the universe, law for men as well as for
things ; and there is no majestic greatness or enduring force except in the line of law. No piece of rock,
no gem, no river, no mountain, could have any beauty,
usefulness, or power, outside the laws of order that
entwine the globe. Let anything in nature set up
for itself and refuse to obey, and it is weak and good
for nothing. We hear a great deal said about instinct
self-reliance, and the virtue of impulse and disposition. It is true that the saintly goodness consists in
this, but it is a virtue that the soul attains and ends
with. Every man must apply a law to himself, before he can be a law to himself. Weeds are spontaneous, fruit is cultivated. It does not depend on a
man's virtues, whether he shall be *distinguished*, but
it does depend on them whether he is *great.*

We must make a clear discrimination, and keep it
ever in mind, between distinction and greatness.

Some persons have one power or faculty of our nature, in greater prominence than the average of of the world, and we call them *great* because of it. One man has more strength, or more mechanical. skill, or more of mercantile sagacity, or more fluent utterance, or a more fertile brain than ordinary men. If there was no moral truth, or moral law in the world, we might decide the greatness of men, as most persons do now decide it, not at all by the uses to which men put their faculties, but simply by the degree in which they possess certain powers.

Some men are distinguished also by a certain fineness of quality; their sensibilities and their brain seem to be made of more delicate and subtile material. Poets and artists are distinguished thus. Others, again, rise above the level of capacity, by the quantity of their nature and attributes. They have vastly more of the common qualities which other men possess, such as prudence, steadiness, common sense, and are eminent by their *mass* of substance. But before the word " greatness " can be applied to any of these, the question must be asked, " What do they do with their qualities ? how do they rule them? in what service are they employed ? "

In the light of these principles it is very easy to see the line in which Washington was great. He was not distinguished from others by the great preponderance of any one faculty. It is said of some great men that they would have been equally eminent in many other careers. Thus Napoleon, or Cæsar, might have been a great orator, poet, mathe-

matician, engineer. But Washington would not in
any line have been a brilliant man. No culture probably could have brought any one power of his nature into such distinction that it could be eminent
in a circle of the most gifted minds which his country or his age produced. As a· speaker, a writer, a
scholar, he could have been faithful and respectable,
but not remarkable, not brilliant, and in no sense original. Neither did he have the second element of distinction, that is, a peculiar fineness of quality or
organization. Of all that passes for genius in the domain of artistic creation, he was destitute. A subtile
thought, an acute distinction, a delicate perception,
a fine and elusive emotion, — anything connected
with the poet's sensibility or the poetic capacity, he
was debarred from by temperament. The distinction of Washington was the great bulk and compact-
ness of his practical powers, the solidity, the strength,
and the poise of those faculties, which we do not
usually associate with genius, but which are the spiritual substratum of every nature that is called efficient and reliable for systematic and practical work
in society. The remark which Patrick Henry made,
after his return from the first Continental Congress,
to a person who asked him who was the greatest man
in that body, comes in play here. "If you mean
who is the greatest orator, Mr. Rutledge of South
Carolina is, no doubt, the most eloquent man; but
for solid information and sound judgment, Col.
Washington is unquestionably the greatest man on
the floor." He was great, that is, distinguished from

other men, by the mass, gravity, and majesty with which, by nature, the strong qualities of our humanity were aggregated in him.

But this does not define his greatness in the true sense of that word, that is, in the sense which every Christian man should use it. With this large quantity of being, Washington could not long have played a subordinate or trivial part in practical life, but he might have made his energy and power of influence ministers of his own aggrandizement in startling ways, and at the expense of general welfare. It is one of the first elements of his greatness to be noted and to be revered, that his powers were subjected to a rigid rule. He had great passions, but he had iron walls and reins of steel for them. Self-command was his prominent trait. The lower flames of his being beat in vain against the ramparts of his will. And this self-command was not merely the discipline of his lower properties, so that they should not interfere with his success. Many men, doubtless, have had the power to smother their flaming passions in emergencies by a cool selfishness; but in his case, the will itself that ruled them was loyal to an idea of right, and all the powers of his nature were subordinated and systemized by the dominion over him of the law of duty. He was a law-giver to himself. From the date of his responsible years he rigidly strove to·put himself in harmony with moral truth, learning to command by being commanded, and through obedience aspiring to be free.

The proverb says, " He that ruleth his spirit is

better than he that taketh a city." A vast proportion of what the world calls greatness has been in
the line of the strong passions of our nature; the
spring, the power-wheel of it, has been some one of
the unruled, riotous, and degrading forces of the
soul. Very seldom is greatness seen that is based
on, and grows out of, self-rule, and the antecedent
conquest of that portion of hell that is contained in
every human breast. If Washington's spirit had
been less orderly, he would doubtless have seemed
greater to a vast many who now see nothing very
remarkable in his nature, because he would doubtless have done many things that would have been
more startling and would have called forth more
applause. Take, for instance, the case of the two men
— Cæsar and Napoleon. In contrast with the brilliant story of their victories and their subjugation
of great nations to their will, the exploits of Washington look meagre enough. But their successes
were all stimulated by selfishness and ambition, and
were thus in the direction of passions, whose gale
they trimmed their sails to take. It is easy enough
to scud before the wind, but seamanship is oftener
displayed in beating into harbor against the breeze,
around the points, and among the shoals, than in a
quick run across the ocean. Who knows what brilliant achievements Washington could have surprised
men with, if his powers had been wildly dishevelled,
and his faculties put to the service of lust for
dominion and aggrandizement? Who knows whether
the temptations to do just such things as have im-

mortalized the imperial geniuses, did not writhe in his brain and swell his breast, to be wrestled down and fettered? If so, he was greater than Napoleon or Alexander, by that rule of his spirit that made him refuse such distinction as theirs. If the temptation to be a despot conquered the genius of Bonaparte, and was conquered by the soul of Washington, all the splendors of the first man's success only show · that, in the region of morals, he was magnificently weak, and the poverty of splendor in the ·second man's achievements, prove him to be magnificently strong.

The very word *passion* implies subjection and submissiveness. No human strength is suggested by the word, but the contrary. Where a passion is violent, and speeds through the soul with irresistible press, no matter what great records of brilliant confusion it may leave in the outward world, the man himself has been acted upon and swung as an instrument. The law-giving, order-appointing faculty at the centre of his being, *the will* in which the likeness of the Infinite Ruler is reflected, has been conquered, so that the soul becomes a subject thing, and not a monarchical lord of the forces in its own realm. The horse hurries the rider in the paths it likes; the mob invades the deliberative silence of the Capitol. For this reason it is that "He that is slow to anger is better than the mighty."

Surely then it is time that we made the most important discrimination between the distinction that comes from lawless yielding to the currents of world-

ly temptation and passion, and the greatness that lies
in stemming these and working in the line of truth,
usefulness, and law. If Napoleon and Cæsar had
been greater men, that is, truer, more loyal men,
they would surely have been less brilliantly distinguished men. They would not have jarred the globe
with the tread of their armies, they might not have
crowned the Alps with their banners and their
eagles, they would not have made so many homes
desolate and so many acres rich by the slaughter of
their foes, for they would probably have kept at
home, and labored to increase the blessings and improve the civilization of their own people, and the
record of their battles would have been limited to
those fought to repel invasion, or to crush the out-
rageous tyranny of foreign despotism. If the present ruler of France were a *greater* man than he is,
the world would have heard far less about him. It
would never have heard of the subtile and comprehensive brutality by which a nation's liberty has
been betrayed, and the sportive fiendishness that has
contrived to make the people themselves parties to
his conspiracy. Had he been a greater man, he would
have respected his oath, or, if forced by the desperate
condition of his country to save it from misrule by
momentary usurpation, he would have used his
power for the broad good of his land, and not to increase, by stupendous rascality, the pomp of his own
state and name. I heard an eccentric but shrewd
man once remark that he never knew a person who
startled people very much, and for whom crowds

seemed willing to throw up their hats, that was not, to a great extent, a humbug. There is much truth in this, for it is often the case that if persons who show brilliant and surprising qualities in the world of action, speech, or thought, had more solidity or good sense, their startling distinction would be less prominent, because their wisdom and general vigor of nature would be greater.

God strives in every way to make us see the greatness of all that is productive of peace and order. The prairies waving with growing wheat, and forests studded with swelling oaks, make no noise; and the electricity which roars in the thunder peal is not a tithe so powerful as that which sleeps in the light and holds the drops of a cup of water in their liquid poise. The world's estimate of power gives greater prominence to that which upheaves and causes disorder. The eruption of a volcano, to almost all minds, symbolizes more strength and grandeur than the silent swing and radiance of a planet. If there could be some splendid confusion produced amid the serenity of the present universal order, if some broad constellation should begin, to-night, to play off from all its lamps, volleys of Bengal lights, that should fall in showers of many-colored sparks and fiery serpents, down the spaces of the heavens, or if some blazing and piratical comet should butt and jostle the whole outworks of a system, and rush like a celestial fire-ship, destroying order, and kindling the calm fleets that sail upon the infinite azure into a flame, how many thousands there are that would look up to the skies, for the first time with wonder and awe, and exclaim inwardly, "Surely there is the finger of God." They do not see anything surprising or subduing in the punctual rise and steady setting of the sun, and its imperial and boundless bounty; and yet there is enough fire in the sun to spirt any quantity of flaming and fantastic jets; it could fill the whole space between Mercury and Neptune with brilliant pyrotechnics and jubilee displays, such as children gaze at and clap their hands. But the great old sun is not selfish, and has no French ambition for such tawdry glories. It reserves its fires, keeps them stored in its breast, spills over no sheets of flame from its huge caldron, but shoots still and steadily its clean, white beams into the ether, that evoke flowers from the bosom of every globe, and paint the far-off satellites of Uranus with silver beauty.

It is a bad sign always for the permanence and beneficence of any power, when there is much clamor in it and excitement about it. Where a school is governed by the frequent accompaniment of loud talk and whippings, there is not nearly so much power at work as in a school where, through respect for the teacher, everything goes on quietly, as it were without direction. So it is in homes; the more noise and scolding, the less parental power. Activity and clamor of the tongue and hand are brought in to supply the lack of that steady, central strength which organizes peacefully. In the same way it is the excess of the violent and degrading passions — which in their dominion really show the weakness of a man, and not his greatness — that usually has made the fame and supremacy of the leading geniuses. If a man is not too great to be unscrupulous, he can, with a fair share of force in him, make headway and considerable noise in the world. There is more power in putting the foot upon a passion, and being unknown through that victory, than in surrendering to it, and thus making a world-wide noise. We may conquer the globe in the latter case, but in the former we conquer the prince of this world. The passion for money-getting, for reputation, for power, for a seat in Congress, often acquires for a man the credit of greatness, through his success, when he may have neighbors that show themselves to be greater than he, by refusing to let a passion absorb them, and are restrained by the delicate bonds of refinement, honor, and conscience, from the tricks, meannesses, and questionable measures that must often be used to be brilliantly successful in the world of wealth and fame.

All true greatness is calm, has a large side of silence, works in harmony with the still and modest laws of truth, and shows symmetrical proportions that prevent its majesty from producing its full impression upon us until we study it carefully. I was talking with a man, not long since, who said that he could not see the remarkable greatness of Washington. "What new thing did he do?" he asked; as if it were not a marvellous instance of greatness that, with such opportunities to do such new and brilliant things as to be the founder of a line of kings on a vast continent, he would not think of it; as if he did not show the very originality of his greatness among the chieftains of history by lifting up the common virtues of honesty, integrity, and regard for the welfare of others, and wearing them instead of a royal robe and princely crown, thus showing that they were broad and ample enough to cover him with majesty; as if that letter by which, from the impulse of honor and devotion to republican truth, he refused the imperial office and name, and rebuked the officer who wrote the temptation to him, was not the most original page in the bloody annals of revolution and war; as if it were an every-day occurrence for a man, by the justness of his motives and the clearness of his sight, to insure liberty for generations to half a hemisphere; as though it were something lightly to be estimated when the devil takes a great nature, such as he has so often conquered by his splendid baubles, up to a high mountain, from which the extent of a nation is visible, and offers the landscape as the prize, if he will kneel and worship, — to hear the answer given that echoes round the world, " Get thee behind me, Satan, for I will serve only truth and my fellows, and the Supreme God."

Mr. Carlyle has been led away by the same false-ness or feebleness of sight to disparage the great-ness of Washington. Because he gained no brill-iant victories, because he made no startling and

melodramatic displays of arbitrary will, because
there were no meteoric moments and passages in his
career, he and many others, doubtless, have thought
him unworthy a place among the great heroes of
the time. "Good enough," they say; "a very good
man,—but over-estimated for greatness." Ah!
was it a small thing; to be turned off in that way
in our rhetoric, that there has been a man who lifted
up generalship from the low purposes and aims
which have degraded it, and in the height of power
showed the world the dignity there is in serving,
rather than lawless seizing? We need not deny, or
detract from, the splendid abilities shown by the great
captains of history in their campaigns that gave or
upheld their despotic power. We see the brilliancy
of such achievements at once. They glare. But
bring them into comparison with the silent greatness of Washington in the first years of the Revolution! Look at those great leaders with their
mighty and well-appointed armies, full of enthusiasm for their chiefs, and eager for war, and then,
then think of Washington, in his humble camp,
so feebly and fitfully supplied; invested with every
sort of difficulty that might dishearten a noble nature; denied the opportunity of doing anything brilliant in the way of battle; compelled to counsel,
argue with, and inspirit the Congress that appointed
him and that watched him; obliged to use the
greatest art, often, to conceal the poverty of his resources from his foes and from his own men; seeing
his ranks thinned just when help was needed most;

doomed to have his head and heart pecked at by
jealousy, detraction, and infamous slander; compelled to keep up courage in defeat, and to look
abroad for light in the thickest gloom; to cheer his
soldiers amid the frost and the famine of their winter retreats, and to suppress their mutinies and keep
alive their patriotism, when their pay failed and
their prospects were black; and yet in the midst of all,
to keep the same calm temper of endurance, and
the same deep love of freedom and serene faith in
success; to feel "though persecuted not forsaken,
though perplexed not in despair, though cast down
not destroyed;" and to come out of it all triumphant, and with the same majesty of joy in victory as
there was of trust in the night hours; and then to
rule with the same steady justice in the cabinet, as
he had shown in the camp, is not this a greatness
that is only too original in the annals of the world's
warfare and struggle? Where is the other great
genius that has been called to stand the strain of
such constant and exciting duties, — the wear and
tear upon temper, hope, confidence, and the last resources of the breast for years, with no absorbing
personal ambition to inspire him, but only a sentiment of duty, and the ardent desire to give freedom
to a land?

In the silence and persistency of the breast of
Washington there was the noblest display of greatness. The spirit which ruled him was the highest
spirit; and the qualities within him to be ruled thus
must have been massive and immense, or they never

could have done the organizing work which they performed. Try to think of any other man, connected with the armies or the councils of our revolution, taking Washington's place, and he performing a subordinate part. We cannot do it. The history of that period, and the fitness of things, would be tortured by such an arrangement. We might as well try to conceive the sun acting as satellite to one of its dependent orbs. Great men, noble men, brilliant men, there were belonging to the camp and to the Capitol, but they show aright, and to the best advantage, when disposed around his Doric greatness. He was the man fitted and made to uphold the banner of liberty on a continent, — the colossal nature representing in his own inward rule and repose the greatness of a nation rising up to proclaim and illustrate liberty founded on law. He towered from the level of the virtue and patriotism of his countrymen, not by any different or more surprising qualities than theirs but as the mountain rises by greater mass and gradual slopes from the plains; and he stood among the cluster of large names that surrounded him and supported the common cause, as the summit which bears his name in the highlands of New Hampshire, rises from the cluster of neighboring peaks, so majestic and supreme in its eminence that at the distance all the rest seem blended into its sublimity, and it is its height that represents the grandeur of the region, and guides the traveller from afar on his way.

Whenever we are grateful to divine Providence for
the freedom we enjoy, and the persistent heroism that
secured it, we ought especially to recognize and adore
the guidance that raised such a nature to be its support and head. Coming a generation before, or a
generation after, there would hardly have been on
this side the globe, the proper work for such a man,
and he would have been a discreet, successful, and
happy farmer at Mount Vernon. Many speak of the
indications of Providence in behalf of our land,
shown by the seemingly miraculous interpositions
that kept him, in his youth, from the service of a
foreign navy, and that guarded him, in forest skirmishes and open battle, from the skilful bullets of
his enemies. But it is wiser and more Christian to
study the comprehensive providence that organized
secretly such a soul in the settlement of Virginia,
and, when the time arrived that called for a leader,
able to conciliate differences, disarm prejudice, inspire confidence and courage, and give weight and
dignity to a popular cause, led forward the man
full-formed, competent to utter without heat the
radical opinions and determinations of an excited
people, and to invest rebellion with the calmness of
philosophy and the majesty of truth. Without
Washington, our revolution, if successful, would
have lost its chief grandeur. No brilliancy of military genius in any other leader, could atone for the
loss of that brave manliness at the head of our
armies that collected and pious patience in reverses
and distress, that chastened and systematic enthu-

siasm which defeated, by wearing out, the haughty
hostility of a foreign cabinet and king, that serene
and stately wisdom from which has floated down to
us the parental counsels of that Farewell Address,—
fitting close to a life of unfaltering devotion to duty
and a country's cause. The man to whom a whole
country looked for support, and on whose inward
resources they relied in war and peace, has not been
overrated for greatness, nay, has not been wisely
enough estimated as yet. Let us bless God for
Washington! And if any man cannot see our indebtedness for his service by looking at the past, let
him turn towards Europe, and study what each oppressed and bleeding land is suffering, because, in
the spasmodic throes of its strength or despair it
has no such man as he to comprehend the justice of
its cause in his brain, and the sentiments of it in his
breast, and to excite in every thinker, in every lover
of God and religion, and in the cottages of every
village, a trust in the clearness of his sight, the
purity of his heart, the soundness of his judgment,
and the republicanism of his sword. When there
shall be fewer metaphysical declaimers and atheistic
brigands in the ranks of the leaders of the popular
cause in Europe, and a few men, yes, even one large
and well-poised nature, to whom manliness and
piety may look up without fear and without shame,
the prospects of liberty will not be so dark as they
are now.

I wish to speak next of the morality of Washington's intellect. Without the due appreciation of this,

any estimate of his genius must be partial. As the great powers of his nature were only the ordinary qualities of good men enlarged and intensified, so the greatness of his mind consisted in his tendency and desire to see the single truth and justice in every question that came before him for consideration and for action. Somebody has finely said that, if you seek the new, you will be likely to miss the true, but if you seek the true you will probably find the new. Simple standards are very severe ones for the judgments of men. How few are there that, in all their inquiries, seek only truth with their whole heart, and in all their actions desire to do purely what is best. Let the bigotries and prejudices, the oppressions, the infidelity, the unfaithfulness of men answer for this ; for they exist simply because men do not pursue truth with singleness of mind, and strive to support in action what they know in meditation to be the right. But there never was a nature sounder to the core of its interest and its will, in these respects, than Washington's. Sincerity and truth-lovingness were in his blood. Morality shot up into every fibre of his brain, and was alive in each sinew of his hand. We cannot conceive of him making any investigations to dress out a subject in any other light than its own, or planning to serve a party, or laboring in any course that did not seem to promise the best results for all. Reference to what is highest in the nature of things had been made a habit so strong by his faithfulness, that it became an instinct. A patriot he was in the highest sense, not because he loved his country with a selfish love, but because he loved justice on the broadest scale, and believed that the cause of his country was that of eternal justice ; and so when he spoke of resistance, it was a command from the very spirit of loyalty, saying " submit no longer," and when he drew his sword, every Christian in the land might safely say " *Amen.*" So lofty was his nature, that he could not stoop to selfish ambition, nor counsel anything that would tamper with the public good, or did not point directly to his country's benefit. If such a spirit is the soul of greatness in whatever sphere, we may see also the breadth of the nature in which that spirit lived, when we consider how naturally we think of Washington as a public man. There are many very good men, reliable men, — men as pure in the spirit of their greatness as Washington, whom we should instinctively consider out of place in any large public capacity. And many who are called to the national councils seem too small for the work allotted to them, not less by the feebleness of their powers than by the selfishness of their spirit. The ample expanse and dignified associations of the Senate Chamber dwarf them; the Capitol does not seem to enclose its masters when they are in it; an empire is too broad a background for their height and bulk. " Pigmies are pigmies still, though perched on Alps." But Washington was emphatically a *States*-man. The home and the farm could not keep him, although his heart was there. He was made for the broad sphere of public action.

The swing of his arm had momentum enough to move a nation ; his presence was for the head-quarters of an army, or for the palace of a people ; his pen was made to transcribe treaties, and his voice to be heard at the limits of a State. His writings have the solemnity and majesty appropriate to the deliberations and decisions of a congress, and nothing but a nation, and a serious revolution for the maintenance of right, could be competent to relieve the plain but colossal proportions of his judgment, prudence, integrity, and love of freedom.

And now, bring into the presence of such a character — thus seated upon the throne of justice and a people's veneration — such men as Cæsar and Bonaparte. We ought to bring them there ; it will do us good to see how they look, and we ought to know how they look, in the light which that brow and that face shed upon them. Do they not look smaller ? What right have we to judge any man, however great, by any other standard than that of *the good ?* If a man is a Colossus in genius, but is a colossal criminal, why not always use the noun to describe him, rather than the adjective ? Is it not time to see that the standard of the just and good flames over *statesmen* as well as over *humble* men, and that if a man who cheats and conspires against his neighbor's right in a small sphere is called a knave, the man who cheats and robs and fetters his country, by whatever brilliancy of achievement he effects it, should be branded as a royal villain ? Let not the purity of Washington's character be considered, as it too often is, an almost supernatural exception to what can be expected of mortals, but let it be looked up to as the pattern of what humanity may attain, and let it shine upon the reputation of these men that are accounted great, that the splendor of their battles may pale in the solemn brightness of his integrity, and that the complexity of their genius, which only offers so many channels for the selfishness of our nature, may dwindle in its charm before the great simplicity of his soul, that was translucent with the immortal brightness of virtue and fidelity.

It is well for us to look up to the height and mass and complexion of such a virtue. The anniversary of his birthday does not come round too often for us to devote some hour of it, whenever it returns, to meditation upon him and to gratitude for his spirit and his work. The Almighty has put him into history, as he put the soul of Samuel into the history of Palestine, to show men the majesty of virtue, its public relations, and to speak to the human sensibilities and conscience through the incarnate eloquence of a life.

The character of Washington is a buttress to every pulpit of America; for it is a character that is baseless, if religion be not true. If men are mere animals, if there is no law of God, no holy duty, no eternal life, his life is a sublime inconsistency. There is a firmer fulcrum for the lever of the gospel against the passions and the worldliness of men, there is greater vigor in the eloquence that denounces self-worship and enthrones loyalty to truth, there is

more intensity in every appeal that calls men not
to be "lovers of pleasure more than lovers of God,"
because such a man has woven the tissue of his fidelity into the half century of his earthly stewardship.
Such a life makes the greatness which the precepts
of Christianity present abstractly, a reality; it
strengthens the laws, and adorns the landscape of
the kingdom of heaven.

The Saviour said that his apostles after their death
should "sit upon twelve thrones, judging the twelve
tribes of Israel." And every great character which,
out of the materials of human discipline, builds up
a shining, greatness, rises after its death to a throne,
and by its eminence judges the world. And so our
subject mounts to a climax of moral authority, im-
pressiveness, and appeal. The character of Washington hangs in the moral atmosphere, for instruction and for judgment, over the statesmen of our
land. How can there be a timeserver, a demagogue,
a trifler with right and the true interests of his
country, a brutal scorner of the laws of virtue and
honor, in that Capitol founded by Washington, and
in which his marble counterfeit still strives to shed
dignity and truth? The people of this land have
before them the incarnate ideal of what a statesman
should be, and they ought to hold the statesmen who
have read his life, and who meet in the city that
bears his name, to the duty of laboring in a spirit
like his for the business and the interests of the great
estates they guard. It is our fault if his name shall
die away into a mere ornament of congressional and

caucus rhetoric, and if it 'is suffered that business shall be postponed, and the courtesies of life trampled upon, and the supreme law of God made a byword and mockery, by puny men who sit in the high places of an empire which his fidelity and religion saved. If any man smiles at the idea of great virtue being possible amid the temptations of public life, and thinks that the standard of the pulpit is not for the conflicts and rivalries and diplomacies of the political arena, and feels that the religion of Christ is good enough outside the storms and stress of the world, let him be pointed to Washington, who went clean and victorious through all, and who, " though dead, yet speaks " to us, that the trouble in gaining a great virtue is not in the strength of the world, but in the feebleness of the soul.

And that character shines down upon all of us, and searches the depths of our hearts to prove our fidelity to truth and heaven. The greatest goodness is imitable and encourages aspiration. What is there in the greatness of Washington that cannot in spirit be revealed in us, and that is not applicable to our circumstances and needed in our breast? If Washington had failed in fidelity to his call ; if he had said " My circumstances are easy enough here amid my parks, and forests, and farms, and I will not hazard my happiness upon the issue of a conflict between my feeble country and the most powerful empire of the world ; " or if, having taken the responsibility, he had used its means and power for himself more than for the great duties to which it

called, we should mourn when we read it, and view
it as another dark page in the history of the frailty
of human genius. And yet, in the sight of God,
what would it be but a record in larger type of the
practical infidelity and failure which so many men
are printing in smaller type upon their allowance of
time? Every private soldier is required to be faithful, as much as every officer who has charge of the
campaign. Every man is required to rule his passions
and to discipline his powers as the great founder of
our freedom did; and although every man is not
required to save a country, yet there is no one that
does not have a soul to save from darkness, depravity, the feebleness of sloth and luxury, and the
powers of hell. Some men say that the divine
character of Christ is too high for them, but what
man has done surely men may do; and the affectionate reverence which we feel and pay towards the
Father of his country, and the gratitude we confess
to Providence for placing his name foremost and
lustrous on the roll of our country's annals, call on
us, in the name of consistency and our own moral
aspirations, to examine ourselves and see if there is
in us, as there was in him, a love of the truth that
makes all falsehood infamous; a devotion to the right
that keeps the ear away from the seductions of the
flesh and the world; and that upward look to what
is best, which fosters in us the desire at all times to
be the servants of that and that only which is supreme and everlasting.

III.

BEAUTY AND RELIGION.

WE propose in the present article to point out a few elements of the relation that exists between the perception of beauty and religious culture. Of course, it will not be necessary for us to prove that a desire for beauty, and a delight in its manifestations, are natural and legitimate passions of our nature. This point may be assumed. Taking this for granted, it is evident, on independent grounds, that *some* relation must exist between the growth of this faculty and the development of our religious feelings. There is an integrity in our intellectual conformation that will not allow a disproportionate degree of cultivation to any of our powers; a secret selfishness at the centre of our being which always appropriates something for general use, levying contributions upon the treasures of every faculty, and commanding the service of all the powers of the soul. We cannot select a single organ of the mind, any more than we can select a single organ of the body, and, by any healthy process of nourishment and training, increase its vigor and develop its strength without also incidentally assisting every other power with which it is associated. A central bond, a mysterious attraction, independent of human will, binds together all our mental as our physical powers, and by fine and secret ties compels the growth of each to subserve the good of all.

But especially is it true that this capacity of appreciating beauty is connected with religion. This, which is the central want and passion of the soul, is developed and strengthened by every degree of attainment in every line of mental culture. As the laws of the natural world may be carried up at last to a single law, of which they are the separate expressions, and in which they meet and blend, so, by a beautiful analogy, the forces of our spiritual nature would seem to be but instruments and servants of religious growth. Towards this great reservoir, our separate faculties, like confluent streams, are ever bearing the treasures collected in their onward flow. The last results of science are religious. The physical inquirer tortures nature with his apparatus, and by mathematical subtlety or logical precision extorts the physical law inwoven in material facts. The aim of all his studies and experiments is to discover the relations between outward objects, the rational ties hidden from the senses, and revealed only to patient observation and laborious thought. Facts are nothing to him, except as he may dispose and classify them; they are valueless, if he be not capable of reducing them to order, and of discovering the plan which they imply. He would translate the hieroglyphics of the outward world into the clear and simple language of the intellect. It is evident, therefore, that the labors of the scientific student do not end with the success and progress of his own branch of study. Incidentally, but really, religion is aided also. The better portion of his discoveries is transferred directly to her immediate sphere. Our acquaintance with the Deity is extended and enlarged by every triumph of law over confusion ; purer conceptions of his wisdom are awakened in us, as evidences of design and skill are detected and unravelled in the minutest facts of being. There is hardly a tenet of the Christian Scriptures that has not been unfolded or confirmed by the researches of science. Copernicus, and Kepler, and Newton, and La Place, by enlarging our views of the grandeur of the universe, have furnished us with something like a scale for measuring the grandeur of the Deity. Modern Astronomy has set at rest the question as to the Unity of the First Cause, and has added an awful significance to the sentence of the Saviour, 'God is a spirit.' Modern Chemistry has proved the omnipresence of the Eternal Mind ; and all the sciences united, with an admirable harmony and common friendship for religion, by the innumerable instances which they unfold of benevolent adaption and arrangement in the forces of the world, point to the testimony of nature for His goodness and His love.

Philosophy, too, like science, has aided us in forming our conceptions of the nature and charac-

6

ter of God. As the movements of human history have been examined by a critical eye, it has been found that there, also, are law and foresight and benevolent design. The same grand despotism that holds in check the forces of physical nature, governs at.the centre of the spiritual universe. We cannot find a more splendid argument for the providence of God, than that revealed in the establish-ment of the laws of the moral world. The metaphysician and moralist, too, have discovered in our inner nature, in the delicate mechanism of conscience and our affections, proofs of a relationship with God that trembles on the very verge of the divine paternity.

Beauty is no exception to this general law of mental cultivation. Progress in æsthetics leads to the same result. Religion is still the summit to which we rise by the severer road of truth, or through the more pleasant and flowery paths of taste. But the progress of æsthetic culture seems to be more intimately associated with the health and purity of our spiritual nature. Not only, as in the case of science and philosophy, does our acquaintance with the laws of beauty, and a familiarity with its forms, react upon, and refine, and extend the sphere of religious ideas, but the very perception of beauty is assisted and quickened by the purity of religious feelings. This will be apparent if we will consider, for a moment, in what the essence of the beautiful consists.

Modern inquiry has greatly simplified this question. The theory of a separate sense, to which the impressions from external objects are addressed, and which decides upon the degree of beauty revealed in their construction, is now very generally abandoned. The diversity of judgments, even among refined critics, as to the existence of beauty in the same class of objects, is fatal to it. If there were an organ in the structure of our sensitive nature, referring simply to objective elements of beauty and specially adapted to that quality in things, as the eye refers to light, and is adapted to the laws of light, a greater uniformity of tastes would inevitably result. At any rate, similar cultivation would tend to reconcile the primitive differences in the judgments of different minds. However the intensity or strength of the organ might vary with age, or circumstances, or careful training; still, like the optic nerve, its delicate fibres would respond immediately to the presence of its exciting cause. Yet we often see that an object beautiful to one person is absolutely painful, or disgusting, to another of equal cultivation. Our estimate of beauty varies, too, with our states of mind, our bodily health, or the circumstances of our present position. Indeed, with respect to objects which elicit from different temperaments, even, a common judgment as to the presence of beauty, we may find the widest disagreement as to the quality that makes them beautiful, the evidence on which the separate decisions rest.

For the same reason, it is found that the theory

that refers the essence of beauty to certain mathematical lines, or peculiar conformations of matter
and adjustment of parts, to delicacy of construction
or softness of coloring, cannot be sustained. It is
not warranted by sound induction. The theory is
not broad enough, and does not cover all the facts
in the case. It may gratify our love of system, but
it sadly perplexes a healthy logic. In the distribu-
tion of beauty, nature exhibits inexhaustible resources and grand impartiality. If we define beauty, and limit it to one line or form, she denies the
definition by presenting an opposite form which reveals the same magical essence. A flower is beautiful, but so is a crystal; a bird, and also a shaft of
granite; a painting, and besides a proposition in
metaphysics. The standard of beauty can be nothing less than 'the entire circuit of natural forms, —
the totality of nature.' Any attempt to bind its essence by sensual or mathematical bonds is worse
than useless. The essence is universal; all definitions must be particular, dogmatic, and exclusive.
Our theory of beauty must be more flowing and
flexible, offering no harsh obstructions to the varied
movements of the goddess, but bending to all the
caprices of her will, and revealing every posture of
her graceful form.

Such a theory we have in the Catholic doctrine,
now generally received among men of taste, that
beauty always is ideal, the expression of mental
qualities, the reflection of spiritual truths. The
contests of all partial sects with regard to its secret

essence, are reconciled by showing that every sect
is right, and all sects wrong; right in what each
affirms, wrong in what all deny. Things are beautiful which recall, suggest, or create a pleasing emotion, in proportion as they are linked with the
affections or desires or hopes of the human heart.
That organic pleasure which the senses feel in presence of harmonious construction and symmetrical
arrangement is not the ultimate charm which interests and attracts the soul. These are the channels
of beauty, often the signs of its lurking presence,
but never the mystery itself. We cannot suppose
that the organs of the brute creation are charmed
before a well-porportioned temple, or a graceful
form, or the movements of a flying bird. The sensible impression, in its integrity, addresses them
equally with us, but they do not possess the key to
unlock the secret treasure. This is the prerogative
of man. He is connected with the universe by
spiritual ties; he alone is related to it by finer laws
than those of gravitation and chemistry and magnetism. That which we call beauty, depends solely
on the associations which cluster around objects in
our minds, thus dignifying them with intellectual
grace, and raising them to a relationship with human
nature. As Coleridge has well expressed it, —

> " We receive but what we give,
> And in our life alone does nature live."

Our spirits are the urns that sprinkle beauty on the
world. It is a sweet riddle which our purer nature

must resolve. Young stated, with admirable precision, the true theory of beauty in those lines, —

> " Objects are but the occasion; ours th' exploit:
> Ours is the cloth, the pencil, and the paint,
> Which nature's admirable picture draws,
> And beautifies creation's ample dome.
> But for the magic organ's powerful charm,
> Earth were a rude, uncolored chaos still.
> Like Milton's Eve, when gazing on the lake,
> Man makes the matchless image man admires."

It is plain, therefore, that, since the very perception of beauty implies a spiritual nature, the exercise and development of the taste for beauty must, in a great degree, react upon our spiritual condition. If we owe the power to that inherent dignity that separates us from the brutes, the growth of the power must elevate us still higher in the scale of being. And so we find that beauty leads us gently to a purer sphere. Religion is aided and quickened by every habit and association which strengthens our spiritual relations and raises us above a sensual view of the world in which we live. Beauty spiritualizes the very objects of the senses, investing them with a certain moral meaning.

> " Fancy is the power
> That first unsensualizes the dark mind,
> Giving it new delights."

It raises the material universe to a higher power, and makes the varied forms of nature hieroglyphics of thought, petrified or incarnate truths. As science has detected the presence of life in every atom of the outer world, and proved that inorganic matter is baptized in spiritual laws, so the imagination has discovered that nature is also permeated with a delicate significance that can be measured and appreciated only by the affections of our hearts.

This intimate relation between beauty and our religious nature will assist us to solve a difficult question which has been raised among modern critics. It has been objected to the theory of the beautiful stated above, that it destroys the existence of any *real* beauty. By making it depend solely on some individual associations, we take from it all substantive character, and make it always *relative* to the sensitive nature, the capricious disposition, or unhealthy state, perhaps, of the percipient. Of course, by the terms of that theory, we cannot expect unity of judgment upon the degree of beauty in an object, as we expect unity upon a proposition in Euclid, or a problem in algebra. But it does not follow that, on this account, beauty is accidental and has no law. On the contrary, we believe that it does obey an infallible law. Always, in its present form, it is religious; and the varying estimates of different tastes are graduated according to the purity of the religious conceptions involved. In the last analysis, beauty is one with truth, and both are written in cipher, which the religious sense alone can interpret and resolve. The significance of things is definite; but it is revealed to us according to a sliding scale, of which religious culture measures the degrees. It is, indeed, our light thrown upon nature which interprets beauty; but if that light be religious, finer elements will become apparent, and beauty become more clear. It is sympathy with the outward universe that unlocks its treasures; that sympathy is born of religion, and is strengthened and deepened by every accession of spiritual life. To the mind of God, undoubtedly, every fact in the material world has a fixed significance, a precise and definite value. The universe is his art, and struggles to express the crystallized and imprisoned thoughts which he has written there. A delicate correspondence connects every beast and bird and tree and flower with some type of thought, or passion, or emotion, present in the Creator's mind at their formation, and of which they are the organized exponents. But we rise towards, and appreciate so much of this infinite art as the purity of our inner life can gauge. Likeness to the divine nature only will admit us to the secrets of the divine mind. The most stubborn matter is plastic and ductile and fluid to the religious sense. All the changing degrees of significance, which the objective world assumes, from that feeling of health and buoyancy and animal enjoyment which the lowest minds experience in a clear and bracing morning air, to the unfathomable inspiration of the poet and the artist, are determined by its presence and its purity. It is to cultivated religious minds alone, that "the laws of moral nature answer to those of matter as face to face in a glass."

The truth of this position cannot be shaken by any seeming contradiction of experience or history.

Raffaelle may paint finer pictures than Channing, by assiduous culture, could even imitate ; but the finer sympathy with nature, the purer delight in her companionship, and deeper suggestions from her inexhaustible stores of truth, will visit the soul of him who has drunk deeper of the elements of moral life. There are few of us that cannot verify this by our experience. The growth of every spiritual mind attests the fact that nature sympathizes with religious progress. Not while our souls remain steeped in sensuality, or fettered by dull and sordid cares, will come the revelations that are hidden in the universe. The lilies of the field have no meaning to the cold eye of avarice, but to the warm spirit of Jesus, they reflect the doctrine of universal Providence. And so, with us, it is in moments of calmer meditation, in seasons of quiet prayer, or after a noble deed, that the awakened energies of our inner life spontaneously interpret the oracles of nature.

> " With an eye made quiet by the power
> Of harmony, and the deep power of joy,
> We *see into* the life of things."

And thus, where we least expected it, we find that law exists. Beauty always is relative to our state of mind, and depends, to us, upon our state of mind. But it has also a definite and objective existence that reveals itself according to our piety and virtue.

There is a certain vagueness which accompanies the purest perceptions of beauty that is intimately associated with religious feelings, and is eminently calculated to foster and sustain them. In our better moments, the inspiration we derive from nature comes in the shape of suggestions and unfathomable intimations, and hints that are inexpressible in the poverty of speech. And thus, by communion with the outward world, the sentiment of reverence is continually quickened and refreshed. While standing before the sea, for instance, the dim thoughts that rise, half-formed and vague within the mind, and die before they are born in the clear light of definite consciousness, suggest to us a grandeur which the scene does not exhaust, of which it is rather but a faint and momentary type. Logic cannot estimate the significance of the ocean in its periods of sublimer strength. The grandeur before us carries us away in meditation on a more awful power; insensibly, from the sublime we are led up to the infinite; an unconscious instinct leads us to muse upon Him in whom alone our ideas of grandeur find repose; and thus we are elevated from material forms to the home of eternal beauty in the mind of God. There is the same indefinable, untranslatable, and perpetually expanding meaning in the stars. Astrology has sprung from it, and they have been supposed to influence human life, and to unlock the secret of human destiny. They have inspired every poet that has written, and yet their tale is not half told. For every condition of spirit they have a ready sympathy, and even in our day, they remain our truest teachers. It is because " the blue sky in which the private earth is buried, — the sky with its eternal calm, and full of everlasting orbs, is the type of reason." A man troubled with doubts, or weary with thought, or faint at heart, has only to gaze upon the heavens in the midnight silence, and a religious awe returns upon the soul, and a strength refreshes every spiritual fibre that is akin to Christian faith. What is it on a moonlight night that "inundates the air" with beauty, that thrills our frame with emotions too fine for utterance, that heaves our spirit with an inspiration before which all words are weak? The spell resides not in the light or air; it is the spirit of religion streaming through material channels, and stirring with a quicker flow the pulses of the soul. The silence of the summer woods is burdened with the same mysterious power. A solemnity broods over them, as though God had preceded us in our walk, and our presence had intruded on the intense and silent worship of the trees. Even in human art, the same vagueness, the same mystery connects beauty with the religious sense. Persons of uncultivated taste instinctively uncover in presence of a statue or a finished painting by a master. It is the unconscious confession of our nature that the marble and the canvas are organs and revelations of truths that belong to the ideal world, before which it is profane to speak too loud, or to stand with irreverent and idle curiosity.

Beauty, too, is linked with religion in another way; it is medicinal. The foe of guilt and sin, it would ever win us back to purity and love. The universe is in league with virtue. No man comes

fresh from sin into the presence of the joyful fields,
or within hearing of the birds, who feels not rebuked
by a gentle influence that arouses the life of conscience, and prompts him to repentance and return.
Calmly we listen, and yield our minds to the sooth-
ing charm, until

> " we stand,
> Adore, and worship, when we know it not;
> Pious beyond the intention of our thought;
> Devout above the meaning of our will."

Nothing but innocence can harmonize with nature,
and, to the guilty heart, she sends the eloquent warning and the balm of peace.

> " Some souls love all things but the love of beauty,
> And by that love they are redeemable;
> For in love and beauty they acknowledge good."

Seeing, thus, that beauty is connected by so many
ties with religious life, we are prepared to solve the
question as to its relation to Christianity. We have
only to study the history of literature and art to
discover that every form or theory of religion has
exercised a powerful sway over mental cultivation.
It would seem that the laws of national progress are
written always in the national faith. By the conceptions of God and duty and providence and immortality, the depth of all philosophy, the spirituality of all art, the soundness of all literature, can
alone be graduated. The beauties, the limits, and
the defects of the Greek religion were plainly written
in Grecian poetry and statuary and architecture.
Indian art and literature sprang, very evidently,

from the Brahmin philosophy and faith, the ideas of which, however, they vainly struggled to reveal. The massiveness and sullen grandeur of the Egyptian temples is easily explained by studying the Egyptian views of God and worship and human destiny. Religion cannot relieve itself from the dignity, nor from the obligation, of being the teacher of the race. This pretension is found in Christianity. On every page of the Christian revelation it is clearly written, or implied, that our religion is final; and it furnishes the true law of individual growth and the only code of social progress and perfection. Its promise is, to furnish for the world a system of universal education. Of course, in this scheme of training, the essential element of beauty cannot be neglected. Provision must be made for that, else the justice of the claim is at once removed, its legislation becomes partial, and an intestine war springs up between the religious creed of Christ and the æsthetic wants of man.

Christianity, we believe, has amply redeemed its promise. A new age began with Jesus, of which there are other signs than the calendar, deeper records than the alteration of our dates. His holy life changed something more than the religious creed of the universe. Follow back all the streams of modern cultivation through the gloom of ages, and, in spite of seeming deviations, and the temporary divergence of their tortuous channels, they approach at last, and, mingling their separate currents into one, lead us, with a silent and solemn and

half-conscious instinct, to the foot of the cross.
Christ is at the head of modern philosophy and
modern literature and art. He refreshed the weary
imagination as well as the languid faith of the world.
How plainly can we trace the influence of the Christian system in unfolding the elements of ideal
beauty! The fine arts in modern times may not
rival the ancient masterpieces in formal beauty, but
their sphere has been enlarged, and their inspiration
drawn from deeper sources. The passions and feelings at the command of the ancient artist were few
and simple, for the most part belonging to the physical relations of mankind; and to the narrowness of
his circuit, may, undoubtedly, be ascribed much of
his success. To modern painting and statuary have
been offered the nobler sentiments of piety and
faith and love ; affections that have a deeper significance, and which, by their very purity, and their
relations to the Infinite, are less easily subdued to
bonds of stone, or the finer slavery of colors. It
surely cannot be heresy to say that the Madonna
of Raffaele exhibits a higher and purer sense of
beauty than the face of the Venus ; or that Gothic
architecture, with its thousand faults, sprang from
a lower deep in human nature than the more perfect
symmetry of the Grecian temples. We can be just
to classic models, and the ancient taste, without
being unjust to the merits or meaning of modern
art. And such a judgment is only to say that
Christian feelings are higher than the sources from
which Grecian taste borrowed its ideas of grace ; it

is only to assert that spiritual beauty is purer than regularity of features or symmetry of form; it is only to confess that heathen mythology is inferior to the purity of our simple faith; it is only to declare that the face of the Apollo, the clearest revelation of ancient moral beauty, that perfect incarnation of lofty scorn, a self-conscious elegance and self-satisfied repose, is, after all, less elevating in its influence upon the artist, and less inspiring to our better nature, than the face of Jesus, refined by religious love, spiritualized by holy sorrow, lighted by unshaken hope, and turned to heaven with a look, not of haughty satisfaction and self-dependence, but of serene and chastened confidence and humble prayer. That face, as we all picture it in our imagination when we understand the real depths of his nature and his character, is the modern ideal of moral beauty. Elements of spiritual loveliness, beyond the conception of the Grecian masters, are collected and centred there. It is the rich endowment of Christianity to the stores of imagination. And, whatever destiny may be reserved for modern art, it is evident that its productions refer to a higher faith than the Greek religion, and that for it, a mightier magician than the ancient priest, has smitten the rock of humanity with a more potent rod, unsealing its deepest springs of feeling and religious life.

Especially may we see this in modern poetry. For everything which gives it a distinctive character, it is dependent on Christianity. The deeper elements of modern tragedy have been borrowed from the purer' revelations of duty through the Saviour, the new revelation which his religion brought of human destiny, and the higher sanctions it imposed on virtue. Hamlet's restless longing, and continually flying ideal of life, are Christian. It is by Christian light that we look down, with such deep emotions of tragic delight, the ecstacy of awe, into the ravines of human nature, the chasms and abysses of human will opened to us in Macbeth. And even in that beautiful imitation of the ancient models, faultless in diction, around which is thrown such tragic horror, and yet such witchery of grace, in Talfourd's Ion, we cannot help feeling that the unities have, after all, been somehow violated; that a little of Christianity has crept into Argos before the time; and, that the finest passages were inspired, not by Greek philosophy, but by the purer element of Christian love.   .

And not alone by purifying moral beauty has Christianity assisted the poetic art; it has altered the significance of nature. Between natural beauty and our religion, there is a sympathy equally apparent. The doctrines of Christianity were caught by the Saviour from the outward world. His finer sense appreciated its hidden meaning; his ear was bent in reverence, and caught the faintest whisper from her mystic oracles. The flowers revealed their doctrine of universal Providence; he followed back the rain to its source in the fountains of Divine benevolence; he analyzed the sunlight, and unravelled from it the splendid truth of God's impartial love. And ever since, has the spirit of Christianity been drawing men into a nearer sympathy with nature and a more intimate communion with her hidden life. The perception of this spiritual sense in the outward universe is now the surest gauge of poetic inspiration. In vain shall we look for it in the elder poets and dramatists. There are fine descriptions of natural scenery in Homer; splendid imagery in the Greek tragedies; and exquisite personifications of physical forces; but nowhere a perception of that delicate bond that binds the outward world to man. Between "Prometheus Vinctus" and the Prometheus Unbound," there is all the difference that separates two civilizations. Shelley was no professed believer, he could not throw off the *unconscious* Christianity that lay around his genius like the air, nourishing his creations with different sustenance, and informing them with a deeper meaning than Æschylus could draw from Greek mythology. The Christian revelation has extended the feeling of brotherhood to all the powers that constitute the life of nature. It would seem that the boldest speculations of modern science, which tell us that men have risen by gradual development from inorganic matter, are hinted there, and therefore is it that, in our better moments we feel such intense and silent sympathy with the fettered consciousness and imprisoned feeling of our former state. This is the soul of the best modern poetry; and it is wholly religious, wholly Christian. How have the best minds of our century

7

striven to grasp the depth of natural beauty!
Wordsworth hears in the outward world

> " The still, sad music of humanity."

In his periods of deeper communion with nature,
he confesses the feeling of

> " A presence that disturbs me with the joy
> Of elevated thoughts; a sense sublime
> Of something far more deeply interfused,
> Whose dwelling is the light of setting suns,
> And the round ocean, and the living air,
> And the blue sky, and in the mind of man."

Beauty reveals to him, besides the sensible impressions, —

> " Authentic tidings of invisible things;
> Of ebb and flow, and ever-during power,
> And central peace, subsisting at the heart
> Of endless agitation."

Shelley's refined and spiritual perception can only
catch

> " The awful shadow of some unseen power
> Floating unseen among us. · · · · ·
> Dear and yet dearer for its mystery."

Mr. Bailey asks, in Festus, —

> " How can beauty of material things
> So win the heart, and work upon the mind,
> Unless like natured with them? *Are great things
> And thoughts of the same blood? They have like effect.*"

And Mr. Emerson, despite the keenness of his
glance, which generally interprets the finest shades
of consciousness, waits for the coming of a greater

master, who shall express what he dimly feels, and show " that the *ought*, that duty is one with science, *with beauty*, and with joy." Thus do we find that Christianity accepts and sanctions the idea with which we started, — that beauty is associated with religious culture by the influence it has exerted in every department of the sphere of taste, assisting us to see more clearly that beauty is one with truth, and that of both religion is the highest manifestation and central bond.

IV.

GREAT PRINCIPLES AND SMALL DUTIES.

It is a beautiful fact in the ethics of the gospel, that great principles do not require great occasions for their exercise and exhibition. The spirit of Christianity teaches us, both by verbal precept and through the embodied eloquence of the Saviour's character, that it is the highest office of great principles to dignify the common experience of men: they are manifested best in trifling acts; they raise the level of daily life to a higher elevation, and reveal their active presence most completely in homely and familiar duties. "Whosoever," said Jesus, "shall give to drink unto one of these little ones a cup of cold water only, in the name of a disciple, verily I say unto you, he shall in nowise lose his reward." We intend to follow out the thought suggested in that passage into some of its present applications to men.

It is not unusual, in our time, to hear complaints of the meanness of modern life. There are many who mourn that existence has become so dull and mechanical. There is no charm, no healthy excitement, no beauty in the common experience of the world around us; nothing to feel an aspiring, imaginative, poetic mind. Everything is prosaic now: the spirit of business, omnipresent, all-active, and omnipotent, has reduced life to square and rule. Surprise, romance, and heroism, have been banished from existence. The stern utilitarian tendencies of the present have degraded life to a lower pláne, and, by connecting society in the simplest relations, and thus bringing men under the dominion of obvious and easy duties, have made experience flat, monotonous, and insipid. Those persons are not few, whose minds are restless under the unpoetic aspect of the life we live ; whose ideal is borrowed from novel pictures, or from the dramatic side of history ; and who, if their imagination is kept alive, lapse into melancholy, sentimental languor, acquire a distaste for all the burdens and duties of our daily existence, and delude themselves with the idea, that they are above their age, of finer mould than their coarse contemporaries, born out of season, ill-appreciated by their dull companions.

All that looks attractive to such minds is seen in the past, or is expected from the future. The present is but a half-built bridge, loaded with the rubbish of degrading toil, which has drawn us away from the Elysium behind, and not yet permitted us to reach the Eden before. The time óf Cæsar, the age of chivalry, or of the Reformation, or of Shakspeare ; the lives of men like Napoleon, or Washington, or Howard, who lived on a large scale, and whose deeds arrest the attention and fill the eye by

their grandeur, seem to them the only desirable
epochs, the only true and worthy lives. Such eras
and such fortunes alone should satisfy the ambition,
the dignity, the ideal, of an aspiring mind. Beside
them, the scenes, the duties, the life o to-day, look
mean and barren.

We have the authority of the gospel to assure us
that such is a false estimate, a mistaken view of life.
It is vitiated by a double error. It is a false estimate,
in the first place, because it attributes an unreal
value to the kind of life by which it is so powerfully
charmed. The grandeur and beauty of such a
seemingly poetic existence are much enhanced by
contemplating them at a distance. Nearness removes
most of the gorgeous hues; the tinsel and glitter
would soon grow wearisome ; familiarity would make
all look poor and mean. It is the creative imagination that weaves the charm. Mountains in the distance, with the rich haze upon them, to soften and
spiritualize and refine their outlines, or when gilded
with the glory of the morning, or the luxury of the
evening light, look tempting and beautiful, fit for
the common residence of gods. But when we visit
them, the spell is broken ; they are rocky, rugged,
cold, and barren ; it tires our limbs to climb their
steep ascents ; we gladly escape from their uninviting sides, to the common, customary comforts of our
less showy and poetic homes. And so with those
tempting circumstances for which so many sigh.
Once attained, we should be no more satisfied with
life. Habit would socn destroy the glossy lustre.

The society of courts, *daily intercourse* with kings and emperors and heroes would soon pall the spirit, and convince it that a worthier, more noble existence must be found to satisfy the craving, grasping soul.

And this romantic estimate of life is false, too, not only because it overrates the charm of its favorite mode, but radically false because it overlooks the object and aim of life, the destiny of the soul. Christianity advises us that we were placed in the world to develop character, to unfold our powers, to grow in moral strength. It is the final purpose of the soul, not to be an ornament merely to some great occasion, not to make a show, not to live on the stage as an actor, dressed in ribbons and spangles, but to be educated, to put forth its strength, to live in accordance with the great principles of duty and and right. Here lies the error in all poetic and overwrought imaginative views of the world. Man was not created for some dazzling end ; but for culture, continual, steady, moral power. The sun was not placed in the heavens to inflame and awe the imagination of men, to spout cataracts of fire, and blaze fitfully, with a grand, poetic splendor, but to radiate an even heat, and call forth continually the energies of dependent planets, by the unvaried bounty of its beams. It fulfils its destiny at every moment, by a life of constant use. It is so with man. The attainment of our destiny is not reached by any particular form of life, but by continual development and unwearied use. We were not made for such or such a good, but for perpetual culture. We must not hope to live at some future time, at some more favorable period, at the end of the next week or the next year, when we have retired from business, or have removed, perhaps, from the city. There are no divisions of periods, no stopping-places, where we may change our raiment and begin to live. The existence is in each moment, however and wherever it may find us; the journey's end is in every step of the road.

The moral beauty of Christianity is seen in this: that it reveals the grandeur of common life and humble virtues, that it throws an infinite value into the smallest actions, that it transfers our gaze from the scale of the deed to the spirit of the deed, that it makes the circumstances of small account, and the motive all; showing us that a cup of cold water, given in the name of a disciple, and from the impulse of love, will bring the disciple's reward.. It shows us that great principles are tested best by the performance of small duties, and that the spiritual development, which is the real end of life, is better attained by continual discipline, than by great achievements.

We estimate life aright, we understand its dignity and its toil, only when we judge it by this Christian standard. The aim of the gospel is to perfect character; and a noble character is revealed in little deeds, and is attained only by discipline and triumphs in common, habitual trials. We ought not to suffer moral judgments to be blinded by the glare of circumstances and scenes. It is easier than we imagine to become a martyr; to die calmly in defence of right when the world is look- ing on, when we are a spectacle to the crowded am- phitheatre of the universe, to an audience of angels and men, and when hope of escape is dead. It is noble — godlike, if you please to call it so — to triumph then ; but it is not the most unerring test of greatness and strength of soul. That is the purest greatness and the firmest strength which overcomes the toughest obstacles to a lofty and holy life ; and those obstacles, every practical Christian will confess, are the little cares and trifling per- plexities and incessant temptations of daily experi- ence. These are the gnats that worry the sturdiest virtue. Goliah was proof against a steel-clad ar- ray, but not against the despicable weapon, David's sling ; and many a moral giant has fallen before as puny an attack. "The finest sense, the profoundest knowledge, the most unquestionable taste, often prove an unequal match for insignificant irrita- tions ; and a man whose philosophy subdues nature, and whose force of thought and purpose gives him ascendancy over men, may keep, in his own temper, an unvanquished enemy at home."

It is easier to fulfil the greatest than the smallest task. It is easier to perform the moral deed which the world must witness than to crush the small temptation which comes in our private hours, invit- ing to a little sin which the world can never know. He is the moral hero — how few who can challenge the title ! — that can resist the almost harmless impulse of selfishness, like that which prompted the mind of Christ to turn the stones to bread ; who can go through the day and feel that he has been faithful to every call of every moment, and has lived in Christian relations with every man whom he has met. And, therefore, small duties are the real test of power. You cannot know a man's temper in company; see him at home. You cannot judge his piety at church ; observe him through the business hours of a single day. You cannot infer his benevolence from his public charities and large subscriptions; watch his intercourse with the poor. It is the frequent gifts, yes, it is the *manner* of giving, more than the charity, the sweet expression, the cordial sympathy, the tone of kindness, which makes the penny of more value then the coldly given pound ; it is these, and the frequency of these, that determine the purity and love of a person's soul.

The common complaints of almost every person, our incessant quarrels with our fortune and lot, attest the value and difficulty of these small duties, and show us that the performance of them alone is the surest sign of moral vigor. "How gentle should we be, if we were not provoked ; how pious, if we were not busy ! the sick would be patient, only he is not in health; the obscure would do great things, only he is not conspicuous ! " It is the great soul only which does not quarrel with its tools, but relies upon its skill. It is the noblest character that can be gentle in provocation, and pious in business, and patient in sickness, and faithful to the humble duties of obscurity. Beauty of soul, like the beauty of a statue, results from the complete symmetry of the smallest parts; and it is minute care and perpetual discipline alone that can bring the spirit to that standard, and which reveal the Master's hand. " Why waste time on such trifles?" said a friend to Michael Angelo, who consumed weeks in the finish of a muscle and the form of an ear. " It is these trifles that constitue perfection," — replied the artist, — " and perfection is no trifle."

They have strangely mistaken life, then, who sigh for propitious or more poetic circumstances, in order to give it dignity. Let them endeavor to live a single day in the privacy of their own homes, obedient to the Christian law of life, and they will learn how needless are all trappings to make a martyr or a hero. For the keenest intellect that ever thought, for the finest genius that ever refreshed the heart of the world, it is a virtue sufficiently arduous, it is a moral triumph brilliant enough to keep the hours true, to fulfil the obligations of daily life, to refrain from slander, to be resigned in sorrow, and to remember the poor. It was said of the great orator and philosopher, Edmund Burke, that a stranger could not stand under a shed with him for five minutes, during a summer shower, without knowing he was in company with a great genius. The power of the man would reveal itself in his casual talk. The die of his intellect was stamped even on his insignificant coin. And so the purity, the power, of a trained and vigorous virtue, depends not on the occasion, but will disclose itself in the slightest and most trivial act. We may not all be Alexanders. His genius was no merit of his; but we may do what, with all that genius, he could not do, — and that is, keep sober and preserve an even temper. We may not be gifted with the intellect of Bacon; but, nobler than Bacon, we may keep our honor pure, and never betray a friend. We cannot become Napoleons; but, in the private walks of life, we may acquire strength to do what the hero of Marengo and Lodi was unable to accomplish, — always to tell the truth. Their *genius* performed their miracles; *they* fell before the plain and simple demands of duty. Truly, Solomon was right: " He that is slow to anger is better than the mighty, and he that ruleth his spirit than he that taketh a city."

We may learn a beautiful lesson on the moral worth of small duties by observing the method of nature, — the wisdom of God in the outward world. Perfection, in nature, is not measured on the scale of magnificence, but by the quality of the work. We cannot exhaust the analogies between nature and the gospel, they are so completely in harmony; and we may say, that the whole universe is the intellectual statement and explanation of the morality of Jesus; — the value of the trivial fact is an expression of the great principle. Men of science are continually surprised to find how the most astonishing results are

crowded into and implied in the narrowest compass. "The whole code of natural laws may be
written on the thumb-nail, or the signet of a ring."
Examine the structure and observe the growth of
a single wild violet, and it will be seen that every
force of the universe, and the vast mechanism
of the heavens, are necessary to the development
of its simple life.   Astronomy and geology and
chemistry 'are all written in its fibres, buds, and
stem.   The roots of it strike deeper into the heart
of nature than into the soil from which it springs.
It lives by the action of laws that are equally essential to the existence of the great globe itself.
It is watered by rain, drawn from the treasures of
the ocean; its nightly blessing of dew is distilled
from the atmosphere which supports all animated
life; it is held firmly in its place by the all-pervading force that gives stability to the architecture
of the sky; it is expanded into beauty by the
warm stream of life that weaves its tissue around
the solar system,—burning on Mercury, and carrying his dim day to distant Saturn.   And thus
the whole universe exists as an inference, a corollary of one simple flower.

Dig a flint from the bosom of the mountain;
and, when it is broken, its sides will reveal to the
microscope the fire which hardened it and the
waters through which it passed, the convulsions
and catastrophes it has known, and the fossil ani-
malcules which it holds; showing us that the history of the great globe may be deduced from the

experience and changes of that single pebble. From a solitary scale of a fish, found petrified in a stone, the naturalist has reconstructed its whole frame, has announced that it belonged to a species become extinct, has stated the kind and temperature of the waters in which alone it could have lived, and so again has discovered, in that tiny vestige, the secret of thè geological epochs. If we go to nature for our morals, we shall leàrn the necessity of perfection in the smallest act. Infinite skill is not exhausted nor concentrated in the structure of a firmament, in drawing the orbit of a planet, in laying the strata of the earth, in rearing the mountain cone. The care for the bursting flower is as wise as the forces displayed in the rolling star; the smallest leaf that falls and dies unnoticed in the forest is wrought with a beauty as exquisite as the skill displayed in the sturdy oak. All the wisdom of nature is compressed and revealed in the sting of the bee; and the pride of human art is mocked by the subtile mechanism and cunning structure of a fly's foot and wing. However minute the task, it reveals the polish of perfection. Omnipotent skill is stamped on the infinitely small, as on the infinitely great. It is a moral stenography like this which we need in daily life. We attain the summit of Christian excellence, when we obey the instructions of nature, and learn, in the common acts of every day, to manifest the beauty of a spiritual character, — to leave in trifling duties the impress of a noble soul, — to reflect on common life the radiance of a pure and holy nature, — to make a cup of cold water, daily given to the suffering in the spirit of love, testify, with eloquent emphasis, to the grace and health and beauty of our general existence.

The lesson of Christianity, then, urged and enforced by nature, is the inestimable worth of common duties, as manifesting the greatest principles; it bids us attain perfection, not by striving to do dazzling deeds, but by making our experience divine; it tells us that the Christian hero will ennoble the humblest field of labor; that nothing is mean which can be performed as duty; but that religious virtue, like the touch of Midas, converts the humblest call of conscience into spiritual gold.

The Greek philosopher, Plato, has left an instructive and beautiful poetic picture of the judgment of souls, when they had been collected from the regions of temporary bliss and pain, and suffered once more to return to the duties and pleasures of earthly life. The spirits advanced by lot, to make their choice of the condition and form under which they should reënter the world. The dazzling and showy fortunes, the lives of kings and warriors and statesmen were soon exhausted; and the spirit of Ulysses, who had been the wisest prince among all the Greeks, came last to choose. He advanced with sorrow, fearing that his favorite condition had been selected by some more fortunate soul who had gone before him. But, to his surprise and pleasure, Ulysses found that the only life which had not been chosen was the lot of an obscure and private man, with its humble cares and quiet joys; the lot which he, the wisest, would have selected, had his turn come first; the life for which he longed, since he had felt the folly and meanness of station, wealth, and power.

In like manner, though in a far different spirit, Christianity teaches us the beauty and dignity of common and private life. It makes it valuable, not as Plato did, for the cares from which it frees us, but for the constant duties through which we may train the soul to perfect symmetry and power. It shows us that the humblest lot brings calls and opportunities which require all the energies of the most exalted virtue to meet and satisfy. It teaches us that, "in the management and conquest of the daily disappointments and small vexations which befall every life, only a devout mind attains to any real success, and evinces a triumphant might." It impresses upon us the solemn truth, that life itself, however humble its condition, is always holy; that every moment has its duty and its burden, which Christian strength alone, the crown of power, can do and bear; and that the perfect character is the character of Jesus, who fulfilled the greatest mission in the humblest walk, and showed to the world that the simplest experience may become radiant with a heavenly beauty, when hallowed by a spirit of constant love to God and man.

V.

PLATO'S VIEWS OF IMMORTALITY.[1]

It is our desire to define in this article, as fully
as our limits will allow, and as clearly as the nature
of the subject and our own ability will permit, the
views of Plato upon immortality, with particular
reference to his doctrine concerning the condition of
the soul in its disembodied state. It would seem
to be an important acquisition to our knowledge,
if we could understand thoroughly the faith, and
appreciate the hopes, of a mind like that of the first
among Greek philosophers, — a mind which had
attained probably the perfection of heathen culture, and whose intellectual development may be
assumed, therefore, to be the goal and limit of
uninspired thought. But the difficulties are proportioned to the interest of the task. We are not
acquainted with any exhaustive examination of the
question, and the conflicting results of commentators only perplex the mind, giving us no assurance,

[1] The materials for the present article are mostly drawn from Cousin's French Translation of Plato's Dialogues, in thirteen volumes, Paris
edition; and the references, accordingly, are made to that work, as the
best modern version of the Greek philosopher, and probably the easiest
of access to those who are unacquainted with the original.

and little valuable aid. Besides, few subjects offer
more perplexities to criticism than a complete analysis of the Platonic writings for the purpose of unfolding a clear, dogmatic, symmetrical result. It is
exceedingly difficult even to give, in modern terms,
an accurate statement of the leading points of Platonism; and probably the variety of opinions inconsistent and even contradictory, which learned
men have evolved from the words of Plato, can
only find a parallel in the variety of creeds and doctrines, which equally learned and honest critics
have unfolded from the Scriptures. According to
his commentators, Plato becomes a Kantian or an
Eclectic, a Gnostic or a Swedenborgian. His works
form a sort of philosophical kaleidoscope: turned by
one man, Plato appears a modern Orthodox; shifted
again, he is a modern Transcendentalist. Cold-
blooded men, like Mr. Norton, find nonsense in a
dialogue where warm-hearted, poetic spirits, like
the German Ackerman, detect delicate filaments of
the Christian faith; so that it depends very much
on the position and relations of the reviewer,
whether we get a dissertation on Plato the sceptic,
or Plato the polytheist, or Plato the Christian, or
Plato the fool. Even the theory of ideas, which lay
at the base of his speculative system, which is at
once the corner and keystone of his philosophy,
has had almost as many interpretations as interpreters, and remains, to-day, an unexhausted subject
for criticism and dispute. It must be an amusing
task for the spirit of Plato to observe the various

judgments of different thinkers; to see his system, as it passes through different minds, receiving from each a subjective hue and form; to range side by side the motley group of Platonisms which the ages have produced, from the dissertations of the Alexandrian school, who found a mystic sense in every name, and a subtile meaning in the number of interlocutors, to Sewell,[1] who detects in the Republic a dim instinct or nisus as it were of the Church of England, and Mr. Tayler Lewis,[2] who grieves that amid so much gospel doctrine of vindictive punishment and eternal woe, he can find "nothing of that great atonement which forms the basis of the Christian scheme."

The cause of this diversity certainly cannot be attributed to any lack of precision in Plato's terms; for his diction is clear and pure, a transparent medium of thought. The English critic, alluded to above, finding a similar obscurity in the Scriptures, takes occasion to hint, as a solution, that Plato possibly is inspired. If we are not disposed to acquiesce in this opinion, we may find a more probable explanation in the nature and design of Plato's works. Perhaps it is needless to inform our readers that no definite, dogmatic statement of his philosophy was ever given from Plato's pen. His writ-

---

[1] Sewell's Introduction to the Dialogues of Plato; a powerfully written, and *very amusing* book.

[2] Plato against the Atheists, or the Tenth Book of the Laws, with notes, etc., by Tayler Lewis, L.L. D., the last classical development of Orthodoxy.

ings were isolated, and form no organic developed whole. ' They consist chiefly of dialogues upon various topics of morality and religion, through the most of which Socrates is introduced as the central figure, for the purpose of controverting the opinions of others ; himself examining and refuting propositions b7 the use of a rigorous analysis and dialectical skill, but rarely proposing positive opinions of his own, or leaving a definite impression upon the reader's mind.   Plato never speaks in his own person, or with a purely didactic aim. ›He loved the dialogistic method ; he was the greatest artist in composition, probably, that ever lived ; and this form offered a wider scope and less restraint to the range of his taste and powers.   When we consider, therefore, that his dialogues amount to more than thirty ; that many of them were written, seemingly, for no other end than a display of logical acuteness or skill ; that, through their *dramatis personæ*, they embody the opinions of almost every prior and contemporary school ; that some may be intended to represent scenes from the history of Socrates, and develop opinions which Plato did not indorse ; and that they were composed at widely different periods of life, — some running back, probably, to his early youth, and others employing his dying moments in their revision, — we may well suppose that it is a task of no ordinary difficulty to condense and arrange his views into a consistent body of didactic statements and opinions, nicely balanced and scientifically evolved.

Besides, at the very outset of our researches into the real nature of Plato's views, we are met and staggered by the question, — Have we any trusty sources from which to draw his secret doctrines? Are his published writings authentic records of his honest thought? Has he imparted in his dialogues, without reservation, the essence of his views as they existed in his own mind, or as they were delivered to his pupils in the retirement and confidence of his school? This is a point which demands more space for a thorough discussion than we can afford for our whole subject; but, as it is an essential condition to critical success in any department of his system, we must give a few words to it by way of introduction.

From the circumstances of the time, from a few passages of Plato himself, and from the spirit and structure of many of his works, we are convinced that while the great body of the dialogues indicate, hint, and suggest the elements of his philosophy, in no one of them, nor in all of them can we find an entirely unreserved and honest expression of his views. He lived among a people who certainly had not shown a great attachment to innovations on the popular creed. Anaxagoras had been banished and Socrates condemned, for the purity of their speculations and the long-established feud between philosophy and paganism had not sufficiently subsided, to render it safe for any man to evince extraordinary boldness in the domain of morals. A wise prudence was the better rule of war; and Plato had every warning in the fate of his predecessors, to deter him at least from a rashness which would have proved fatal to success. The long life and quiet death of the philosopher would seem themselves to indicate that he used some policy in his public dealing with the popular faith of the time. Moreover, we find in some of his works expressions, which, if rigidly interpreted, forbid us to expect any thorough exposition of his philosophy in written disquisitions. In the Phædrus, for instance, Socrates makes a decided and somewhat lengthy attack upon writing, as a medium for imparting clear and solid knowledge. He labors to show that severe dialectical discourse is the only method of instruction. Written statements can be moulded into any form, according to the reader's mind; they know not with whom to speak, or with whom they should maintain silence; unjustly attacked, or misunderstood, they cannot answer, but, like a weak child, constantly need their father's aid; and therefore the best written compositions are useful merely to awaken reminiscence in the minds of those who know already the subjects of which they treat.[1] The letters of Plato, of which thirteen are left, would seem to be explicit on this point. In the second and seventh he expressly declares that the deepest science cannot be taught in words; that after a pure life of meditation it bursts forth like a spark, like gold becoming pure only after long years and toil, and that every

---

[1] Vol. vi. pp. 123, 124.

man seriously occupied with things so serious, should restrain himself from treating them fully in writings intended for the public.[1] He confesses that his writings are not without merit, but declares that they do not contain that deep and pure science which conversation and reflection alone can bestow. It is proper to state that the genuineness of these letters has been questioned and severely tested by many modern critics. The whole evidence of antiquity, however, is in their favor, and they have been rejected mainly on account of those passages that speak of an esoteric wisdom which the dialogues do not convey.[2]

If we take these declarations of Plato in the sense which probably they require, namely, that no one of his works contains a full and exhaustive treatment of his system, and that in them are many accommodations to popular prejudice and superstition, they

[1] Vol. xiii. Letter 2, p. 61. Letter 7, pp. 96, 100.

[2] Cicero quotes from the fifth and seventh Letters, and in the Tusculan Questions remarks, "Est præclara epistola Platonis ad Dionis propinquos;" also, Ad Atticum, I. xiii. mentions that a certain Hermodorus was accustomed to publish the books of Plato. (See Tennemann's Lehren der Sokratiker über Unsterblichkeit, page 22, note.) Plutarch uses the seventh Letter very freely in his life of Dion; quotes twice from the fourth, and mentions the thirteenth. (See Langhorne's Translation of Plutarch, vol. vii., Life of Dion, pp. 144, 147, 149, and throughout.) Cousin boldly rejects the Letters, although he includes them in his translation of the Dialogues. As in many other cases of critical difficulty, however, he cuts the knot without unloosing it, settling the question by a bold French generalization, an eclectic leap. He calls them "more affected than profound," "superficially Alexandrine," etc. (See Cousin's Plato, vol. xiii., note on page 229.) Boeckh regards the seventh alone as genuine, which is the most important as connected with our question.

are certainly sustained by the evidence of the dialogues themselves. Most of these are plainly intended to be guides and aids in the acquirement of
precise thinking, and the attainment of the dialectic
method of philosophy. They are admirable as hints
and suggestions of truth which they do not state.
They shine with what Heraclitus would call a humid
light. We can account for and explain their artful
obscurity only by keeping in view the Acadamy
where they were more clearly unfolded, or the severity of whose lessons they were perhaps intended
to recall. In different dialogues, opinions entirely
contradictory are unfolded, with seemingly equal
honesty. He speaks at times, too, of the popular
worship in terms of great respect, although the
whole was the antipodes of his own belief. Often
we are led through the most intricate avenues of
metaphysics in chase of a sophism, and frequently,
after tiresome discussions, and when the light seems
ready to break upon our vision, the curtain falls and
the discussion ends. The most important dialogues
close with gorgeous myths drawn either from tradition or the sources of his own rich mind, and through
these, as through a highly-colored transparency, he
throws his light upon the imagination of the reader, impressing by symbols upon the fancy what he
refused to do by words upon the reason. And no
reader, even now, can study his works without confessing with Ast, that " the peculiarity of Plato's
compositions is that he has no peculiarity," that they
are valuable chiefly as exercises in mental gymnas-

tics, to train the mind to habits of patient thought, hinting truths which they will not tell, leading us up ideal heights and refusing at last to be our guide, but pointing the way to higher progress, making us feel indeed that the Platonism which they teach is inferior to the Platonism which they inspire.

Taking this view of the Platonic books, the only one, we believe, capable of explaining them, it is evident that mere verbal or textual criticism cannot succeed as a method of interpretation. It finds itself confused at once with a thousand embarassments.[1] The clew to the Cretan labyrinth, or the solution of the Sphinx's riddle, were easy in comparison. The only proper and successful method is a free, liberal treatment, with a single eye to Plato's method and the general spirit of each piece. Like a tangled skein they yield easily to a loose and patient handling, but if forced or strained at all, become knotted into an inextricable mass.

Especially must we bring this liberal and patient spirit to an examination of Plato's views of the future state. For it is over questions connected with the nature and destiny of the soul that the greatest obscurity is thrown. We might readily suspect it would be so. Upon these points he was brought im-

---

[1] An amusing instance of the beauties of this method may be seen in Mr. Norton's expositions of Plato, scattered throughout vol. iii. of his "Genuineness of the Gospels." The final cause of the spirit that wrote the preface to the "Statement of Reasons" certainly was not to be the expounder of the Greek Transcendentalist.

mediately in contact with the popular religion, and there was great temptation to a guarded and incomplete publication of his opinions. Besides, Plato had a highly poetic mind. He had determined in early youth, previous to meeting Socrates, to devote himself to poetry ; and throughout his works we discover a marked relish for allegories and myths, to which he always turned with eagerness, not only as a relief from the dryness of abstract discussion, but as a medium through which to hint ideas which reason could not grasp. Nothing was better fitted to feed this poetic turn than speculations upon the condition and fate of the dead. It was a question removed beyond the boundaries of science ; revelation had not dispelled the gloom and mystery which lay around the future world ; it offered, therefore, a fit field for the revels of a highly imaginative and spiritual mind. The mythology of his country and of the East, too, was rich in fables illustrative of the future destiny of souls ; and therefore policy, together with the severe temper of his scientific method, compelled him to adopt that allegorical and legendary dress for his speculations, which his poetic genius so dearly loved to weave. The Platonic myths and stories are often contradictory with each other, embracing materials which it is impossible to harmonize by verbal criticism, and thus our only method is a poetic abandonment of mind to the influence of the pictures, rather than a microscopic analysis of words. No two writers whom we have ever consulted agree in their abstract of Plato's

views of immortality; scarcely can one be found
who is entirely consistent with himself. The trouble
has generally arisen from a false or too rash method
of interpretation. It is a hopeless task to extort
the meaning of poetry by logic. "Spiritual things
are spiritually discerned."

In passing, then, to a direct consideration of his
views concerning the soul and its destiny, we must
remark that the writings of Plato form an epoch in
ancient philosophy. Socrates impressed a new tendency on speculation. He brought into use the
psychological method. Before his time the philosophy of Greece was conversant with little else than
physical inquiries, explanations of the origin of the
universe. It was entirely ontological. Speculation
seems to have been lawless, busying itself with the
mysteries connected with the genesis of things, unrestrained and undirected by any rules of scientific
thought. Philosophers were mostly physicists; no
base had been laid for a moral system; science was
dissipated into theories and hypotheses, based, however, on no facts, at the mercy of the next thinker,
and held together only by the speculative ingenuity
of the author's brain. Socrates swept it all away.
He saw that it was aimless, profitless, and barren.
He brought back philosophy to its true starting-
point,— the human soul. His motto, his method,
the Alpha and Omega of his system was — "Know
thyself." He made psychology the portal to the
temple of science, and thus gave to speculation a
moral aim. Socrates left no works. His greatest

legacy to the world was Plato's mind. The scholar was thoroughly imbued with the master's method, and in his works for the first time do we find the true canons of philosophy observed, and a rigorous moral system raised upon the results of psychological analysis, and induction from the facts of consciousness and experience.

At first sight, we are struck with the spiritual character of Plato's system. He has no compromise, no sympathy with materialistic views. With him man was a living soul, the body merely an organ, instrument, and slave. The natural order of things, reversed in most of the schools of Grecian speculation, was restored by him. Spiritual interests in his philosophy are always supreme. So far from the spirit being dependent on material organization, it existed before the body, sustains the body, and is in its very essence immortal, indestructible. That Plato held to the prior existence of the spirit, no student of his philosophy can doubt. It is a fundamental point of his moral system. But when we go beyond this fact, and seek to define his view of its former state, and the manner of its passage into an earthly form, we are embarrassed by a crowd of contradictory statements entirely insoluble. "To know the soul in itself," said he, "requires a divine wisdom, and dissertations without end." Plato seems clearly to have understood and recognized the boundary line between science and speculation. His mind was poetic but not mystic. Strange as it may seem, we see proof of this in his treatment of the

question of preëxistence; and it is on this ground
alone, we believe, that the contradictions, so perplexing to most commentators, can be explained. In
establishing the fact of preëxistence and the superiority of the soul, his method is scientific. He draws
his argument from the facts of our mental experience
and the laws of bodily organization. The sources
of this proof are found in the Phædon and the Meno.
By an examination of the principal ideas of the
mind, such as the true, the good, the beautiful, equality, etc., Plato discovered that their characteristics
are such as to forbid the supposition of sensual origin.
They cannot be traced to sensible impressions; they
are beyond the reach of our bodily organs. The
sight of material things awakens them immediately
in the mind; and therefore, since their origin is not
in this state of existence, they come into consciousness by reminiscence, and must have been acquired
in some former state, and brought with us here as
part of our mental furniture.[1] The ideas of science
and duty also, both demanding freedom of the spirit
from the ties of sense and matter, imply the independence of the soul, and hence its priority.[2] The
evils of life, moreover, spring from too intimate

---

[1] Vol. i., Phædon, pp. 219-231. Vol. vi. Meno, pp. 174-191. In studying the genesis and comparative anatomy of philosophical schools, relationships and affinities quite unsuspected may be brought to light. Thus
it was the existence in the mind of *certain* and *super-sensuous* knowledge which led Plato into his theory of reminiscence and *ideal realism,*
Kant into his discovery of the categories of pure reason, and his system
of *subjective scepticism,* and Cousin into the doctrine of *impersonal reason,* and the possibility of arriving at absolute, ontological science.

[2] Vol. i., Phædon, pp. 200, 205.

union of the soul with flesh, and moral order is attained only as the soul acquires and feels its native superiority to earthly bonds.[1] The soul also is the principle and source of motion, and therefore prior to material organization, which is merely the channel and instrument of motion. The body dissolves at death; but dissolution is possible only with the composite. The soul is formless, substantive, and simple, hence indissoluble and superior to all organization.[2] Neither can it be the harmony of the body, a result of the arrangement of its forces, dependent on matter like the music of a lyre upon strings. A harmony has no substantive essence; it exists only in the conditioning elements; — while the soul is conscious of substantive existence, can distinguish and separate itself from bodily elements and make war upon them.[3] Hence it is a prior individual unity.

All these arguments are based on psychology. The logic is wretched, but the method true. ·The fact of preëxistence, then, we believe to be a firmly established element of Platonism.[4] But beyond this mere fact, to the *manner* of preëxistence, and the worldly origin of souls, induction could not reach;

---

[1] Vol. i., Phædon, pp. 209, 210.   [2] Ibid. 283-300.   [3] Ibid. 263-271.

[4] Coleridge (Biog. Lit. ch. xxii.), in a note to Wordsworth's beautiful "Ode on Immortality," referring to the doctrine of preëxistence, hinted there, remarks, that a competent reader "will be as little disposed to charge Mr. Wordsworth with believing the Plantonic preëxistence, in the ordinary interpretation of the words, as I am to believe that Plato himself ever meant or taught it." If this refers to the mythic description of the soul's former condition, the remark is just; if applied, how-

then Plato designedly abandons himself to speculation and hypothesis, sporting freely in a poetic element, careless, of course, about the consistency and harmony of his fanciful plays. Accordingly, in the gorgeous imagery of the Phædrus, he shows us the cars of the original souls, moving in the train of the Deity, and borne around the heaven in contemplation of ideas. In the Timæus we see the elements of human souls, at the command of Deity, mixed by demi-gods from the remnant of the first creations, and scattered upon the stars, where they first become acquainted with ideas ; while, in the Philebus, the souls are emanations from the great world-soul, the first creation of the Almighty.[1] Plato founds, however, no important doctrine on the tenet of preexistence, and in all the poetic passages as to the circumstances of the soul's former state, he warns the reader against receiving them as truths or as anything more than fanciful guesses and badinage.[2]

ever, to the fact of the priority of spirit to bodily forms, the scepticism is too sweeping and indiscriminate.

Teouemann, (System der Platonischen Philosophie, vol. iii., p. 109,) makes a distinction between the *hypothetical* and *mythical* in Platonism, which, he says, must not be overlooked. Thus, " when Plato admits the preëxistence of the soul, on account of super-sensuous knowledge, it is an hypothesis; when, however, he seeks to represent the *condition* of preëxisting souls, their dwelling in the stars, and their travels through various bodily forms it is a myth." This *hypothetical* hypothesis does not, we think, explain all the allusions to preëxistence in Plato so well as our own theory, that the *fact* is scientific, the *details* mythical.

[1] We have made no allusion to the Tenth Book of the Laws, because there, evidently, the passages on preëxistence refer to the general priority of mind to matter, and not to individual preëxistence.

[2] Vol. vi., Phædrus, p. 96; vol. xii., Timæus, pp. 118, 203.

Holding fast to the *idea* of preëxistence, as a fact of his philosophy, a wise criticism, instead of trying to reconcile the irreconcilable, will transfer the *details* of the soul's former state from the region of scientific to that of poetic Platonism.

Passing from a consideration of the nature, to the duration, of the soul, we may say, that Plato undoubtedly had firm and constant faith in immortality. It was with him, not merely a matter of speculation, but of science. The same arguments which decided his faith in a preëxistent state, were conclusive in favor of the soul's independence and enduring life. We read him with perfect confidence. There is no hesitation, no wavering, no insecurity of faith betrayed in any of his dialogues, where mention is made of immortality. The idea is involved and connected by numberless nerves and fibres, with the whole scientific structure of his philosophy. For aught in his writings to the contrary, it was as much a matter of certainty, as his belief in God, or his confidence in present existence. To him belongs the honor of first placing the idea of immortality on a rational basis; to him alone, throughout the ranks of ancient philosophers, is due the praise of holding to it firmly, as the only solution to the mysteries of our moral nature, and the ever-present sanction of the moral law. It is a difficult and quite unwelcome task to proceed to a critical analysis of his views, concerning the future condition and destiny of the soul. Could we collect and arrange the passages that refer to the subject,—which would be the proper

method for the treatment of most authors, — and
thus present the tenor of his views in his own language, we might hope for some success, notwithstanding the mass of materials it would be necessary
to sift. But this is impossible. There is no outward
unity or consistency in his statements. It would be
comparatively easy to work the vast Platonic mine,
and disclose to general view its rich veins of moral
speculation, if they ran in any order. But a strange
caprice governs their development. They break off
so suddenly, and branch out in so many directions,
and with such lawless irregularity, that there seems
to be no possibility of tracing unity or plan. The
impressions left upon the reader's mind, by a first
and hasty reading, of Plato's various passages on
future life, are extremely confused and chaotic. Not
only are we perplexed by different treatments and
developments of one fundamental conception, as in
the case of preëxistence, but different and entirely
hostile modes of future life, are posited with equal
freedom and seeming indifference. In attempting a
solution, we must bear in mind that it is this part
of his philosophy, probably, which Plato treated
with the greatest artistic liberty in his writings, re-
serving a clear and consistent development for the
retirement of his school. Although the same distinction between the scientific and poetic, to which
we referred in the remarks on preëxistence, may be
equally applicable here, still there are many inconsistencies and troublesome questions concerning
Plato's conception of the soul's final destiny, which

9

we think, a patient examination can reconcile and solve. At any rate, we are confident that it is possible to establish a negative, to show what he did *not* believe, and thus to rescue his system from being implicated with doctrines sometimes imputed to it, but for which it is not at all responsible.

The first difficulty that presses on us, relates to the tenet of metempsychosis, or transmigration of souls. From many passages in his works, it would seem, that he held to this theory as the mode and form of eternal existence. The dialogues which contain allusions to, or statements of, the doctrine of transmigration, are the Phædrus, Meno, Timæus, Phædon, the Tenth Book of the Republic, and the Tenth Book of the Laws. In the Phædon, which contains the last conversation of Socrates with his friends just prior to his decease, and where the subject is, the soul and its destiny, we find it alluded to in the following manner. After having argued for the independent nature of the soul, from conscience, the idea of science, etc., Socrates, in passing to speak of its eternal duration, commences[1] by referring to " the very ancient opinion, that souls in quitting this world go to the unseen state, and thence again come back to life after the passage of death." This gives rise to a discussion upon the law of contraries; all things spring from their opposites, as the colder from the warmer, smaller from greater, quicker from slower, night from day, etc. This ceaseless flow and change is

[1] Vol. i., Phædon, p. 213.

the law of nature.   Things are continually returning into, and reissuing from, their opposites.   *Cir-
culus arterni motús.*   Existence is an active circle,
whose extremities perpetually return upon themselves, and thus, in order to maintain the stability
of this universal order, death also must give place
to life, birth must be the compensating opposite to
dissolution, else all being would finally become stag-
nant and dead.[1]   The natural complement and
climax of this argument, of course, should be, that
the number of souls is limited, that the series of
earthly lives is continually refreshed by the spirits
of the departed, and that natural birth in this
world is the immediate return of the spirit to existence.   But Socrates, as if conscious of the tendency of this theory, and recoiling from its logical
results, artfully breaks the discussion, and passes
immediately to the argument for the soul's independence from reminiscence, and after settling that,
resumes[2] the consideration of its future condition.
But here the demands of his rigid law of contraries
are forgotten.   The theory of metempsychosis has
itself experienced a metamorphosis from a scientific
necessity as before, to a moral condition of punishment.   " The soul, which is immaterial, goes to an
abode like itself, pure, excellent, and immaterial.   If
it pass pure, without dragging with it anything corporeal, it returns to the divine, immortal, and wise,
and there is .happy, delivered from error, folly,
fears, dissolute love, and all other human evils ; as

[2] Vol. i., Phædon, p. 218.   [1] Ibid. p. 289.

they say of the initiated, it passes, truly, eternity with the gods. But if souls withdraw from the body corrupted and impure, loaded with the bonds of the material envelope, they fall, and, dragged anew towards the visible world by terror of the immaterial, and of that world without light which is called hell, go wandering, *as they say*, among monuments and tombs as a punishment for their first wicked life, until the natural appetite of the corporeal mass which follows them, leads them back into a body, and then they reënter, probably, into the same habits which made the occupation of their first existence."[1]   Those who were abandoned to intemperance and sensual excess go into the bodies of asses and like animals; those who loved injustice and tyranny, into wolves and hawks; peaceable, mild souls, undisciplined by philosophy, pass into social and peaceful animals, as bees, wasps, and ants, or perhaps return to human bodies and form good men.   But to attain the rank of the gods is permitted only to the philosopher.

A careless reader, unacquainted with Plato's method, and the license of his art, would at once conclude from the above-cited passage, probably, that the tenet of metempsychosis formed an element of his creed.   In fact, we have given the most perplexing passage first.   Generally his allusions to transmigration are veiled in mythic dress, and form a rich embroidery, an ornamental fringe to his abstruser speculations, while here they seem to shoot

[1] Vol. i., Phædon, substance of, pp. 239-248.

like a golden thread across his logic. A thorough
study of his works, however, is fatal to the theory.
Not only, as in the very instance of the discussion in
the Phædon, does he artfully elude an implication
of his argument with the natural consequences of
transmigration, but he is so entirely inconsistent
with himself in his different modes of representing
it, as to force upon us the conclusion that he used
it for an artistic embellishment, borrowed from his
favorite, Pythagoras, and as a convenient vehicle
through which to impress upon the imagination the
moral results of sin. A careful examination and
comparison of the passages where the theory is introduced, we are confident, will substantiate our
position. In the Phædon, as we have seen, no notice is taken and ño solution offered of the question,
how the souls are united at birth or reunited at
death with an earthly form. In the Phædrus, the
most poetic unscientific, as well as one of the most
gorgeous and fascinating of the Platonic dialogues,
the first appearance of the spirit in a body is ascribed to sin. The soul in its preëxistent, empy-
rean flight, becomes heavy and dull through forgetfulness or vice, loses its wings and falls to the
earth. But it is forbidden to animate the body of
any beast at the first generation. The fallen spirits
consist of nine degrees, and make up, accordingly,
nine different ranks of human character; the first
and purest rank entering philosophers and men
whose lives are consecrated to Love, Beauty, and
the Muses. The others are arranged in the follow-

ing order:—just kings and warriors, statesmen, athletes and doctors, priests, poets and artists, artisans, sophists and demagogues, and, lastly, tyrants. After death, the souls return to the other world for judgment, and, according to their improvement of the first probationary state, are punished or rewarded for a thousand years. At the expiration of this period, they make choice of a new earthly existence : each being free to select the condition which it prefers, whether of beast or man. And only through a circuit of ten lives and a disciplinary and retributory punishment of ten thousand years, can the souls regain their heavenly state ; except the philosopher, who, after three successive virtuous lives, and a discipline of three thousand years, may recover his wings and resume his flight.[1]

All other reasons set aside, this passage would be valueless as a sober, trustworthy statement of Plato's belief, from the fact that it occurs in a discourse attributed to Stesichorus, a celebrated author of lyrico-epic poems, which Socrates recites to Phædrus while seated upon the banks of the Ilyssus, and yielding to the luxury of dreamy musing and contemplation. In accordance with Plato's mimetic art, the ideas and form of the address are suited to the imaginary author, philosophic severity being sacrificed to poetic license and consistency of character. No reader of Plato can fail to remark, besides, the discrepancy between this statement as it respects the fate of the philosopher, and his usual

---

[1] Vol. vi., Phædrus, pp. 53, 54.

dogmatic positions on that point. Always in his dialogues and myths he allots to the lover of wisdom an *immediate* return to the life of the gods; while here he subjects him to a probation of three worldly existences and a discipline of three thousand years. The nine lives and return to purity after the tenth cycle of punishment, shows us that he is using a Pythagorean doctrine, under their mystical veil of numbers. Almost all commentators are agreed that this is among the earliest, if not the very first of Plato's written works, marked by the luxuriance of youthful fancy, betraying throughout a lack of art in subordinating properly the poetic and mythical to the philosophical and scientific elements, and so ill balanced that the author found it necessary to warn the reader against an undue fascination with its form, with the twice-repeated confession that it is a poetic myth, " a kind of mythologic hymn to Love who presides over beauty." [1]

The work most commonly cited to substantiate the theory of metempsychosis is the Timæus, a composition which pretends to give a solution of the origin of things, and to embody Plato's speculations upon nature and the theory of the world. Here, too, the details of the statement are entirely different. After the creation of higher orders, the souls of men were mixed by demi-gods from elements furnished by the Almighty, and were then divided among the stars, one great soul to each

[1] Vol. vi., Phædrus, pp. 96, 189.

star. Before the first birth, which is the same to
all, the souls are made to mount upon a chariot,
" that they may see the nature of the universe, and
observe its inevitable decrees."   After death, if the
soul has lived justly, it returns immediately to its
proper star.   If it sin, it is changed into a woman
at the second birth, and if then it does not improve,
it passes through a lower round of change, corresponding to its vices, until by discipline it becomes
worthy to recover its first and excellent condition.
The creation of lower animals is ascribed to this
degradation of human souls by sin; each degree of
evil and debasement manifesting itself in the creation of a new and appropriate bodily form.   The
apparent freedom of the passages in the Timæus
from any mythic mixture, and the dogmatic form
in which the doctrine is stated, have caused greater
stress to be laid upon it as authority for Plato's
faith in transmigration.   Too much credit has been
given, however, to the Timæus as an exposition of
Plato's sober views.   The whole structure and form
of the work remove it from the category of his
severe scientific productions.   It is not cast in the
dialogistic mould ; the dialectic method employed
in his other great works, such as the Thæetetus,
Philebus, Gorgias, Phædon, and Republic, and
which Plato declares to be the only medium for
conveying truth, is abandoned. Moreover, his usual
mouthpiece, Socrates, is thrown aside ; and the
substance of the work is given as a long recital
upon nature, from Timæus, a Locrian, and a cele-

brated teacher of the Pythagorean school. Consistently with Plato's usual aim after dramatic propriety, therefore, we discover in it much of a peculiarly Pythagorean cast, and accordingly, as in the case of the Phædrus, we find that Plato introduces a caveat, lest he be held responsible for the literal statement of opinions, confessing that all which he has said is a philosophical recreation, a wise and moderate amusement for the mind when it lays aside the study of what is eternal.[1] That the Timæus discloses many physiological views which Plato really held, we have no doubt; but its transcendental speculations bear all the incidental and positive testimony that can be given to prove that they were mere philosophic myths and *jeux d'esprit*.[2]

---

[1] Vol. xii., Timæus, pp. 118, 174, 203. The passages in this dialogue which refer to metempsychosis may be found pp. 137–141, and 242, 243.

[2] Mr. Norton (Evidences of the Gospels, vol. iii., p. 104) calls the Timæus a mere work of imagination. Tennemann, noticing the inconsistency between the Phædrus and the Timæus relative to future life, with a short-sightedness unusual in him, places greater stress on the representations in the Timæus as a riper and later book. The Timæus, it is true, is a later book, but lateness has nothing to do with the *veracity* of *poetry*. Afterwards, however, he refers to the Timæus for proof that Plato held his speculations to be mere guesses upon questions removed from knowledge. ("System der Platonischen Philosophie," vol. iii., pp. 96, 97.) And further on (p. 124), speaking of Plato's statement that the soul at its second birth enters a female form, he adduces evidence from the Republic, where Plato allows an equal dignity to the male and female natures, for proof that he did not affirm the doctrine "in full earnest." Again, referring to the return of the wicked into the souls of beasts, Tennemann contends that Plato "held it not as rigid truth, but as a feasible mode of representing the moral condition of the soul after death." (See his "Lehren der Sokratiker über Unsterblichkeit," p. 478.)

Stallbaum, a German editor of Plato's works, and who has been

In the tenth book of the Republic, we have still another poetic statement of the theory of transmigration, clothed in all the luxuriant drapery of Plato's inimitable art. The details differ from those of all the rest. According to the recital, the information concerning the future state was communicated by Er, an Armenian, who had been slain in battle, but whose corpse was preserved from the funeral pile until the twelfth day after his decease. When all preparations had been completed for his obsequies he suddenly revived, and related what

called "one of the greatest living scholars in the Platonic writings," in criticising the mythical passages relating to metempsychosis scattered throughout the Phædus, Phædon, Timæus, and Republic, contends that a serious study of them all easily demonstrates that they are mere plays of fancy; to use his own words, — "Philosophum in hoc argumento tractando ingenii lusui nonnihil indulsisse, ut in re quæ mentis humanæ intelligentiam superaret." (See Cousin's Plato, vol. xii., p. 345, note.)

Cousin himself is not committed to any decisive opinion. His criticism is remarkably eclectic, or rather *synchretic*. He touches both sides. In his preface to the Phædon, he hints the idea that the tenet of metempsychosis may be only a symbolic envelope for the dogma of the unity and incorruptibility of intellectual substance, (vol. i., p. 181.) This opinion is still more decidedly advanced in the notes to the Meno, (vol. vi., p. 480.) In the notes to the Timæus, however, he rejects Stallbaum's view, and inclines to the opinion that it is neither *a jeu d'esprit,* nor a doctrine Plato would be willing to indorse, but "a specious noted opinion, more or less true, borrowed from his favorite Pythagoras, and constituting his own mythology through which he addresses the imagination and the soul, after having arrived at the limits which separate the certain from the probable, and having exhausted rational demonstration," (vol. xii., p. 346.) It is hard to define the difference between this view and Stallbaum's; and at the close of his notes on the Timæus, Cousin protests against the tenet of animal transmigration in good earnest, calling it *mal à propos,* and declaring that "we could very well have spared *an ornament* which degrades instead of elevating the majesty of Plato's ideas of the animal kingdom and the universe."

had been revealed to him in the other world. We
have not room to present even an outline of this
statement, the particulars of which would fill sev-
eral pages. The substance, however, is, — that immediately after death, all souls, according to their
characters, are despatched by different routs to the
abodes of the happy or the wicked. In these dwellings they remain a thousand years, each soul receiving tenfold reward or punishment for the deeds of
its earthly life, and, at the end of this period, the
spirits are permitted to make choice of a new existence. In working out this gorgeous picture, one
of the finest gems of imagination which literature
contains, and upon which Plato seems to have bestowed more artistic labor than on any other, he
seems not to have restrained his fancy at all by the
desire to be consistent with his other statements,
but rather to have constructed it without reference
to them and from new resources. Accordingly, no
moral distinction is made between the value of animal and human forms, as in the Phædon and Timæus, and they are selected not in obedience to
spiritual necessity, but from considerations of con-
venience, or at the suggestion of arbitrary whims.
The spirit of Orpheus selected the soul of a swan,
from his hatred of women who had once caused his
death, not wishing to be dependent again upon that
sex for birth. Ajax, son of Telamon, disgusted
with human life, and remembering the judgment
which deprived him of the arms of Achilles, took
the nature of a lion. Agamemnon, too, averse to

the human race because of his past misfortunes, selected the condition of the eagle. Ulysses, cured of ambition by the memory of his severe reverses, chose the tranquil lot of a private man, which the other souls had disdainfully refused; while Thersites, very properly, concluded to reanimate the body of a monkey.[1] No difference is posited between male and female as in the Timæus, for sexes are changed at will. Atalanta had a strong desire to become an athlete, and Epeus, son of Panopeus, returned into the lot of an industrious woman. No peculiar fate is reserved for the philosopher, and not a hint is dropped relative to the point whether this return is part of a long system of purification, as in the Phædrus, or whether it is the general law of earthly existence and reproduction.[2] The beauty with which the whole myth is wrought out cannot be surpassed; art everywhere shines through the story, and we can imagine no more thorough cure for a tendency to believe that Plato really held the doctrine of metempsychosis, than a study of this fiction in a proper attitude of mind.[3]

---

[1] Vol. x., Republic, Book Tenth, pp. 291, 292.

[2] Cousin thinks, that the substance of the whole fable is Oriental, embellished, but not originated, by Plato, (vol. x., p. 377.)

[3] The mythic passages in the Meno hardly require a passing notice. This dialogue, as we have before stated, is one of the chief sources for the doctrine of reminiscence and preëxistence. Before the discussion is introduced upon the question that all knowledge is merely memory, Plato weaves in, as a sort of poetic prelude and preface, "the opinion of Pindar, and many other men skilful in divine things, that the soul is immortal, sometimes becoming eclipsed, sometimes reappearing, but never becoming totally extinct. For Proserpine, at the end of nine

These inconsistencies in working out the details
of the soul's future condition, and the poetic license everywhere betrayed in the treatment of the
separate myths, seem sufficient to condemn them as
expositions of Plato's views. For surely he would
have evinced more care, and would have shown
more anxiety about the consistency of the outline
and form of his pictures, although he might be arbitrary as to his materials, if he really intended to
convey through them his decisive views as to the
future state of souls. But it may be objected, that,
although Plato might not have intended the myths
to be clear and accurate expositions in detail of his
religious views, and, therefore, in his treatment of
them, very properly subordinated scientific precis-

years, returns to the light of the sun those souls who have paid to her
the debt of their ancient sins; and from these souls spring illustrious
kings, celebrated for their power, and men remarkable for their wisdom," — vol. vi., pp. 170, 171. The passage is left thus in its poetic
form, — the latter portion quoted, being, probably, a fragment of some
lost ode of Pindar, and the scientific investigation into the nature of
knowledge begins. The whole bears marks too plainly stamped to be
mistaken, that it is poetic embellishment, an artful management of
the transition in discourse, and a relief of dialogistic skill.

In the ninth book of the Laws, (vol. viii., p. 185,) occurs another allusion to metempsychosis, unimportant, however, in our examination,
since it is a reference to the doctrine of the Eleusinian mysteries, and
is introduced for illustration. Plato, in speaking of the proper punishment for the crime of murder, and in a preamble to his legislation upon
that point, remarks, that it is proper to include in it the doctrine of the
mysteries, which many men religiously believe, that in hell are reserved
punishments for these murders, and that the guilty man, commencing a
new life, is condemned to undergo the same punishment, and thus ter-
minate his days by the hand of another, and by the same kind of death.
The design of the allusion, of course, is to strengthen the force of the
law, by adding to it the sanctions of the popular religion.

ion to imaginative freedom, still they may be authoritative as expressions of his faith in the fundamental fact of metempsychosis, on which they rest,
and which they reveal. That the myths may be
received as hints of a progressive and ceaseless
activity of spirit in its freer life, and that under
the picture of continual changes, he may have
intentionally vailed the theory of a moral cycle of
conditions in the soul's future history, is a somewhat plausible, though we think an indemonstrable
hypothesis. The allusions to future life in the
Tenth Book of the Laws would seem to favor it.
For there, a gradual progress of souls towards
higher degrees of happiness, or lower degrees of
misery, is hinted as the result of the experience
" of this life, and of all the deaths we successively
undergo." It is impossible, that a single soul can
escape the established order of heaven, " were it
small enough to penetrate into the recesses of
earth, or great enough to soar even to the sky; but
it must bear the punishment awarded by the gods,
either on earth, or in hell, or in some other and
still more frightful abode." [1] The theology and
theodicy of the laws, however, present so many inconsistencies between the principles and the details;
they are adulterated by so much that is palpably
exoteric, that it is not safe to draw a conclusion
upon such a point from their testimony alone. [2] But

---

[1] Vol. viii., pp. 266, 267.

[2] The Tenth Book of the Laws is a perfect riddle. No person can read
it without feeling elevated by its noble views of God's omnipresence,

that in such a cycle, a return to *earthly* life under a
bodily vesture was not really included, we think is
evident on other grounds. * A mind so critical as Plato's would not have entirely overlooked the physiological question suggested by transmigration, namely, how is the return to mortal life effected, and
what connection exists between departed souls and
human generation?   Even if no solution should be
hinted in scientific form, a myth might easily have
suggested to the mind some probable explanation.
But Plato is entirely silent on this point.   In the
Republic and Laws, he treats at length of marriage
and the true method of sexual union ; and it would
hardly seem possible that, holding such a theory
of birth as must necessarily be involved in metempsychosis, he should not even allude to it in such
a treatise.   On the contrary, all his directions and
laws are hostile to the view of transmigration ;
the two theories cannot be reconciled ; and since
in such passages we may, of course, presume that

and the moral providence which reaches all men, and which is never
withdrawn for an instant from the soul.   The imagery often recalls passages from the Psalms and Isaiah; and the statement seems at times as
clear and pure as the language of Paul.   In its fundamental principles,
the book is a complete system of Optimism, and recalls at once the
Theodicy of Leibnitz.   And yet before it closes, the popular worship is
sanctioned; the evils of life are assumed to he greater than the goods, —
just the reverse of what had before been definitely proved; and the
hypothesis of two souls is introduced to account for evil, when the
whole preceding argument had been directed to exhibit the complete
and ceaseless agency of God in the government of human life, to show
that "He, who directs all things, has disposed them for the preservation
and good of the whole; that each part experiences or does only what it
is fitting it should experience and do."

Plato unfolds his honest views, his silence with respect to metempsychosis may be taken as decisive evidence against the supposition that he held the theory as a scientific dogma.[1]

As yet, however, we have left the main argument against metempsychosis untouched. It is not included in some of the most elaborate myths. In the two which form the conclusion of his severest moral dialogues,— the Phædon and the Gorgias,— the idea of transmigration is not admitted. The mythical elements of the picture at the close of the Phædon, although artistically treated, are borrowed from the popular faith. The common distinctions between the realm of the blessed and Tartarus are affirmed ; punishments are expiatory, except for offenders of the last degree ; and philosophers are reserved for a purer life, entirely bodiless, in dwellings more beautiful than those allotted to innocent but less cultivated souls. Socrates closes his description with the politic warning to his friends, that although things may not occur precisely as he described, still, the only wisdom is in piety during life; " for the prize of the combat is beautiful, while the hope is grand." [2] At the close of the Gorgias, which is the loftiest, the best sustained, and the

---

[1] Schleiermacher, who seems to hold to the tenet of metempsychosis as a Platonic fact, mentions this difficulty in his notes to the Republic, and says, " We cannot suppose it escaped Plato." He attempts a solution of it, which is quite ingenious. as a German hint, how the matter might have been reconciled, but which, unluckily, has no foundation in the Platonic books.

[2] Vol. i., Phædon, pp. 312, 313, 314.

most terrible of all his works, the same facts are used as a basis for a myth. Nothing can exceed the sublimity of the scene into which Plato introduces the disembodied soul. The chief topic of discussion in the dialogue had been justice, and its relation to rhetoric. It is a masterly attack on the ethics of the time. Socrates, in a personal conversation with three distinguished rhetoricians, had completely riddled the morality of the sophists and pleaders, and had shown that their whole art was false, having no relation to the moral wants of men. Justice, he showed to be the greatest good, and its administration disciplinary, and therefore the unkindest act which a wise man could commit would be to save his friend from a punishment which he deserved. And at last, to prove the final impotence of the sophist's office, he shows, that if it be able to protect from righteous retribution in this life, it is powerless with the terrible judges of the lower world. The soul nor the body at the moment of separation — says he — is different from what it was as a living man. The body preserves its character, the well-marked vestiges, both of the care it has received and the accidents that have befallen it. If a person in life possessed a great frame, the gift of nature or the result of training, his corpse is large. If he were fleshy, his corpse is so. If he delighted in the cultivation of his hair, many locks remain. If, living, he bore upon his body scars of the lash, or any other wound, all will be found there after death. If any member were broken or dislocated in life, when dead these failings are still visible. And so with regard to the soul; when it is disrobed of the body, it preserves evident marks of its character, and of the accidents it experienced in consequence of the life which it embraced. When, therefore, men arrive before their judge, he examines the soul of each without knowing who he is; and often, having in charge the great king or some other potentate or monarch, and discovering nothing healthy in his soul, but seeing it all cicatrized with perjuries and injustice by the stamps which each action has engraven there ; here the windings of falsehood and vanity, and nothing symmetrical, because it had been nourished away from truth ; there monstrous deformities, and all the ugliness of absolute power, effeminacy, licentiousness, and debauchery ; seeing it thus, he sends it ignominiously to prison, where it will no sooner have arrived than it will undergo fitting chastisement. This punishment is proportioned to the offence, and sinners of the deepest die, who cannot be reformed, are used as warnings for the rest, and condemned to eternal pains.[1] The whole picture, which seems a dramatic transparency, lighted by the fires of the abyss, reveals no hint of the metempsychosis ; punishment prepares the soul for more spiritual life, and the scene is closed without any reference to a return to bodily form and worldly state.

With regard to the much vexed question of transmigration, then, the whole facts are these: The

[1] Vol. lii. pp. 408, 408.

theory is developed in a mythical form, dressed in
the drapery of imagination ; or it is introduced as
an ancient opinion, in accordance with the usual
license of Plato's dialogistic art, which induced him
at times to quote Homer and Hesiod, as authority
for moral truths ; or it is communicated through
the lips of some poet or Pythagorean, from whom
it proceeds with dramatic propriety, and accompan-
ied by a warning from Plato to the reader, against
receiving it as anything more than a probable statement, devoid of scientific value.   It is inconsistent
in its details ; is unsupported by any allusions to it,
or any provision for it, in his physiological system ;
and is, moreover, entirely absent from equally elaborate myths, which are introduced to reveal the
future condition of the soul.   Besides, it is never
connected, for a moment, with the idea of a pre-
existent, bodily life on earth, as is said to have been
the case with Pythagoras.[1]   Many discrepancies in
the Platonic dialogues have been reconciled by reference to the time of composition ; statements, in the
earlier and less severely constructed works, being
made to yield, very properly, to the more authoritative and careful passages of the later writings.   But
this solution is denied to us in the present instance ;
for the Phædon and Gorgias, whose myths contain
no allusion to transmigration, are universally classed

---

[1] Mr. Norton in the third volume of his " Genuineness of the Gospels,"
attributes this opinion to Plato. He quotes no passages, however, and
makes no allusion to any; but nowhere have we discovered a trace of
such a doctrine.

with the most trusty sources of his philosophy.
Keeping in view, therefore, the great freedom in the
scope of the Platonic dialogues, remembering the
poetic character of Plato's mind, and his artistic as
well as scientific aim, and balancing, with an even
hand, the testimony of all the sources, an impartial
criticism must decide. that the theory of transmigration borrowed from the East and from Pythagoras, together with the details of the popular mythology of his country, were indifferent to Plato as
poetic materials for the clothing of his views, and
that he used both with a license which his followers
could easily interpret, as media for impressing upon
the imagination, by over-statements and highly-
wrought pictures, ideas which reason and dialectics
could not clearly establish or convey.[1]

[1] Ritter, in his History of Philosophy, vol. ii., p. 373, throws his influence in favor of metempsychosis, as a clear and decided opinion of
Plato, and not a merely figurative or mythical exposition of the soul's
life after death. He thinks it in accordance with Plato's physical system. But he takes the details of transmigration entirely from the
Timæus, without attempting to reconcile the conflicting forms of the
hypothesis, and without previously settling the claims of that dialogue
to credit as a scientific work. Moreover, in order to harmonize the
theory, as stated in the Timæus, with what he calls Plato's physical
system, Ritter is obliged to deny a fundamental, ethical position of Platonism, viz., that the soul of the philosopher may expect an entirely in-
corporeal existence, and return to immediate communion with the
divine. The license of criticism, which allows him to reject that, is not
required to dissipate the whole theory of transmigration as a dogmatic
element of Platonism. Fries, on the contrary (Geschichte der Philosophie, vol. i., p. 329), contends for the symbolical treatment, and, without reference to Ritter, since his work was written first, asserts that
there is no physical background for it in the Timæus.

No point of Ritter's exposition of Plato is more unsatisfactory than
the pages on the future state. He fails as a critic of Plato, by reason

In criticising a system like Plato's, in which the scientific and poetic are so closely blended, considerable importance should be attached to the harmony of a tenet with the general moral spirit of the whole. Applying this canon to the two forms in which he has left his speculations on the future state, we should at once conclude in favor of that which speaks of a final, future condition, entirely separate from earth, and should therefore be inclined to accept the mythical statements of the Gorgias and the Phædon as the truer sources of his religious creed. It is rather dangerous, we know, to rely too confidently on such a rule ; but the mysticism, which could hold honestly the tenet of transmigration, would be very apt to betray itself in moral speculation ; and therefore the clearness, the severity, the admirable purity of Plato's ethical code, furnish strong collateral testimony against his faith in a literal succession of bodily forms. Pres-

---

of that quality of mind which fits him for an admirable exponent of Aristotle, — a lack of imagination, and too exclusive reliance on words, without appreciating the former spirit of a piece, which the words do not exhaust, but which pervades them magnetically, and gives them form. Platonism, in Ritter's pages, is like beauty anatomized, — the flesh and bones and nerves all there, but the *beauty* gone. From a note of Cousin's, (vol. vi. p. 480), it would seem that Ritter, in a separate history of the Pythagorean philosophy, indorsed the view that the metempsychosis in Platonism was merely a symbolical statement of the persistence of intellect under the mutability of forms. We have never seen that work; but in Ritter's exposition of Pythagoreanism, (Hist of Phil., vol 1,) he intimates that with Pythagoras the theory was a holy myth, " much of it obscure, and indicative only of the soul's immortality. It is a queer freak of criticism to attribute the theory as a myth to Pythagoras, and as a dogmatic tenet, to Plato.

ent to the mind of an impartial judge, acquainted
with Christianity, but ignorant of Christian parties,
the three parables, — the prodigal son, the rich man
and Lazarus, and the sheep and goats, — and it would
not require much critical rashness to decide their
comparative value as expressions of the moral spirit
of the gospel. The two last mentioned would be
accepted, of course, as equally appropriate with the
first to the object they were designed to illustrate ;
still the first is immeasurably superior as an exposition of the central idea of Christianity, the love
of God, while the others contain elements designed
merely for a local application, and are given in a
form suited only to the culture of the time. And
we cannot but feel that the same injustice is done
to' the symmetry of Platonic ethics, by fastening
upon it the tenet of transmigration, as would be
done to the purity of Christian theology, by literally
applying the imagery of Abraham's bosom, and the
impassable gulf, and the details of the judgment to
the eternal world.

Great value too, in an examination of this kind,
must be attributed to incidental allusions, and side-
way hints, and unconscious intimations, with respect to the future state. For in these we are more
apt to detect the real opinions, the stable faith of a
mind like Plato's, than in more labored artistic passages. We observe his mind in its undress, when it
is not taking attitudes for display. And these allusions, which are very numerous throughout his
works, are hostile to the view of transmigration.

They refer always to a coming state of continued, but severer discipline. The form in which these allusions are conveyed belongs to the popular mythology, but the key-note to the whole is, the declared belief of Socrates in the Phædon, that " there is a destiny reserved for men hereafter, and which, according to the ancient faith of the race, must be better for the good than for the wicked."[1] In the discussion in the Gorgias, too, it is stated that "the greatest of misfortunes is to pass into the other world with a soul loaded with crimes."[2] The allusions to the future world in the "Apology of Socrates," all imply a disembodied being,[3] and in the Phædon, previous to the introduction of " that ancient opinion," as to metempsychosis, Socrates speaks of the occupations of the spiritual state when, "freed from the follies of the body, we shall converse, I hope, with free men like ourselves, and shall know, by ourselves, the essence of things."[4] In the eleventh book of the Laws, also, the souls of the departed are spoken of as " taking still some interest in human affairs;" and in the twelfth book, speaking of the soul, he says that the body is its temporary image, its *simulacrum*, and that it passes at death into another state, to find other judges, and, " as tradition says, to render an account of its actions, — an account as cheering to the good as it is frightful to the wicked."[5]

[1] Vol. i., p. 198.   [2] Vol. iii., p. 403.
[3] Vol. i., pp. 118, 119.   [4] Vol. i., p. 206.
[5] Vol. viii., pp. 810, 876. See also Epinomis, vol. xiii., p. 2; Republic, book i., p. 9; Book iii., pp. 122 *et seq.;* Book vi., p. 33; Timæus, p.

Our excuse for dwelling so long upon the point of transmigration must be the strange diversity in the judgment of commentators respecting it, the fact that no thorough examination of all the passages referring to it has ever fallen under our notice, and a desire to rescue the moral system of Plato from the stain of a doctrine so absurd, and so foreign to Plato's honest thought. As the review of this question has brought out nearly all the allusions in the dialogues to the future state, the nature of Plato's views relative to man's final destiny may be readily anticipated. We have no data to warrant the positive assertion that he held to the final purification of all souls from sin. It will be readily

---

143. We cannot refrain from alluding, in this connection, to a celebrated passage in the seventh letter of Plato, which is hostile to the idea of transmigration. As the letters have been suspected by many critics, and rejected by some as spurious, we have hardly been willing to strengthen our argument by giving great prominence to their testimony. Our own opinion is in favor of their genuineness, and as we have before stated, Boeckh has thrown his ballot for the authenticity of the seventh, which is the only one we quote. The testimony of this document, if received, is the more valuable, as we may fairly presume that opinions expressed in the frankness of social correspondence may be more safely trusted as an honest expression of Plato's views. "Inanimate beings," says he, "can experience no good or evil; but every soul must experience them, both during its union with the body, and after it shall be separated from it. We must confide in the holy doctrine that the soul is immortal; that after its release from the body it finds judges who are strict, and punishments severe, and consequently, that it is a more trifling evil to suffer than to commit injustice. . . . . . Unhappiness is inseparable from all injustice, and a fatal law condemns the unjust soul to draw with it this impiety wherever it may sojourn in this world, and during its wandering courses under the earth, providing for it, everywhere, the most shameful and miserable experience," (vol. xiii., letter 7, pp. 88, 89.)

seen, from the tenor of the passages we have introduced, that future conscious existence was not only
with him a speculative belief founded on pyscholog-
ical analysis, but also a demand of our spiritual nature, to satisfy the claims of the moral law.   Under
whatever forms, or with whatever poetic license he
depicted the circumstances and fixed the details of
the soul's future condition, that condition itself was
never arbitrary in his thought, but always a necessary result of the soul's moral development.   The
severity of his ethical views involved the idea of
immortality as indispensable, not indeed to *restore*,
but to *perfect* the order seemingly violated here.
He looked upon the spiritual life of men as a circle,
of which the present state is but an arc, but whose
full sweep requires and includes the progressive experience of futurity.

It has been charged upon Plato that he held to
the immediate efflux of all souls from God, and to
a reabsorption of spirit into the divine essence.
We do not know a single passage which gives even
plausibility to such a view.   Everywhere the future
life is posited as a state of spiritual development, as
personal agents, either in an upward or downward
course.[1]   This is the soul of his moral system; and

---

[1] Mr. Norton asserts (Gen. of the Gospels, p. 109, note,) that "as regards the generality of men, Plato's scheme was wholly inconsistent
with a belief in their personal immortality." This is the most monstrous perversion of Platonism that can possibly be framed. There is
no justification for the remark in the letter, or the spirit, of a single dogmatic or mythical passage throughout the range of Plato's works. In
fact, the very next passages of Mr. Norton's note are inconsistent with

it was to express this fact that the metempsychosis and the imagery of the popular mythology were used with such poetic freedom and complete indifference.   Accordingly, whenever they are introduced, no matter what sacrifices may be made to the demands of dramatic propriety or to elegance of form, the idea of retribution and of continuous moral development is preserved as the central and stable fact.   Neither can it be denied that generally he affirmed the punishments of the coming state to be disciplinary.   His view of the relation between this life and the future was not that of modern orthodoxy.   Nothing is farther removed from the spirit of his philosophy than the idea that life is a probationary state, and that the experience of the future is to the guilty an unalterable penalty for sin.   Under the veil of transmigration, in the successive manifestations through forms, the cycles of whose changes would at last restore the soul to purity and spiritual freedom, was hidden Plato's view of the future as a disciplinary state.   This reappears in every myth; and in the Gorgias and Phædon especially he shows the efficacy of punishment in reclaiming the great majority of souls to a life of pu-

the statement.   Plato held firmly to the personal immortality of every soul, and to a graduated scale of disciplinary punishments, applied to individual sinners according to the nature of their crimes.   Many other instances of misapprehension might be quoted from the allusions to Plato in the third volume of "The Genuineness of the Gospels." Mr. Norton, though apparently well read in the Platonic writings, very rarely seizes the spirit of Platonism, and, on the whole, is one of the least trustworthy of Plato's commentators.

rity. But, in the last-mentioned dialogues, he speaks
of some who are too far gone to be reclaimed, and
whose punishment is continued, not with the hope
of benefiting them, but as a warning to other offenders. It is somewhat singular that it is tyrants
mostly who are thus delivered over by Plato's justice to eternal woe as incurable. "I think," says
he, "that the greater part of those thus used for
spectacles, are tyrants, kings, rulers, and politicians.
For it is they who, by reason of the power with
which they are clothed, commit actions the most
unjust and impious. Homer, too, is on my side.
Those whom he represents as tormented eternally
in hell, are kings and potentates, like Tantalus and
Sysiphus." [1] In the Phædrus, too, as we have seen,
the ninth and last degree of fallen souls become tyrants; and in the tenth book of the Republic, those
whose crimes are remediless and who are tormented
by devils, are said to be Ardys, and others, "of
whom the most part were, like him, tyrants." [2]
When we bear in mind the frequent accommodations
to the prevailing religious conceptions of the time,
which are scattered throughout the Platonic dialogues, it is somewhat difficult to decide the value
of the few passages that speak of eternal punishment. The theory of transmigration, certainly, is
more favorable to the idea of universal restoration;
for in the mythic forms under which that is conveyed, although no picture is presented of a complete return, the language is generally favorable to

---

[1] Vol. iii., Gorgias, pp. 408, 409.   [2] Vol. x., p. 288.

the hypothesis, and no degree of corruption is spoken of as too stubborn to be cured. The idea involved in the metempsychosis is the one expressed in the Timæus, that condemnation to successive animal forms "will not cease till, governing by reasoning its grosser nature, the soul renders itself worthy to receive its first and excellent conditions."[1] The power to amend is given to the soul even in its most degraded state, and a fair inference from the general language used in stating the theory of transmigration, would be that a return to virtue will finally be effected. Accordingly, it may be doubted whether — since punishment in the coming life is so generally stated to be disciplinary — the exception in the case of tyrants, while it was necessary in order to preserve the consistency of the myths, as representations of the popular belief in eternal woe, may not have been intended to express Plato's horror at unjust and arbitrary government as the most heinous and least expiable of crimes.

And, certainly, if Plato really held the doctrine of utter perdition, there is a dissonance, an insoluble discord, between the outward artistic form and the inward moral spirit of his philosophy. Looking at his religious principles when abstractedly stated, they are pure and lofty, above, we must say, much of the theology of the Church to-day. Good, in Plato's system, is the fundamental quality, the essential character of God. He is the author solely of good. In his model state, Plato would permit no poets to

[1] Vol. xiii., Tim. p. 189

ascribe the misfortunes and calamities of men to the
design of Deity, unless they should maintain that
chastisement is no misfortune, and that punishment
has turned to the advantage of the criminal.[1] All
natural phenomena are so ordered as to subserve
some purpose of good. "There is a Providence
which extends to all men. Thyself, mean mortal,
insignificant as thou mayest be, art of some account
in the general order, and related to it incessantly.
If thou murmur, it is from lack of knowledge how
thy private good is related at once to thyself and to
the all, according to the laws of universal existence."[2] To a mind animated with such views of
Deity, of course the problem of evil must have presented itself as a knotty subject of speculation.
There is abundant evidence, in the dialogues, that
it troubled Plato exceedingly, and that he grappled
with it often, anxious to obtain a clear solution.
His explanations of it are various; many of them
visionary (such for instance as the myth of "the
Statesman,") and destitute, doubtless, even to his
own mind, of scientific value. But he always clung
with invincible tenacity to the entire freedom of the
human will. He is *ultra*, uncompromising on this
point; and in no dialogue has he, to our knowledge,
attempted to show the consistency of this entire
freedom with a controlling Providence. It is always
stated in the boldest form. Plato's piety would not
suffer the character of Deity to be implicated for a
moment with the question of evil. "God leaves to

---

[1] Vol. ix., Rep., p. 118.   [2] Vol. viii., Laws, p. 268.

the disposition of our will the causes on which the quality of each depends."[1] "Virtue has no master; it cleaves to him who honors it and abandons him who rejects it. Each is responsible for his choice. God is guiltless."[2] And with this responsibility was connected the dignity of the soul. "No man," said he, "is willingly evil." This is a fundamental and continually recurring point of Platonic ethics. He borrowed it from Socrates, and was faithful to it throughout.

No man desires to be subject to evil. The end of every volition is not the act committed; but that for the sake of which the act is committed, and this in every undertaking is ultimate good.[3] In the last analysis, the true and the good are one. Evil, therefore, is moral ignorance; and since the soul is essentially reason, it cannot voluntarily be subjected to ignorance, and is not therefore voluntarily wicked.[4] The virtuous man is the true artist who has his aim and can attain it; and vice must be attributed, not really to the will, but to lack of art.[5] The only consistent theory of eternal punishment then, for Plato, is eternity of sin, which is itself contradictory to the last-mentioned view of the harmony of the soul with virtue. We see, therefore, that the idea of eternal punishment as depicted in the Gorgias and the Phædon, is entirely hostile to Plato's declared views of God and man, and moral

---

[1] Vol. viii., Laws, p. 265.   [2] Vol. 10, Rep., p. 287.
[3] Vol. vi., Meno.   [4] Vol. xi., Sophist.
[5] Vol. iv., The Second Hippias.

order. It is contrary to his views of God; for he must not be charged with the commission of any evil, but arranges all things for the best; of man, since the very essence of the soul is free causality and natural harmony with good; of moral order, since to suppose that God removes from the soul this freedom, or that it loses this love of good, would not only violate his scheme of human nature, but would destroy the very principle which solved for Plato the origin of evil. Olympiodorus, one of the Alexandrian commentators of Plato, takes up the passage in the Gorgias which teaches eternal punishment, and attempts to account for its introduction there. "Punishment," says he, "cannot be eternal; much better to say that the soul is perishable. An unending pain can do no good, for it is useless. But God and nature do nothing in vain." He accounts for the passage by contending that Plato used the word *eternal* with reference to the order of the heavenly spheres. The moral cycle of the world corresponds to the motions of the planets, and when the whole system shall have returned to the same relative positions from which they started with respect to each other and the sun, a new period will commence. The cycle includes many thousand years, and it is to this period that Plato refers in his use of the term *everlasting.* The criticism does honor to the benevolence of the commentator, who, with all the Alexandrine school, we believe, rejected the doctrine of eternal woe.[1] But

---

[1] See the whole commentary quoted by Cousin in the notes to his

it is entirely fanciful as a solution of the passage in question, and we must fall back upon the inconsistency of the tenet with Plato's ethics and theology as affording reasonable proof that, like the whole myth in which it occurs, it was borrowed from popular superstition, and was preserved, in obedience to the law of artistic consistency, as an embellishment to the severe moral discussion of the Gorgias.

translation of Plato, vol. iii., Gorgias. We cannot help contrasting this view of the ancient philosopher with the glee which inspires a modern Christian critic — Dr. Tayler Lewis — in detailing the facts of Plato's myths. He seems quite delighted with the aid which Plato brings to his theology, and more than once forces him into the field against "modern semi-infidels and neologists." We doubt whether Plato would be elated with the honor of a doctorate in Calvinistic divinity; at any rate, when modern orthodoxy shall become Platonic, Christianity will have occasion to rejoice over her freedom from many a theological excrescence; and the world of woe, at least, may expect to be visited and cheered by some rays of mercy from the throne of Love. Dr. Lewis's admiration seems almost equally divided between Plato and the Bible. He defends some of Plato's wildest flights of fancy by the letter of Scripture, as in the case of the animation of the heavenly bodies. Plato at times seems to imagine that the planets had souls and are intelligent beings, which Dr. Lewis considers a very plausible idea, and seeks to defend from the Old Testament. "The Bible teaches us," says he, "that even the ordinary courses of physical events are under the controlling agency of angelic beings. *He maketh his angels winds, his ministers a flaming fire.* Why not an angel of the sun, of the moon, and of each planet? Was it simply a sublime personification, when it was said, *He bringeth out their host by number, he calleth them all by their name?* or when we are told that, at the creation of our earth, THE STARS OF THE MORNING *sang together, and all the sons of God shouted for joy?*" And yet with all Plato's orthodoxy, Dr. Lewis's mind seems not entirely at ease upon the question of his salvation. Could he trace anything of the doctrine of the atonement "in the lives or writings of Plato and Socrates," he should "indulge more hope of their salvation from it than from any of those moral lessons — truly beautiful and sublime as they are — which have been left to us in their immortal dialogues."

It may easily be seen, from the rapid survey we
have taken of Plato's passages on immortality, that
the task of criticism is no pastime.   And so far as
results in plain black and white, in dogmatic sentences, are concerned, it certainly is unsatisfactory.
"Myths," says Cousin, "can never be translated."
It is almost impossible to convey by analysis the
fresh impressions produced by the perusal of an
author like Plato.   He is an artist.   In his dialogues, as in his mind, the philosophic and the
poetic, the beautiful and true, unite and blend.
No author is less likely to be appreciated, or more
likely to be misunderstood by a cold, severe, and
unimaginative thinker.   He must be read by an
eye that can look beneath the words ; he must be
criticised by a spirit in sympathy with the author's
aim, and which can resign itself to the influence
of the dialogues, often trusting to feeling as its
guide, rather than to a microscopic analysis of sentences.   Such a mind, while from the diversity of
the materials, and the various poetic developments
of the thought, it feels the difficulty of stating with
precision the form of Plato's views, will rise from
the study of them impressed with their power and
elevated by their purity.   It will no more impute
to Plato the literal views developed in many of his
gorgeous philosophic poems, than it would judge
the theology of Phidias by his head of Jove, or the
faith of Goethe by his picture of Mephistophiles.
The results to which a criticism fitted to disen-
tangle the Platonic dialogues would arrive, as to

11

their doctrine of immortality,. would be immeasurably more accurate, we believe, as they would be
more noble than could be developed by any textual
harmony. It would grant that concerning everything connected with the soul and man's spiritual
nature, Platonism is vastly superior to any other
form of ancient, we may almost add, even of modern speculation. For Plato never faltered in his
spiritual view of man. The superior principle and
governing agency of the universe was one infinite,
controlling Mind, entirely independent of material
forms. And so the spirit in man, with him, was
superior to its fleshly envelope, an indivisible, eternally subsisting entity. The proofs brought to establish this point may seem futile to modern logic ; but
the moral end and aim of existence, the relation of
the soul to duty and the moral law, everywhere
implied in Plato's system, compel us to rank it
next to, though far enough removed 'from, the
ethics of the gospel. Plato keeps the soul ever in
the light of eternity. His theory of life is based
upon a consciousness of the enduring nature of the
spirit and its nearer relation, in its disembodied
state, to eternal justice, the discipline and retribution of impartial wisdom. The limit which divides
the abstract theology of Platonism from the abstract theology of Christianity is the boundary line
which separates the intellectual principle of justice
from the higher quality of love.

Looking 'about in modern. times for some man
with whose views to compare Plato's theories of the

future state, we should say that it has a nearer affinity with the speculations of Swedenborg than with those of any other thinker; inasmuch as the central idea of most of the Platonic myths would seem to be that the soul creates its own objective circumstances according to its inner character, with the difference, however, that, with Swedenborg, the condition of the soul in future life is fixed and final from the beginning, while with Plato there is a constant development of life, the successive cycles of its discipline promising at last to restore the soul to good. The man who reads Plato, expecting to find logical arguments for immortality, applicable to the present state of science, will certainly be disappointed. There is no danger that the Christian will be anxious to exchange the grounds of his belief for the supports of philosophy alone. Still, no man can become thoroughly imbued with the spirit of Plato's views, without being better able to appreciate the simplicity and purity of the gospel; and it is a valuable and inspiring truth which Platonism sufficiently reveals, that the human mind, in proportion as it becomes more spiritual, and learns to live within itself, feels a witness of its dignity and destiny, and is elevated to a sense of certainty as to its enduring life, which logic, though it may not be able satisfactorily to establish, is utterly unable to weaken or remove.

VI.

THOUGHT AND THINGS.

St. Paul has said, "The things which are seen
are temporal; but the things which are not seen
are eternal." And, apart from the special reference
of the passage to the superior stability of spiritual
interests and treasures, a consideration of it may
lead us to alter our general estimate of what is
truly transitory and what permanent in life. It
represents the relations between spirit and matter,
between the ideal and impalpable, and the gross and
sensual; between *thought* and *things*.

The common philosophy of the world ascribes
true permanence and substantial persistence to the
objects of our senses, to the whole outward universe,
to what we see, hear, and feel. Thoughts, sentiments, perceptions of right and beauty and truth,
the soul and affections, systems of philosophy, liter-
atures, views of religion; — these are *abstractions*,
they are fleeting and variable; they are ghostly,
speculative, *unreal;* while houses and estates, the
stomach and brain, armies and money, the visible
deeds of men, and whatever we can discover of the
world by the aid of our eyes and our instruments;
these are impregnable *facts*, about which there can

be no mistake, stubborn and solid as the stones that pave the streets. A piece of rock in the hand is *felt* by any one to be a pretty substantial thing; to institute a comparison between it and a perception of truth and beauty, as to real power and durability, would be taken by a majority of people as an evidence of insanity.

Without denying now the correctness of this estimate of material nature, and the sensual side of life, we affirm that it is not *so* real, so *substantial*, in the highest sense, as the realm of thoughts and feelings and abstract principles. For, when we study rightly, we shall see that all outward and material nature, and all the facts and appearances of life, are but the manifestations and forms through which hidden, subtile, abstract thoughts and forces are revealed. We must not think to determine true reality and strength by weight and measure. The stream of fire that splits the oak is hardly a ponderable thing. That is the most durable and real, we will all, I think, allow, which *moulds* and *causes* and *creates*, which subjects other things to its influence, and determines their character and form. Now, the side of nature which seems to the senses so firm and enduring is not the *causal* side, but only the *passive side*, the *effect* the product, the transitory case or shell of deep, underlying, active, permanent powers. It is the veil of a more delicate, refined, but greater presence, the obedient body of a subtile, indwelling soul. What we see is temporal; it is the unseen always that possesses the essential life, and is permanent and eternal.

The subject may be illustrated on the broadest scale by reference to the outward universe itself as presented to us by modern astronomy. How sublime is the spectacle revealed to the imagination by the physical glories with which space is filled! I will not attempt to convey, by words, a picture of the magnificence of the visible universe. The effort would be futile. And yet the whole scene is only the picture of ideas, the imagery of thought, the hieroglyphic record of the art and meditation of the Deity. There is not a planet that wheels a tiny circle around its controlling flame; not a sun that sheds its steady radiance upon the dark depths of neighboring space; not a comet that rushes through its eccentric track; not a constellation among all that burn like fantastic chandeliers upon the dome of heaven; not a firmament that hangs like a ragged fringe of light upon the confines of infinity, that is not merely the visible statement of a conception or wish which dwells in the mind of God, from which it was born, and to which alone it owes its present form and being. It was the thought of the Almighty that first gave meaning to universal chaos. Darkness hung over the deep of things till the spirit of God moved over it, and infused its essence into nature; and it was in answer to the silent will of the Invisible, that light burst like a wave of glory over an orderly creation.

Science impresses deeply on the student the lesson that there is a causal force, a stability in the ideal world, of which the material is only the transitory show. The curves and circles and ellipses, which the planets cut in space are the geometry of God. The oscillations which at times disturb and threaten to destroy the stellar harmonies, reveal the intricate method of eternal order, when we see them compensating each other and mutually controlled into the most stable concord. The chemic, electric, magnetic forces that preserve the universe in constant activity and sustain its life, are nothing else than the immediate agency of the spirit that is hidden in its frame. Take these away from our conceptions of the outward world, and what would be left? The sensualist feels the ground to be solid beneath his feet, and calls that substantial. And yet we tread only on a subtile, invisible force. What is it that makes the earth compact, and binds the hardest rock into its firm consistence? Nothing ·but the forces of cohesion and gravitation. Withdraw these from matter and instantly it becomes a mist of finest sand; it crumbles and dissipates into motes smaller than an animalcule's eye, it flies off into nothing. And these laws and powers are God's will and thoughts; we *tread* on abstract principles. It is overwhelming, the revelation which modern science gives of the impalpable and spiritual forces that underlie, surround, and enclose us all. Strike the ideal element from nature and the whole frame of things would dissolve and die. The golden-fretted roof of night was stretched by an omnipo-

tent thought; the suns are but points and lines of
splendid diagrams; the planets, beads rolled in the
grooves of law; the beauty of nature, which so
haunts and inspires the poet's soul, is the struggling
of matter with a hidden meaning which will rise in
subtile exhalations from its bonds; the solidity of
matter is the continuance of a divine resolution.
Everything we touch or see is but the shape and
color of a mental force that lies behind. Let the
pleasure of the Almighty or his thought change,
and the universe will instantly, and by necessary
response, change its order, hue, and form. The
things which *are seen* are merely the temporal,
accidental manifestations of secret, intellectual
powers, which are unseen but eternal.

Shelley has finely said, —

> " Earth and ocean,
> Space, and the isles of life and light that gem
> The sapphire floods of interstellar air,
> This firmament, pavilioned upon chaos,
> With all its cressets of immortal fire,
> With all the silent or tempestuous workings
> By which they have been, are, or cease to be,
> Is but a vision;
> Thought is its cradle and its grave, nor less
> The future and the past are idle shadows
> Of Thought's eternal flight — they have no being;
> *Nought is but that it feels itself to be.*"

And so in outward nature there is but one substance, *God*, — a spiritual force of which all apparent being is the emanation and form.

And history also reveals the same law; the working and persistence of ideas and spiritual principles

behind the outward facts which strike the eye. If we look behind us, upon the nations that have occupied and ruled the world, we shall learn how impotent are all the material implements and appliances of strength, if there be not a groundwork of right and ideal power as the support of greatness. The fortunes of the chief nations of the past seem like camera shadows thrown upon the mists of time, chasing each other rapidly across the scene, and melting at last into the dark. Nineveh, Babylon, Persia, Meroe, Egypt, Macedon, none of these obtained a rooted being. In history, they appear like a dream. As we read their annals under the light of a chronology in which the philosophy of history must always be studied, and in which centuries are the hours of a providential cycle, they all ' come like shadows, so· depart.' Physical power they had, impregnable cities, splendid palaces, countless wealth, powerful armies, and yet there were no elements of permanence and firmness. They were only massive forts thrown up in nature, but ungarrisoned by ideas, which the elements played with as they would. They had no hidden moral and mental life, no abstract existence that dwelt in them like a guiding soul. Not that they were generated by accident, without a cause ; but, like gigantic mushrooms, they were animated only by a feeble, feverish, quickly-expended life, and therefore sprang up full-formed in a night, to perish in a night. The solemn political lesson to which history points us, written on the tombstones of kingdoms that are·

buried in the sands of time, declares that truth, courage, genius, integrity, temperance, self-denial, all intangible, spiritual, unseen elements, are the only bonds and bulwarks of nations. Where these fail in the mightiest physical monarchy, it is like severing the living, fibrous sap-roots of a giant tree, and drying the sap within its bark. A blight will fall upon it. The process of decay will rapidly go on. Its leaves look sickly, its branches shrink and wither. It can no longer wrestle proudly with the storm. A passive subsistence is all that remains, and it depends only on the pleasure of God whether it shall fall, crashing before the angry blast, and uprooted from the soil of time, or rot and moulder into oblivion by the more silent and terrible visitation of the worm. It is not by wealth, or walls, or muscles, that a nation can intrench itself securely, but by enterprise devoted to some mental and moral culture, by free absorption of the unseen, spiritual elements of health and vigor. It is not the area of political freedom, but the spirit of moral freedom on which a state can build secure. History preaches continually to understanding ears the phrase, "the things that are seen are temporal and transitory ; it is the ideal and unseen that endures."

Do we need a more impressive revelation of the fact that truth and thought alone are permanent, than the bare conception of the fortune of the beings that have inhabited this globe ? A thousand millions of intelligent forms now people our planet, with busy hands and scheming brains. While we, too, are active on the scene, life seems something quite secure ; we do not realize how busy is the scythe of death. Every fifty or sixty years, like a vast array of ghosts, they flit, these myriads, over the stage of life, almost with an audible wail over their unsubstantial vanity, and vanish, we know not where. How few from among this spectral array of our fellows, leave any record of their being to remain in the memory of the world ? And who are those few ? Not the wealthy, the haughty, the despots who ruled by force. Scarce one of these, except it be for the scorn and execration of posterity. Those who pass away to leave behind an earthly immortality, are they who brought into the world more of the enduring elements of spiritual power. A Homer, Shakespeare, Dante, Burns, — poor, untitled, and obscure, — sends forth from a spirit finely organized, a thrill of melody, sweet, sad, or cheering, in response to the experience that has swept over his heart, and the bodiless tone goes down the ages when the creative soul has fled, rising above the noise of wars, the crash of falling empires, and the harsh discord of a conqueror's fame. From the mind of a David or Isaiah gushes a lyric psalm or gorgeous prophecy of good ; and those die not, though all traces of the Hebrew state, and the rich pomp of the ceremonial worship, the grand temple structure, and the millions who bowed within its courts, have gone into a common grave. Raffaelle and Angelo, during their earthly stay, caught gleams of a more than earthly beauty, and left slight sketches of it in color or in stone ; Mozart and Beethoven, with finer ears, reported symphonies which had never before been published in this grosser world ; Bacon and Newton pointed to the method, and shed over the race the radiance of higher and sublimer truth ; Washington and Howard yielded their hearts to the guidance of perfect principle and holy love ; and thus out of the thousands of myriads of spirits that are driven across the stage of being like snow-flakes before the storm, some half a score from every century endure because they have caught the elements of permanence from the ideal forces of nature into which they had baptized their souls.

We may draw some useful instruction from history also, concerning the greater stability of thought compared with things, by observing how the inward life of every people — its ideas and aspirations — reveal themselves in its outward institutions, and create its outward institutions. Precisely as the thought of God expresses itself in the order of nature, in the harmonies of space, and the plan and parts of the material universe, does the genius of a nation reveal itself in its government, its laws, its schemes of conquest, its poetry, its religion, its art.

> " And what if Trade sow cities
> Like shells along the shore,
> And thatch with towns the prairie broad,
> With railways ironed o'er? —
> They are but sailing foam-bells
> Along Thought's causing stream,
> And take their shape and sun-color
> From him that sendsthe dream."   .

The institutions of no two nations are the same, because the intellectual structure and the prominent ideas of no two nations are the same. When the historian observes the outward complexion and forms of life of different kingdoms so unlike as Hindostan and France, China and England, Greece and Persia, he knows that it is not by accident, but by necessity; he sees that the superficial dissimilarity is but the sign of a difference in the moral life and spiritual structure of the people, and he seeks to know the habits, feelings, religion, aims of the nation; because then only can he understand its true, essential character. These visible forms are but the casing of ideas, the fibrous wood and bark that enclose the living organic currents that flow within, and from which the case is generated. " The things which are seen are temporal." It is from the intangible, permanent, ideal elements that the outward appearances are born.

I have often, in standing upon one of the bridges that connect the city of my residence with the metropolis of Massachusetts, and while reflecting upon the scene there presented to the eye, felt the force of the motto which was written by Paul. A little more than two centuries ago, no foot of any representative of the present possessors of the soil had trod the surrounding shores. The river flowed in a beautiful, broad current to the sea, unbroken, except by the sea-bird's wing, or the swift, noiseless motion of the picturesque canoe. The stillness of primeval nature rested in benediction over the scene.

Year after year the morning dawned upon a monotonous landscape, while the setting sun gilded
the smoke that rose from humble cabins, and the
deepening twilight gave a sombre gloom to groves
and forests that enclosed the homes of the simple,
unaspiring, dusky tenants of the soil. They were
content, and nature remained undisturbed. And
so it would have remained forever ; but another
people, with a deeper, more creative inward life,
are directed to its shores; and the powerless
natives melt in their path, quickly trodden down
into forgotten graves. And now see how a magic
ideal wand changes the whole aspect of the picture!
Before their strong ideas, the forests fall as if swept
away by a resistless flame. Institution after institution springs up amid the solitudes, to answer an
inward want in the new dwellers' breasts. Their
emotions of worship dot the scene with temples, each
consecrated to some slight difference in the ideas of
God and Heaven ; the river is bridged by their skill ;
their enterprise lines the shores with masts, and
whitens the water with sails that are to take the
breezes of every sea ; from one summit looks down
the dome that represents their justice, government,
and law ; from the blood-stained soil of another
shoots the shaft that bears witness to their patriotism
and heroic valor ; on a third is set the shrine of
learning, where the principles of freedom may be
perpetuated in cultivated minds ; where the deer
roamed undisturbed, the university springs forth in
obedience to an intellectual call ; towns grow popu-

lous along the track of the steam-car, the splendid triumph of their restless, cunning labor; and from a thousand points arise the structures that proclaim the existence of refinement, health, luxury, and an ever-active Christian love. What an organic revelation is such a panorama presented every day to the dwellers in American cities, teaching the causal power and creative energy of ideas, and feelings, and faith, and aspiration. These are the permanent forces of being, the substantial base of things. All history has been pliant to their moulding, leavening power. They work in the centre of empires; they heave up the embankments of social and political existence; often they shake, with a sudden earthquake throe, the rotten thrones of kings and the hollow pillars of licentious palaces into ruin; and at times, when the pressure of force and fraud and falsehood becomes too desperate, they burst through some yawning revolution, rend all the strata of conventional resistance, and send forth a volcanic, fiery stream to overwhelm the obstacles which have too long restrained their natural and peaceful play.

The eternal, permanent side of nature is always unseen; all force is spiritual; causal, creative, enduring power resides only in abstract things: in truth, virtue, emotions, thought. When we would prophesy in relation to the prosperity or downfall of a kingdom, our calculation is always founded on the moral and intellectual vigor that is in it. This, rightly directed, will hold it up; when this begins to fail, we know that the nation begins to die.

Our whole civilization, too, is nothing but a network of invisible, spiritual, but most potent bonds which preserve society from anarchy. The power of law,—what is it but the respect for law? Sturdy patriotism,—what is it but personal love of freedom? Refinement of manners,—what is it but a practical feeling of the beauty of courtesy and the dignity of man? Social order is built on these subtile elements. Should they fail, civilization itself would crumble.

The process of reform, also, is nothing but an expulsion of degrading sentiments by the infusion of a purer spirit. If the philanthropist would stifle intemperance, he must plainly inspire the popular heart with a nobler self-denial, or an affection for a higher than sensual gratification. He labors to smother wars. Could an entire reverence for the Christian law of life possess the hearts of rulers, armies might be disbanded, and navies used for commerce. He struggles against the horrible enormity of slavery. If a divine miracle could but infuse a proper sense of justice, a hearty recognition of the fact of brotherhood into the South to day, to-morrow's sun would not set upon a single bondman.

Wherever a higher idea, a worthier principle goes forth, it goes to renovate and conquer and reform. And all those events and epochs of time that are connected with the birth and development of a greater truth, are the important epochs, the immortal events. The salient vital periods in history have not been the times of widest tumult,—the wars of Napoleon, the crusades, the great political storms, and social convulsions, and temporary anarchy. It is astonishing how soon, when no great principle is involved in them, when it is mere brute struggle, these pass away without a trace from history, and leave the surface calm again.

Great epochs begin with the birth of a new truth, with a new discovery, with the development of a higher character. When the idea of the printing-press dawns on a mechanic's mind ; when Columbus fancies the round shape of the globe ; when Luther utters an impregnable principle; then the fortunes of the race are gently turned into a different channel by the mild pressure of necessity.

It is the great conceptions of noiseless birth, not the roaring effervescence, that change the face of things. "The meek, silent light can mould, create, and purify all nature ; but the loud whirlwind, the sign and product of disunion, of weakness, passes on and is forgotten."

The most notable period of the ages was that when a Galilean peasant uttered by the way-side, and in humble homes, to artless listeners, to dull disciples and wondering ears, his simple, winning thoughts. He trusted his words to the air, to the memory of his hearers, to the providence of God. He knew they would not die. They were feeble sounds, articulated in a decaying language, but in no fact seems his spirit greater than in his serene confidence that they *could not die*. "Heaven and earth," said he, "shall pass away, but my words shall not pass

12

away." What a calm statement is this of the superior permanence of a fleeting thought, if it be a truth, over all material nature. No, they have not passed away. They are still stronger than all the resistance of the world. They are the chart of life, the cement of society, the pillars of our welfare, the hope of the race.

If we study life aright, we shall never sneer at abstractions — at speculative or ideal principles — as visionary and unreal. If they are false, they are unsubstantial as the coruscations in the northern sky. If true, they are permanent, — omnipotent as God. "Solid as a rock," is a common proverb among men; a more expressive sentiment would be "solid as truth," "impregnable as principle," "resistless as right."

These thoughts are religious teachers. If it is ideal and mental forces only that are permanent, then the spirit within us, when rightly educated, is the most substantial fact in nature. *If rightly educated*, for the lesson which our subject teaches is, that there is just so much substance to us as there is truth, virtue, spiritual life within. The soul is *ideal*; all there *is* of us is ideal. A man may have as much soul as he pleases. By culture and discipline it will *grow* as the muscles harden and the flesh grows firm by healthful food and exercise. And just in proportion as he believes in the permanence of ideal things, and endeavors to build an inward temple of them, does he become a solid fact, a stubborn *something* among these transitory shadows. If he neglects this work he is a ghost, an airy apparition, long before he dies. The world is filled with these spectral men, with lean, lank, hazy spirits, which have become thin and unsubstantial by neglect. We see it in the common aims of life, in the kind of ambition that fires the popular heart, in the temper of the market, the etiquette of the exchange, and the morality of the crowd and the Congress hall. The all-engrossing care of the body, the absorbing desire of wealth, the craving for a life of easy and superficial show, the sensualism entrenched behind every phase of society, betray the fact that we are animated bodies only, that we have little faith in the greatness of inward sentiments, in the wealth of cultivated affections, in the bliss of devotion and self-sacrifice.

Men feel and know that pain is a fact, although it is unseen; they need to learn that peace of mind is a *fact*, and comes by a well-ordered soul; that reverence is a fact, and brings us near to God; that elevated sentiment is a fact, and raises us into a higher society than earth; that sober faith is a fact, and gilds the horizon of our being with a heavenly glory. In the absence of this faith we read the barrenness of soul there is in the world.

We read it too in the prevailing, lurking, practical scepticism in immortality, a scepticism that " haunts with fiend-like stare the uplifted eye of faith and love." I do not wonder at this scepticism. The body weighs us down; we are contented prisoners in it; we forget our native realm, and so easily believe that the grave is the goal.

Every argument for immortality that can be brought is of little avail; even the resurrection of Christ is a wonderful story merely, to a thorough sensualist whose aspirations have never reached beyond pleasure and the present, — whose meditations, sent forth like doves from the floating ark of life, have never brought back a green and budding promise of that solid land. To feel a conviction of immortality we must *live* for it. Let any one firmly believe that the soul is permanent, and live from that belief, and soon existence will seem permanent too; the world becomes the veil of a brighter glory that lies behind it; the condemnation of unbelief is lifted off, since the mind, conscious of its own rooted being, does not wait for immortality, " but is passed from death unto life."

VII.

TRUE GREATNESS.

IT is recorded by Matthew that the disciples once went to Jesus with the question, — "Who is the greatest in the Kingdom of Heaven?" and to-day the world needs to be enlightened in regard to the elements of true greatness. Greatness may be predicated of mental or moral qualities. A man may be great because of natural abilities, or on account of vast acquirements. There is the greatness of gifts, and of energy; of splendid genius, and of ardent faithfulness.

If we ask who is the greatest as a poet, one answer will be appropriate! It is he who has easiest access to the richest treasures of imagination, whose perception of beauty is keen, and who knows how to entrance the human heart by the magic of his creations, and the music of his lines. Do we inquire who is greatest as a preacher? The definition should be, he who can enlighten most clearly the minds of men in regard to duty, thrill them with a conviction of responsibility, and draw them by the sweetest persuasion to the love of God and to purity of life. Would we know who is greatest as a statesman? Evidently, he whose mind is broad enough to comprehend great interests,—the structure of society and governments, and the precise bearing of projected measures upon the welfare and glory of a whole nation ; while his mental resources, vigor of will, and suppleness of temper, are equal to the necessities, perplexities, and dangers of any crisis in the State. Who is greatest as a farmer ? He who has complete mastery over the tractable elements of nature. Who as a mechanic ? The man of most cunning brain and responsive hand.

But these are only fragmentary answers to the question we are considering. We do not ask who is chief or preëminent among different kinds of men, but, who is the greatest *man?* What is central or total greatness of soul ? The answer, of course, depends upon the standard which rules our judgment.

There is the world's standard, which has always been partial. Its test has been power, influence, splendid abilities, worldly success. It has judged the claims and capacities of men by the mental qualities they possess, and the force of these qualities has been gauged by the outward and dazzling results which they have wrought, without any reference to the inward mastery of those qualities, and their stern subordination to a noble aim.

Strictly speaking, the world has never had any idea, or complete ideal, of a great man. Its only estimate of greatness is the possession of conspicuous qualities. Its great men have been great instruments merely, and their relative rank has been determined by their comparative efficiency for certain visible ends. If a person exhibits some one quality in sufficient brilliancy to throw that quality of others in the shade, the world immediately awards the palm of greatness. In its vocabulary the term great is merely the equivalent of noticeable. Hence the heroes of the world are the most remarkable warriors, artists, poets, statesmen, lawyers, etc., — those who can most easily win a battle, carve a statue, write a drama, control a kingdom, and save a desperate cause. Now this is just the method to gauge the force and degree of special qualities, and therefore, the list and rank of the chief poets, warriors, scholars, etc., of the world need little revision. But there is a vast difference between a conspicuous quality and a great man. Alexander was an organized military quality, but he was not a great man. Byron was a brilliant poetic faculty, but not a great man. Lord Bacon was a consummate intellectual energy, but not a great man.

We cannot construct a complete definition of greatness without including a moral and spiritual element. The chief characteristic of man is, that he has a soul, and possesses privileges and incurs responsibilities by reason of this endowment. And if the soul be the distinguishing trait of manhood, the exercise of the privileges and recognition of the responsibilities which this trait imposes and bestows must be at least one part, if not the chief part, of the constitution of true manliness. To leave these out of the estimate is to slight the noblest gift and function of humanity, in a description of humanity in its highest form. The comprehensive definition of greatness should be, — the highest exercise of all our powers in their true order and harmony. He is the greatest man who is most of a man, and he is the most of a man who faithfully cultivates in due proportion all the distinctive qualities and force of his being. A great man, therefore, is not one prodigious element, which acts as a single instrument, but a concordant congress of powers, all working with a composite unity to a noble end. And so we must look in at his hidden life, as well as outward at his special work, to test the merits of a man.

It is an indispensable requisite to true and total greatness, then, that a clear and accurate perception of the real aim of life be present to the mind, and that all the faculties bend steadily and strongly to the attainment of it. And here a religious element is directly involved. For it is the province of religion to introduce a supreme, disposing element into the heart. Greatness as a man is impossible till this supreme principle is recognized as an idea, and when it has been recognized, greatness is impossible till whatever genius or talent or endowment we have obeys it, and becomes its minister. "The faculties and affections of the single mind are no democracy of principles, each of which in the determinations of the will is to have equal suffrage with the rest, but an orderly series, in which every member has a right divine over that below." " Greater is he that ruleth his spirit than he that taketh a city." The great man's soul is a " realm of order." The will drives all the faculties in harness towards a changeless goal. He rules, and is not ruled by his genius. The whole man will not be a mere lever to work some peculiar quality. If he feels the ability to be artist, poet, statesman, scholar, he will not let his special ability run away with him, and present itself as the whole business of life, nor exhaust the energies of his nature, but will keep it in strict subjection and easy service to the supreme end. Relatively to each other, those men seem great who dazzle the sight, and attract most notice. Content with seeing the glare, we do not think to inquire how strong and productive is their dominion over their gifts, and how proportionable is the development of their being. We are all only partially developed, and can hardly appreciate wholeness of manhood, and so he who is most brilliantly partial carries the day. But in the view of God, before whose infinite reason the distinctions of mere human genius are of no account, greatness is measured by a proper standard, and means the dedication of the whole nature to the service of right, and the harmonious labor of all the powers to make that service valuable. The men whom this test brings out from the background of human life, form the class of great men of the world, because there is most of merit and most of man in them. He who is preëminent in this class, is "the greatest of the Kingdom of Heaven."

'It may be objected that, by the definition we have given, greatness is reduced to mere goodness, since genius, brilliant properties, and strong powers are left entirely out of the account. If it were so, the definition would be fatally partial. What we wish to establish is, that greatness is something *distinct* from mere brilliancy and power, and embraces the idea of inward self-rule, faithfulness, and spiritual culture. A man may be remarkable for brilliancy, and eminent for power, but if he merely displays these qualities without any inward order of spiritual life, an order generated by a faithful will, — if his eminence consists solely in the possession of these qualities and their natural play; if they be not constituent parts of a proportional breadth of character, and are not used as implements of a commanding sentiment enthroned in the soul, — that man is only an exaggerated faculty; he is not truly great. This is a necessary result from the principles of Christianity.

But it by no means follows that all good men are equally great. There is room for all differences and degrees of greatness in Christianity. It puts no iron rule upon human nature. It is not a levelling system. It is generally supposed to be so, but it is a pernicious misapprehension of the gospel to suppose so. We often talk as though the unlearned Christian, the humble and faithful widow, and the exalted sage, are on the same level in the school of

Jesus. We must not think so. If they are equally
Christian, the spirit of their greatness is the same,
but its degree varies with the richness of their gifts.
" One star differeth from another star in glory."
Though genius alone is not greatness, but only good
fortune, the greatest genius can still be the greatest
in Christianity, and keep its natural bent. The
hasty, passionate Peter, the blunt, plain-spoken
James, the mild and loving John, preserved their
individuality uninjured by their devotion to Christianity. One found a sphere for his impetuosity,
another for his calm, reflective powers, and John for
his serene insight and sweet meditations in the service of Christ, and they were his three chosen friends.
Each was great; he was greatest whose genius
blended most beautifully with his character, and
who had the most genius to use in his Master's
cause.

Goodness can employ far-reaching thought, intense ambition, vigorous will, and splendid abilities
of every kind. They are its natural allies; it needs
them all. There is no reason why a great poet
should not be the greater, if he be a Christian, and
because he is a poet. He may make his taste for
beauty subservient to culture of character; it may
become, besides refinement of perception, refinement
of virtue; and his genius may not only help him to
appreciate the works, but to serve the will, of God.
It has been the curse of poets that they have worshipped their poetic faculty, have considered it their
chief distinction, have been slaves to it, and suffered

its development to be lawless and wild, if only it could be brilliant. For this reason, so much of our finest poetry is cold, barren, or licentious. It has come unconsecrated from men who have recognized no orbit to their career, who have not sought to make their poetic power one element of a grand and healthy life, who have not felt their responsibilities for genius, and put no rein upon it, but have prostituted faculties given to be the allies of heaven, to the service of hell. What sight more sickening or painful than splendid gifts unregulated by principle, or sold to the profane and willing service of iniquity. It is time that the deeper insight of the world made a distinction between showy qualities and greatness of soul. Let us look more for a complete development of manhood, in those so bounteously endowed, and not praise the beauty of the mermaid's face, while we say nothing of the monstrous, disgusting shape from which it grows. Let genius be tried before the full bench of human faculties, for its manhood as well as its intellect. Genius should be the adjective, and character the noun that describes men. When Byron's brow is honored with the richest wreath as a testimony of his poetic powers, let him be branded as a spiritual dwarf. There is no reason why genius should lose any of its inspiration, because it is the minister of goodness and of God. Must the inventive mechanic prove his skill by the construction of infernal machines? Literature shall vindicate itself before the moral sense when its great high priest shall come, —

he who shall disdain to seek the inspiration of intemperance, or gild the rottenness of profligacy, and whose praises of virtue shall be dictated by the glowing experience of his heart. Nay, has it not been already shown that vast acquirements and gorgeous abilities are not cramped by the control of integrity, purity, and truth? The world has seen one spectacle of brilliant and solid powers incorporated into vigorous character. It was in the case of Milton, who considered all his powers mortgaged to the support of freedom and right, — Milton, whose youth was spotless, whose pen, in the full fire of his fancy, never soiled a page with a licentious line, whose virtue was beyond temptation, as his genius was without a mate, the prime of whose years was devoted to the service of his distracted country, and his hours of age, neglect, and blindness given to the composition of his lofty poem, and who, after a most checkered life, all spent " as ever in his great Taskmaster's eye," died in poverty and worldly disgrace, leaving to his country the glory of his unappreciated greatness, and to posterity the assurance, not merely of a poet and a politician, but of a Christian and a man.

So should it be with genius, whatever may be its field. Whether the opportunity of service in public life is afforded or denied, be its possessor, artist, historian, novelist, pleader, he may rule his faculties, may make them the ministers to goodness, the cause of God and man, and thus earn the meed of greatness, by the self-development of his powers in their proper order and natural proportion.

A statesman needs forfeit none of his reputation for great abilities by being a Christian. In fact, if he has not Christian principles,—if his integrity, his purity, and the establishment of the right, be not the highest aim with him, to which his abilities are made to bend, he may become celebrated as an insidious, wily politician, but he cannot be honored as a great man. If anything could justify misanthropy, it would be the spectacle of the intellectual grandeur set off against the moral hollowness and barrenness of life in those who have ruled the world. Who can read the shameful annals of diplomacy, or look in upon the trickery of council-rooms, or mark the relations between the highest dignitaries of the earth, or observe the under-current of private jealousies, malignant motives, selfish expectations, that seem to guide the stream of national affairs, or gaze upon the solemn foppery of courts and palaces, and repress with ease the rising sneer at the meanness and depravity of our kind ? If this be the height, and such be the haunts, of greatness and power, where virtue, honor, friendship, and the highest interests of life are slighted, perilled, shipwrecked for forms, ambition, pleasure, self, who can help questioning whether it is right for the Almighty any longer "to glut the innocent space" with so poor an article as man ? This is not greatness. We abuse the word when we apply it to such characters. Would that we could see a Christian statesman,—

one who could feel his humility and obligations rather than his human station and his gifts, and who would sit in the cabinet as in the presence of conscience and God. What a display of greatness would such a spectacle present! The wide theatre of his action, and the great interests with which he dealt, would seem to be the natural field and proper work for the exercise and grasp of such a soul. He would not look like a pigmy on a tower, but, like the lofty pedestal of a colossal statue, his place would be the fitting setting of his powers. His judgment would not be prepledged, nor his opinions pawned to party, but with religious accuracy they would be formed and swayed by right and evidence alone. The mind of such a man, spurning the narrow track of ordinary legislation, and fired by the generous hopes of a Christian heart, would be filled with noble constructive schemes for the elevation of his fellows, and a better progressive organization of the social world. His sense of right could make no distinction between public criminality and private turpitude. The light of heaven would fall on his state-papers, and make a falsehood of the pen, or a trickery of phrase, as black and heinous as a falsehood of speech, and a paltering in words. He would shrink from war as from the encouragement of private murder, and would feel that national honor could never be compromised in shunning it, till it became the only method of vindicating a vital principle, or a present necessity of self-defence. Passion, feeling, interest, would never dare profane the

sacred shrine of conscience by their treacherous
counsels, but intellect, energy, ambition — all the
resources of brain and breast — would be consecrated to the duties of his position, the service of God
and man. Could not Napoleon have found free
scope for his Titanic powers on the field of Euro-
pean politics, if he had been a Christian statesman ?
Could he not have applied his Herculean energy to
the work of human melioration, and proved a genius
equally vast, yes, infinitely more grand, by pledging
his abilities to the service of right, and sweeping
away from Europe its rotten tyrannies only to or-
ganize a deeper justice and establish a healthier
freedom ? Would not his work, instead of fading
away like the smoke of his artillery, have acquired
the perpetuity of truth, and his name have become
immortal as the giant benefactor, rather than the
disturber of mankind ? An approach to this ideal
our own country saw in the character of Washington, and perhaps again in the political patriarch
whom our own State still deplores. And wherever
exhibited, such is true greatness ; it is devotion of
vast abilities to proper ends ; it is such culture of
soul that total manliness, while it is aided by, yet
envelops and governs genius.

Let us banish the thought, then, that Christianity
has brought a lower standard of greatness, or has
banished its degrees. We must beware, too, lest
we enthrone some one quality, such as charity, purity, meekness, as the Christian measure of its existence in the soul. It is not a quality, but the right

development of the whole nature, and its consecration to the holy, pure, and true.

God demands not only purity, but greatness of us all. There is not a person so humble or so feebly gifted that the call is not to him or her. If we have few qualities that can influence, and but a narrow sphere to fill, still we have ourselves to develop, and ourselves to rule. We have the inward realm to put in order, so that, whatever we do, be it never so humble a deed, shall be an instrument to limit the evil of the world, and advance the kingdom of heaven among men. And when the feelings, thoughts, and powers of the least gifted soul by private faithfulness are thus attuned to concordant action for right and truth, the conditions of greatness and the call of God are answered. And then, let us not be sceptical as to our value in the universe. Such greatness will be felt. It will reach some soul. It will preach to some charmed auditor. In the press and throng of life, though it be unassuming and obscure, virtue will go out from it, as from the hem of Jesus' robe, to heal some fraction of the world's disease.

18

VIII.

INDIRECT INFLUENCES.

THE objects of the physical world continually exert indirect influences upon each other. Each tree, shrub, flower, and spire of grass reacts upon the quality of the air, and in that way affects other trees and flowers, and thus, finally, the health of animals, and of the men and women of the globe. The carbonic acid with which our breathing floods the atmosphere, to-morrow will be speeding north and south, and striving to make the tour of the world. The date-trees that grow round the fountains of the Nile will drink it in by their leaves; the cedars of Lebanon will take it up to add to their stature; the cocoanuts of Tahiti will grow riper upon it; and the palms and bananas of Japan change it into flowers. The oxygen we are now breathing was, in part, distilled for us, some short time ago, by the magnolias of the South, and the roses and myrtles of Cashmere; and, in part, forests older than the flood supplied it.

Every particle of matter, by reason of the various laws of mechanical and chemical influences, exerts unseen and undetected influences upon other particles. The smallest planet, or satellite, in the solar system has some effect upon the orbit and motion of huge Jupiter and far-distant Neptune ; and so nice is the adjustment of the celestial forces, that, if these indirect and humble services of the lesser orbs should be lost from the mechanism, the poise of the system would be disturbed, and the motions that now produce such beneficent harmony, would drift towards wreck and ruin. The physical order, stability, and beneficence we behold, are not the result of a few glaring and easily-comprehended arrangements, but the products of a myriad indirect contributions and intricate influences, which deep and patient study discloses to the scientific mind.

In the structure of society, also, the most power-ful agencies for good are indirect, and seldom con-sciously recognized. What a complex thing is that which we call *civilization !* Of how many delicate and different influences is it compounded ! There are times when we are able to see, for an instant, what terrible passions smoulder in the bosom of our Christian society, what savage feelings can be started beneath the placid order of common life, and how coarse the temper and moral sensibility of large portions of our community really are. And yet all this is generally restrained from destructive fury by subtile influences which are intertwined so skilfully, that the whole strength and pressure of them are no more seen than we see the power and momentum of the wind. The fierce elements of human nature are controlled by civilization, as a lion is entrapped by a net,—each line of which is but a straw in comparison with his strength, but whose knots and meshes bind every muscle, and entangle his feet, and distract his energy, so that his vigor is· soon exhausted, and he is no longer a dangerous foe. The best government is that which *seems* to govern least; whose power and motives and control reach us indirectly, and press upon us as steadily and unconsciously as the weight of the air.

That which we call the power of conservâtism in society, and which gives permanence and force to all institutions, — to many that are bad, — is an *indirect* power. All institutions and customs have many and wide relations with the feelings, habits, and hearts of the people among whom they exist. They throw out fine tendrils into the soil of the senti- ments, which we do not like to have disturbed. And hence it is that, after the upper leaves of some great institution have begun to die, and its trunk has rotted, and it is seen by the sharpest eyes to be a cumberer of the ground, — and even after the storm has madly despoiled it, and the hot bolt of intellectual indignation has smitten and shivered it, — it will stand in· some semblance of worth and majesty, because of the unseen and indirect sup- port that is yet afforded from the tap-roots that strike down into the subsoil of feeling, and the. fibres that are twisted in some corners of the social heart.

So much for the broad law, and the *general* man- ifestations of it., Let us notice, next, some of the indirect influences which, as individuals, we are continually receiving from society, and from our companions and friends. We cannot tell how much we derive in this way. A great part of what we know and of what we learn of our opinions and general views — the tone of our judgments, etc. — comes to us and is formed through the spontaneous action of our faculties upon the materials thrown in our way, and the experience which the world forces upon us, rather than by the deliberate reflection and intentional activity of the intellect. We are but slightly conscious, at the time, of the complicated influences that surround us, the various motives that besiege us, or impel us, and the diverse materials that help to build up and draw out our characters. Society is continually acting upon us, not only through our voluntary absorption, but through all the pores of our spiritual nature.

Past ages have an indirect effect upon us, through the institutions they have bequeathed and the general spirit of the civilization they have helped to form. The author of "Euthanasy" and "Martyria" has finely and truly said, "In my character there are the effects of Paul's journey to Damascus, and of the meeting of King John and the barons at Runnymede. There is in my soul the seriousness of the many conflicts, famines, and pestilences of early English times. And of my enthusiasm, some of the warmth is from fiery words which my forefathers thrilled to, in the times of the Commonwealth and of the Reformation. There is in me what has come of the tenderness with which mothers nursed their children, ages ago; and there is that in me which is holy, and which began from a forty days' fast in a wilderness in Judea, now eighteen hundred years since." Every man we meet, every emergency in which we are thrown, leaves its impress, slight or palpable, upon the soul. Just as every particle of food we take, and every breath we inhale, contributes something to the nourishment or injury of the frame; just as we are unconscious of the play of the lungs, the flow of the blood, and of the operation of the forces that digest and assimilate our food; so our characters derive some elements for healthy or unhealthy growth from each of the occasions of life; and all these are digested and worked into our spiritual substance by forces that play without our knowledge, and independent on the control of our will.

The most precious parts of education are those which men do not derive from books, and which they *cannot tell* how they acquired. Take that practical wisdom which we say comes from experience, and how is it acquired? or take that faculty which we term a shrewd and solid common sense, and how is it developed? Not by books, academies, and the apparatus of study, so much as by intercourse with society, and the training of every-day life, — the indirect culture and discipline which the street, the exchange, the market, the church, and constant communion with the many-sided world, pour sideways, as it were, into the intellect and heart.

And looking at the subject in a more exclusively religious light, how many indirect influences are experienced by us in favor of virtue and Christian goodness! There is the moral law, there are the abstract principles of right ;— we hear them often expounded and enforced, and our souls recognize their truth and authority. But who can tell how they are interpreted, fortified, and recommended by the conduct of those who are honest, disinterested, and Christian ? Who can tell how the glory and divinity of Jesus' religion are impressed upon us, and how our reverence for virtue is deepened by all that, we witness and hear of the beneficence, self-sacrifice, purity, and devotion of the true men and women in society ? or by what we see and know of the sensual, selfish, and depraved persons with whom we come in contact ? Conscience, and the moral sensibilities, and our moral *ideas* are quickened, refined, and confirmed, silently and unconsciously, by the indirect influences of experience, full as much as by conscious and self-directed efforts to train them. I know not that it would not be safer to strike down all the pulpits of the land, and to blot out the influences of the sanctuary from society, than to lose the secret instruction and circuitous support which the integrity of noble merchants, the charities of good Samaritans, and the radiant sanctity of unquestioned saints afford, or to be deprived of the impressive sermons, which a thousand spectacles are ever printing upon our eyes, of the peril and misery of the broad and slippery way. Certainly, rather than lose these, we could afford to spare all the critical and philosophical defences of Christianity which the libraries of the world contain.

We may ·sleep under the proclamation of the verbal gospel; but here is the incarnate gospel. We may question the logic, and slight the preaching of Sunday and the church; but here is the preaching of fact, the eloquence of week-days and of the world. Men respect realities, and will not quarrel with them. We cannot see good characters and bad characters; we cannot observe the beauty of virtue, the peace of goodness, the nobility of integrity, and contrast them with the repulsiveness of vice, the meanness of avarice, and the downward tendency of unrestrained pleasure, without feeling the difference in the principles they reveal, and acknowledging that they are enforced by eternal sanctions, and are as wide apart as heaven and hell. Thus every good act preaches; every pure and true word is a sunbeam; every Christian life is a rampart against evil; and all the virtue which is visible and manifested among men — going to make up the sum of influences that undulate over the whole surface of society — is an indirect but powerful emphasis to all the eloquence and the arguments that would win them to goodness and warn them from sin.

The amount and value of a man's influence, for good or evil, upon the world, will generally depend upon the character of his indirect and unconscious influence. Personal perfection, — the Christian refinement of feelings and sentiments, faithfulness to all the duties of the more private relations we sustain, are inexorably demanded by the Almighty, and by the spirit of Christ's gospel ; and demanded the more rigorously because the effect of such fidelity does not end with ourselves, but goes forth, and wins results that are precious in the sight of Heaven, and which we may never know.   The *spirit* of a person's life is ever shedding some power, just as a flower is steadily bestowing some fragrance upon the air. Do you think that a pure and earnest prayer, in the sacred privacy of home, does not steal through the walls and vivify the atmosphere beyond ?   Do you doubt that a word of sympathy and a gift of charity, in a desolate chamber, publish a sweet influence upon the frosty air of human selfishness ?   Such things reveal and confirm character, and make the power of the person's presence who performs them more intense and beneficial.

Indirect and spontaneous influences always reveal the measure and spirit of character.   One man may discourse to me most eloquently and impressively, in words, of virtue and duty, and I attend with listless ears and untouched breast ; and yet my soul will glow with love of truth and duty, and a thousand new impulses will struggle and burn in me, when I am in the society of some choicer spirit, while his calm eye sheds serenity, and his conversation on ordinary themes is saturated with a religious tone.

Influence depends less on our activity than on the qualities that lie behind our activity ; as the planet

attracts, not by its motion, but by its weight. If
we but lived as we ought to live, and as we might
live, a power would go out from us that would make
every day a lyric sermon, that should be seen and
felt by an ever-enlarging audience.

A living English poet—Mr. Browning—has por-
trayed the indirect, unintended, and unknown influences which pure goodness, even though obscure,
exerts, in a singular poem, or drama, called, "*Pippa
passes.*" It represents one day — a New Year's holiday — in the life of a young girl who worked in an .
Italian silk-mill. She is a sweet singer, and determined to pass her day of rest in strolling through
her native city, seeing its sights and singing her
songs. Early in the day, she goes slowly by a palace where a murder has just been committed for
gain and unholy love. The murderer and his female
accomplice are endeavoring to support each other's
spirits, when the closing lines of the silk girl's song
are heard in the darkened room. The man's ear
catches the lines, —

> " God's in His Heaven —
> All's right with the world."

The singer passes ; but something in the sweet, fresh
melody sends that thought " God's in his heaven,"
into the polluted man's soul, startles his conscience,
chills his vile passion, and compels him to renounce
the objects for which he had stained his hands with
blood.

Soon she loiters near a splendid garden, in which

a mother is striving to dissuade her noble son from joining a party of patriots, who have vowed to rid their country of oppression. The young man has been brought to doubt and pause, when a timely song from the silk girl, as she passes, rallies his courage, and sends him away at the only moment when success would be possible. And twice again do her songs produce effects as striking upon persons whom she knows not, who, as she "passes," are just in the crisis of important emergencies, and are inspirited by her notes to do what is right and noble.

At last the day is spent, and at night the poor, tired girl, as she sinks to rest, wonders how near she may ever approach the great people she has thought of during the day, — " approach them so as to touch them, move them, do good or evil to them in some slight way." She did not know that she had reached them more powerfully than any of their equals could do ; that her melodies had been woven into the fabric of spiritual and political destinies ; that her artless songs had risen to the office of prophet, monitor, and friend ; and that her nature had shed sunlight into the deepening darkness of breasts, into which she could not have dared to dream that any direct influence from her could enter.

Who then can estimate the uses and agencies of one true word, or of an humble, holy life ? To God it is precious, and with men it is more powerful than we believe. For the indirect influence of small things is often much more important, for wide and lasting good, than the direct influence of what we suppose are the important things. A wise man once said, "Let me write the popular ballads of a nation, and any statesman may indite the laws." Who that thinks of the subject carefully will not confess that the homes of a people — the spirit nurtured there, the graces that bloom there, the duties that are discharged there — exert a more powerful effect upon their prosperity, power, and destiny than the senate-house or the capitol? And no strong mind will have to reflect long, in order to be convinced that the ministry of childhood — the indirect influence of little children in softening the nature and refining the characters of men and women, and in preparing them for higher influences — is an infinitely more efficient ally of Christianity than all presbyteries and synods and Episcopal councils and evangelical leagues. It is as true of empires as of individuals, — "He that despiseth small things shall perish little by little."

We may carry our subject to its highest expression, and exhibit the truth of it in its most impressive and triumphant form, by calling attention to the indirect influence of the character of Jesus upon the world. When he was on the earth he produced the deepest effect upon his disciples, less perhaps by what he said (for they could not always comprehend the depth and spirituality of his instructions) than by the inexplicable charm of his presence, and the effluence from his ripe and fragrant graces. And even now, the proportion of the Christian world that study his career, and see the height and depth of his

character, and reverently propose the spirit of his
life as the ideal of effort, is very small. But the
blessed ministry of his life is not confined to these.
Some gleam of its beauty streams through the rifts
of the most beclouded and benighted soul. Some
tone of its pathos steals across the discords of the
foulest breast. Some whisper of its pleading, in
hours of unusual silence or unusual agitation thrills
the nobler chords of natures that have long wandered
astray. The sight of human suffering enforces its
appeal to selfish hearts by the sanction of his compassion. The most heinous guilt pleads for mitiga-
tion of a cruel judgment by the great authority of
his pity and hope. If men have a large idea, or a
comprehensive project of philanthropy to urge, they
instinctively seek the shelter and the commendation
of his name. Millions who know nothing of the
foundations of right, or of the nice shades of obligation, feel no perplexities about duty when the picture
of his career is called up by their fancy. And even
children appreciate the spirit of religion, and feel
the finer sensibilities warm and expand in the light
of his radiant and lovely perfection. The oppressor
is uneasy when he hears of Christ's sympathy with
the people, and his estimate of the human soul.
The slave-dealer, whose conscience is barricaded
against arguments that deny the right of property in
man, must feel the infamy of his traffic, if the vision
of the cross is ever painted on his dreams, and the
pale, blood-spent brow that crowned a life of toil for
the redemption, not only of men of every hue, but

even of souls that are most deeply stained with the
black leprosy of sin.   It is by the blessed contagion
caught from the character of Christ that the law of
duty keeps its hold in some way upon all hearts, —
" Thou shalt love thy neighbor as thyself."   The
indirect influence of Jesus' life, feebly as we have
obeyed it, is the hope of modern civilization.   He
reveals the deep hues of our sin by the radiance of
his spotlessness, and the light of divine goodness he
casts upon it ; he prompts and encourages to good
and holy works for humanity by the constant and
gentle pressure of his recorded life upon the consciences and sympathies of men ; and through the
ordinances that commemorate him, in the lull of
worldiness, and the sacred silence of communion, he
sheds comfort and strength and faith and peace
into hearts that are wounded, and bosoms that long
for help.

IX.

LIFE MORE THAN MEAT.

Jesus, in the Sermon on the Mount, asked the question of his disciples, "Is not life more than meat and the body than raiment?"

The answer of most of the world to this question is, *No!* A great portion of mankind *cannot* live for anything much above physical wants, and a majority of those who can, do not. Is it not sad to think, that of the myriads born every generation upon the globe, most are under the doom of the animal nature by their birth and social circumstances, and are compelled to drudge for material food and raiment? But it is a sadder truth that the interest of the favored classes of the world is so largely expended upon meat and raiment.

Even in the most literal sense, how much of human effort and aspiration is so expended, — for appetite and fashion, for what is eaten and worn! What a force in the world is the dinner-table! We may almost say that commerce, which spots the seas with sails, is the purveyor of human taste, and keeps its fleets of naval bees sweeping across the latitudes, and roving from port to port, to gather the honey of the climates, and enrich the dishes on which fastidious hunger feeds. How many thousands are there who, if the feast were stricken from their day, and they were compelled to nourish themselves on homely and wholesome fare, would feel that the great attractions of life were blotted out; would miss the seasons and the solace which ennoble and adorn their time. So intensely is it true with many that meat is life, that they live to eat instead of eat to live. And as to raiment, — how many thousands who have leisure and every opportunity for deepening an inward life, reckon the value of existence by the dress and jewelry with which they may captivate superficial admiration, and dazzle in the atmosphere of show and pride! Does not the Saviour's language have a solemn cadence in this nineteenth century since its primal utterance, when we think of the hosts of spirits delicately formed, and in an age, too, when the rights and the true position of woman are so earnestly discussed, who would find life empty of charm and stimulus if they were compelled to dress like Quakeresses; if the ambitions and rivalries of fashion and personal ornament were stricken from their experience; and who, so far as any great objects of living are practically entertained, might as well be the figures in a milliner's window, — compounds of wood and wax, made to show the pattern of a silk, the tracery of a lace, the style of a bonnet, the artistic folding of a shawl, and to rotate before a crowd which is gazed upon, through days and weeks, with the same painted smile?

And when we turn from these extreme and most literal illustrations, to the numberless inhabitants of christendom who live in some way for pleasure, self, and external things, we are impelled by sorrow to the question, " *Is* not life more than meat? " Is there no wide recognition of what human life is? Let us look at this more minutely. Physical existence — the play of the animal organs in the frame, the flow of the blood, the sensitiveness of the nerves, the capacity of sensation — is not life only the background or possibility of human life. The Creator made us for the exercise of the great capacities of our humanity, each of which brings us into communion with some sphere of his wisdom or goodness; and if we neglect any of these we fail, to just that extent, of the possession of life. In fact life, everywhere, is a matter of degrees; it depends on the number and the dignity of the functions that are exercised. The elm has more than the flag of the marsh, because it has more vegetable forces at work upon the treasury of nature. The lion more than the elm, because he has more endowments still, and vastly higher ones. So that life, as a privilege and a power, rises, through a series of stages, from the plant whose unintelligent vitality appropriates the materials of earth and air, to the shell-fish that has merely gained the boundaries of sensation, and thence, along the ascending scale of animal development, to the soul of man, which is open to infinite truth, thrills to the charm of eternal beauty, and may inspire something of the grace of the all-pervading God.

We ought, therefore, to feel that life is more than meat, in this sense; that the privilege of life outweighs all the circumstances that may attend our existence. Such a sentiment is essential to any religious estimate or improvement of our being. When a parent places a son in a university, what wise man thinks of estimating the youth's good fortune by the elegance with which his room is furnished, or the costly and delicate meals provided for him? These are slight incidents, well enough if they do not absorb interest; disadvantages if they do. The great privilege of being there lies in the vast means that may be brought to bear upon the intellect, and make a man eminent in the world of truth. That privilege is for all who enter there. No differences among the students are important or substantial but those of faculty and advancement. Is it not so in a still higher sense with regard to our position in this universe? Are not all differences of social position, money, fame, and luxury abased before the fact that we are in the universe, endowed with great faculties, set amid the mysteries of God's being, overhung with starry immensities, capable of conversing with infinite truth, of loving the right, and of giving birth to hopes that travel out into eternal vistas? Though you are a king and lose your throne and crown, though you are lord of a palace and lose your proud estate, what a slight misfortune has befallen you, so long as you

are still a living soul in God's everlasting realm,
under the dome of his boundless cathedral, glori-
fied yet by his image, endowed with his eternity?
Though you are poor, and may be lifted to opulence
and power, how slight the change when set against
the fact that, at any rate, you are rich with the
blessing of conscious and spiritual existence, and
that no money can give you a new faculty, no
earthly power make you anything higher than a
child of God!

The moment we look at it religiously we see that
the great common privilege — life — reduces all conventional distinctions to insignificance. The glory
of the oak is that it can root itself in the soil, appropriate the air, and feed upon the sun; and the
humblest shrub, each yellow buttercup, has the
same birthright, and rejoices in it equally. An East-
ern sage once said, " O God, pity the wicked; for
thou hast done everything for the good in having
made them good." So a deeply wise man might
say that God has done everything for his children in
having given them being. And if a *true* prayer
could go up to God to-day, from every spirit of the
myriads on this globe, the form and hue of each
would betray the differences of circumstances and
trial and sorrow that distinguish our mortal careers; but the common spirit and burden would
be, — the point in which they would intermix into
one dialect of gratitude, — " I thank thee, O thou
Lord and Father of souls, for the gift and glory of
life in thy creation; life under the equity of thy

government and the light of thy love; life more precious than the wealth bestowed upon me, or the earthly good denied; life whose privilege overbalances adversity, sickness, sorrow, and distress; life the opportunity of growth and goodness, and the promise of joy and progress forevermore."

We may measure the defect of religion as a fundamental sentiment by the prevalent poverty of this estimate of existence. So few of us prize it for what it *essentially is*, so · great a majority of us for its incidental, external, temporary, conventional prizes and acquisitions!

The Bible asks, with serious emphasis, "Why should *a living* man complain?"—as though no burden can be loaded upon the soul heavy enough to crush the secret sense of privilege and the great *hope* that life should feed. And yet, those of us do complain of life who slight its central benefaction and count its common opportunity nothing. Those complain of it who ask and strive for excitement to make the days acceptable. They complain of it, who labor for gold as the sole thing worth having. They complain of it, who count their existence a a failure if they do not gain the position and the means to gratify earthly appetites and vanities. They complain of it, who fret and repine inwardly under ordinary hardships and sorrows incident to our lot, and see no vast preponderance of good established in the very fact that souls remain to them, powers of thought, love and service, and hope that may invade the sky.

But we have wandered somewhat from the point I would keep most prominent, namely, that the reality and depth of our life must be measured by the number and eminence of the faculties that are active. That nature in which none of the high powers are exercised, no thought, no taste, no aspiration, no reverence, no love, can only be said to *exist*, — it does not live. It has no actual life that is more than meat and raiment. It might be turned into a plant — if only sensation could be continued to it — without any conscious irreparable loss; it might be lowered into an animal, without any serious protest from a spiritual quarter, if perfect physical satisfaction be guaranteed.

Just as much life is there in us, higher than that which comes from meat and raiment, as there are faculties in exercise that import intellectual, moral, or religious sustenance into our being. Those are our days of true vitality, — those our experiences of *human* life when we gain a new truth; think a noble, exalting thought; receive a better motive; cherish a more generous, catholic, or devout sentiment; feel our mental horizon widen by acquaintance with a good book or conversation with a wiser soul; thrill with admiration of some master-piece of genius; form or encourage an aspiration for more wisdom, virtue, and charity.

No matter in what splendor of circumstances we are placed, everything about us is only the show of existence, not the symbol of a rich, human life if some of the faculties that are related to the Infinite world are not awake and active. And when we think of the wonderful endowment of powers which heaven has made upon us, is it not sad to put in contrast with them our estimate of their worth, the amount of our fathfulness in their discipline, the results that have come from them? If we could listen to the honest prayers, that is, to the deep and steady desires that rise to God from the most favored souls on this planet, how seldom should we hear those that express a longing for more of the substance of life, more knowledge, more reverence; more love;—and of the satisfaction and thankfulness which human hearts are conscious of, and which God regards, how constant would the expression of it be for the attainment of some accident, related only to the surface of our nature,—a little more money, an increase of luxury, a position somewhat more eminent, a competitor for some earthly prize distanced and defeated;—and only here and there a psalm of gladness from a soul that God has created it in his image, and opened to it, in the worlds of nature and revelation, such a treasury of satisfaction and delight.

And yet there is a call to such gladness and thankfulness, not only that we have the privilege of a life that is more than meat and raiment,—a life intellectual, virtuous, and spiritual,—but also that there are such free and ample opportunities for gaining and enjoying it. It is easier to secure the good that belongs to substantial life than that of the senses and the superficial nature. If the energy that is now expended in the interest of avarice, or for show, or excitement, or reputation, or a fleeting power, were expended for any line of *real* good, — in the stimulus and enlargement of any of our immortal faculties, what might not human nature be! It is hard to heap up a great fortune, to get an official position that will not be insecure, to win a long lease of sensuous pleasure; — how many are baffled in their efforts, sick at heart by their defeat, and how many more sick at heart in finding how little comes of even brilliant success, — how great the array of means and labor to insure what will not satisfy as it promised to, what looks attractive in the distance but pales and dwindles in the actual grasp! But whoever heard of toil for truth being without result, or the appetite for wisdom turning to weariness and disgust, or any effort at the culture of a faculty being fruitless, or pure taste for beauty disturbing human peace, or intercourse with nature yielding no satisfaction, or the soul returning unfed and disappointed when it has swept off into the great fields of wonder and mystery?

There is no uncertainty of success in the region of true life, and that region is open to all alike. An earnest thought will go out from a small house as from a splendid one, and bring back its blessings to the mind. The power to love, to meditate, to aspire, is not dependent on the scale of our living. Titled and fashionable people may not visit us if our sphere is humble, our purse small, and our name unfamiliar to the world's lips, but God will

visit us if we invite him; the great deeps of truth
arch over our roof as over the palace, and any exercise of any faculty will as surely be successful
there in deepening our life, as if it was made in a
princely abode. The phrase is often used in fashionable society of persons approaching their majority, that they are going into life, that they are about
to see what life is, — meaning by this that they are
to begin a personal acquaintance with the gayeties,
amusements, superficial strifes, rivalries, shows, and
scandals, which break like elegant and empty foam
on the solemn sea of human experience. But
every young person really begins to enter life, and
to have part in it, when the mind begins to develop,
the taste to refine, the conscience to grow sensitive,
the heart to enlarge, the soul to aspire and grow
reverent, and the whole nature conscious of its divine relationships and of some portion of that peace
that flows in from the infinite. The life of show, —
of meat and raiment, parties and balls, may begin
in a demonstrative, dazzling, and costly way, but
real life beings thus silently and inwardly, and independent on any scale of wealth and fashion.

It is inspiring to think how freely the opportunities for true living are offered to all of us. Not
only is nature free and open, not only are the splendors of the morning and the pomp of the sunset,
the gush of beauty in the spring, and the solemn
magnificence of midnight, given equally to the poor
and the wealthy, the lowly and the great, — but it
is really strange to think how the best things of the

human world travel to all. How many gifted critics have exercised the subtlety of analysis and the resources of eloquence in sounding and celebrating the greatness of Shakspeare and the rich benefaction of his genius to mankind. And yet Shakspeare may be owned by everybody. Very little is asked by the genius of traffic for the privilege of his society, the best talk of his oceanic mind and the acquaintance of the characters with which he has enriched humanity. Milton, too, may be a guest in every house, and recite his sonorous fable of the angelic rebellion and the loss of Paradise. For a trifle, Homer and Dante will repeat their verses to the poor man who cares to ask them, after his day of toil ; or Newton and Herschel will come and tell him of the scale of creation, — its mighty forces, and accurate laws. And when a great gift of eloquence is imparted to a statesman, the large halls must be open for him that the people may freely hear. Great geniuses do not have a long line of children to perpetuate a copyright and inherit their fame, for it is meant for the world to own them and rejoice in them. Luxuries, fine dresses, the entertainment of senses and the pampering of pride are costly ; but the topmost literature of the world — the fountains and inspiration of all thought — can be owned for fifty dollars, and the wondrous Bible, museum of history, poetry, philosophy, and revelation, goes to the meanest hut, introducing Isaiah and David and Job and Paul, to say nothing of the highest name — if the door will be open to it — with-

out money and without price. The best things of
the world, the resources of inward life, are so
cheap that we may almost say they can be had for
the asking.

When I have reflected upon the wonderful results
of human power and genius that are represented
in a *great city*, I have thought of the beneficent
laws that assured everybody, the poor as well as
the rich, the highest advantages that are to be derived within its walls. The organic life of Boston,
for instance, the civilization that has accumulated
from the generations since the Puritans, the social
order and good government that are maintained,
are for the humble, as for the high. The schools,
with every advantage which private institutions
offer, are for the children of the poorest ; — and
long may it be before priestly subtlety shall be suffered, here or anywhere, in our land, to break down
the great bulwark of freedom, — a common unsec-
tarian education assured by law. The best architecture, Gothic or Grecian, will feed any eyes that
choose to look upon it. The most glorious grounds,
infinitely superior to any rich man's estate in the
vicinity, where the crimsom pomp of evening displays itself, when " the sun wraps his robes about
him, Cæsar-like, to die," is truly a *Common*. Private
sculptures and paintings may be shut out from our
sight, but a quarter of a dollar will introduce any
eyes to works of genius in colors and stone which
no man is rich enough to own. A great master-
piece of Handel or Haydon, worthily interpreted

by voice, chorus, and instruments, may be listened
to for the price of a common meal, or on a winter
afternoon a symphony of Beethoven and gems from
other masters are offered to thousands for a trifling
coin.   Suppose that all these were privileges of opulence, high birth, and fashion, — how glorious we
should consider it would be to be partakers of them!
But that which is highest in the life and opportunities of the city cannot be monopolized ; it is free,
or at least cheap enough, for the poor.   It is thus
God would abase and eradicate the spirit of envy,
by showing us that the best is for all.   Everything
that may feed our faculties and deepen our true
human life — everything but luxury of show and
pride — is almost without cost, in order that we
may not blame Providence if our minds and souls
are barren, but praise him for his bounties while
we take the discredit of our shallow living to
ourselves.

And now, having seen that life consists in the play
of our deeper faculties, that it is higher than meat,
more substantial and cheaper than the gratification
of worldly appetites and the strife for show, let me
say, in conclusion, that life is more than meat and
raiment in the sense of compensation.   Men should
be judged by the kind of life they inwardly are conscious of and enjoy, not by the scale and station of
their career.   This is the point from which God regards them, and from that point more order is visible
in the world than we sometimes believe in.   The ine-
qualities are very much slighter than they seem.   Do

you point to differences of wealth, reputation, and
ease in proof of serious injustice in the world?
What do they amount to, think you, in the estimate
of God, in comparison with the development of those
powers that were kindled from his life? So far as
difference of circumstances enables one, and for-
'bids another, to cultivate his moral, mental, and
religious powers, there is disturbance of order, but
no farther.

To know how fortunate a rich man is, we ought
to ask — as higher natures ask — not how splendid
is his abode, but how much domestic love and happiness, which make the human home, does he manifest or receive? — not how much glitter surrounds
him, but what grade of faculties bloom upon his
nature, and are fed from everlasting realities? —
not how many parties can he give, but how friendly
is his intellect, or heart, with the giants of genius,
or the saints of faith? — not how spacious and
beautiful is his country estate, — for the magnificence
and mystery of nature are for everybody, — but
how much pure taste for beauty has he, how deep a
serenity of heart, how peaceful a conscience, how
vital a faith that goes out beyond this world, lays
hold of eternity and appropriates in a filial joy the
great Paradise as the home of the soul? Within,
within is the seat of order. Meat and drink — the
incidents and accidents of existence — are unequally
distributed, but the meat and drink of the soul, the
life that is more than raiment, — life such as great

natures have enjoyed it, and which they have prized supremely, — these are independent of circumstances, they come from our faculties, depend upon our inward culture, purity, and reverence, and decide whether if rich, we are to be congratulated, whether if poor, our state is to be coveted and honored.

X.

INWARD RESOURCES.

CHRISTIAN strength consists in the possession of internal stores which will enable us, in a measure, to maintain an independence on outward circumstances for happiness.

And first, let me speak of the need that men should have some mental possessions which they have stored away by the activity and fidelity of their minds. I do not say that a man cannot be a Christian unless he is educated. The Christian life and character is determined by our *loves*, our aspirations, the state of our *hearts*, — not by our intellectual development and acquisitions. But the more mental culture a man has, other things being equal, the more resources he will have in himself, and the nobler will be his life.

God did not give us this exquisitely ordered reason as a toy. He has not surrounded us with the riches and mysteries of his wisdom that we might be indifferent to them. He would have us cultivate our mental gifts, and inquire into the majestic methods of his infinite reason, and ennoble our spirits by an acquaintance with the beauty and order, the skill and goodness, which the sky and the sea,

the depths of the earth, the vaults of air, and the
sweep of his moral providence, enfold. When the
mental faculties are awake and vigorous, if the
heart is consecrated by a Christian temper, the character is more massive and complete. It is more independent; it has deeper and fuller communion
with God. A man has more stores in his own nature. The strength of two strands is greater than
that of one; and when God gives us a noble faculty,
we may be sure there is no danger in training it to
the utmost, if we but keep it in subjection to the
true spirit, and dedicate its activity to the highest
end.

Some of the most inspiring suggestions and pictures of history are those which teach us the power
of the mind of man to conquer adverse circumstances, and vindicate its royalty over fortune.
Poor and blind Homer! What mental stores had
he as a foundation against the neglect of men.
And how liberally, with a Christian spirit that
moved him to return the richest good for evil, has
he blessed the world that slighted him, from that
intellectual treasury which poverty could not drain,
nor scorn impair! How noble a picture, too, is that
of Washington, upheld in adversities, and uphold-
ing the spirits of a nation in times of utter darkness,
by his inward store of plans, hopes, and visions of
brighter hours! And shall we forget the experience
of him, the great Christian poet, who sang of the
lost, and of the better paradise? The outward

world was shut out from him. With sad, sweet melody did he sing, —

> " Seasons return, but not to me returns
> Day, or the sweet approach of even or morn,
> Or sight of vernal bloom, or summer's rose,
> Or flocks, or herds, or human face divine;
> But cloud instead, and ever-during dark
> Surrounds me, from the cheerful ways of men
> Cut off, ...
> . . . .
> And wisdom at one entrance quite shut out."

But his soul was filled with the riches of thought which he had stored away. Penury, disgrace, and blindness did not leave him without resource, — could not prevent his feeding " on thoughts that voluntary move harmonious numbers." Swarms of glorious, majestic visitants were with him, since his aspiration was answered, —

> " So much the rather thou celestial light
> Shine inward, and the Mind through all her powers
> Irradiate; there plant eyes, all mist from thence
> Purge and disperse, that I may see and tell
> Of things invisible to mortal sight."

No character is complete that has not some mental treasures on which it may draw during the treachery of fortune. It is a mournful spectacle, *morally* mournful, to see a person retiring from the world with treasures of wealth, or one who has perhaps been shipwrecked by the chances of trade, or an old man whose bodily faculties have failed before his energy, either restless or melancholy, or listless and unhappy, because the customary excitement of activity, or the fashionable position, or the sight of the crowd is denied to them, — to see that no love of truth, in a world so full of wisdom, no taste, in a universe so full of beauty, no mental appetites, where nature offers to them such bountiful repasts, have been quickened during a long life of constant toil; — and therefore, that when the horn of plenty runs over, or when luck plays false, or the limbs fail the stronger mind, there is no independent manliness to assert its proper majesty, no inward resources to attest an educated soul. By every consideration of noble self-interest, and gratitude to God for the gift of reason, every person is called upon to lay up some store of knowledge, and to form some pure mental tastes, as a foundation against the evil fortunes that may lurk in the time to come.

Again, — and here we approach the spiritual elements of our subject, — every person should have within a store of moral power, affections, principle. Every man whose virtue is secure must possess a fund of moral strength which is *more* than equal to all the demands upon his will. It is not enough to establish the purity of any soul that it can just rub and go, in keeping clear of sin. It must have stores of spiritual force upon which it is not compelled to draw. God would have our triumph over evil an easy conquest, one which does not fret and wear our hearts away by keeping them always at their toughest strain. It is a bad sign if we have to wrestle long with ordinary temptations. A man ought to feel, not only that he is *equal* to ordinary

15

trials, but *superior* to them, equal to the greatest
trial that may come, yes, *superior* to that. Not
·that a good man will be or ought to be proud of his
strength ; not that there should ever be a haughty
and complacent self-reliance in his breast. The infinite richness of his resources should lie in pure
affections that seek, and love, and are attracted to,
and live in, the right and good. His experience of
virtue should be so deep, his holiness so vital, his
piety so constant, that goodness and holiness become
the food of his spirit. His reliance, therefore, will
not be on granite strength of resolution and Titanic
vigor of will ; he never will cherish a spirit of bra-
vado, and desire to play the pugilist with evil ; his
resources should be so vast that base suggestions
will pass by him without leaving a soil upon his
heart, or finding any chance to hold parley with his
will, — pass by him as a temptation to sinful indul-
gence would have flitted before the upraised eye of
Christ, without disturbing the serenity of his prayer.
The good man's resources of power, like his mental
stores, are cultivated faculties, right instincts' that
naturally seek the good, holy affections abiding ever
in his heart; and which, by their positive attractions, do away, at last, the necessity of any vigorous,
visible, or conscious conflict with sin.

And such inward resources, thus founded, form
the good man's support in seasons of trial and suffering for virtue. He is sustained, then, by the
treasures of his heart. The internal resources of
power which would not suffer him to be false to

duty, become resources of support and pleasure in
the crisis. and the need.   The spirit of sacrifice,
wherever found, or in what manner soever shown,
is always a spirit of illumination.   Stephen and
Peter, and the prophets, and the great missionaries
of the church, have found their support, not in a
miraculous grace, but in that grace which insures
to every faithful spirit a treasury and foundation of
solace and strength, which " moth and rust cannot
corrupt."   It was the buoyant inward stores, developed by long faithfulness to conscience, that
made the bearing of Socrates so serene before his
judges, and filled his prison with the mystic light
of immortality ; it was Paul's earnestness, his consciousness of a well-spent life, the long and glad
devotion of his will to the service of a higher law,
which whispered that grand assurance of immortality to his dying spirit, and made him welcome
the axe as the friendly instrument that should release his spirit from its prison, and permit it to seek
the society above.

In order to impress us most deeply with the fact
that holiness is the highest good of life, God never
bestows any richer blessing upon faithful hearts
than their own holiness.   He never draws any
nearer to the spirit, or by any other medium, than
in and through its holiness.   He has appointed so
that goodness shall be our joy in cloudless times,
and our strength and comfort when the sky is dark ;
and there are no other resources to uphold a
wronged and persecuted good man in his seeming

desertion by Providence itself, and he *needs no other*, than the good treasure of his heart."

A good man, too, has treasures in him of *memory* and *hope*. It is a beautiful and beneficent ordinance of God that we love to remember only the good and holy. No person does or can take pleasure in recalling or dwelling in meditation upon the evil, the base, the vile. The pleasures of memory spring only from the recollection of something noble, worthy, and pure. And it is a universal law of souls, that what seems unpleasant and arduous when we have to face it and resolve to do it, looks delightful when contemplated as a treasure of memory, a fact of our past existence. In *prospect* and *retrospect*, good alone looks winning and delightful. Say to any man that next week he will perform some splendid heroic deed, some act that will thrill the hearts of men, and win the approbation of God, and it will delight and inspire him. Prophesy that he will do some mean, selfish, treacherous deed, however profitable in a worldly view, and he will recoil from it, and prefer, before the terrible temptation comes, that it should be otherwise. We give to holiness the vote of our aspirations, as we contemplate it; we condemn vice by the judgment of our regrets and shame, when we look back upon it. Can you conceive such an anomaly as a memory delighted or happy in the recollection of its once pleasant misdeeds? Ah! we would throw a pall — a pall as of midnight darkness — over the unfaithfulness and unhallowed pleasures of the past.

We would make the miserable moments of those once welcomed joys a blank in our being; we would hail with rapture the spell that could wipe them forever from the tablets of the brain. Go ask the satiated sensualist what he would give if the foul blots upon his soul's history could be exchanged for acts of purity and honor, — if his past years, so spotted with infamy, could unroll themselves before the eye of meditation, filled with winning pictures of useful, holy deeds; ask the murderer, whose passion for vengeance has been quenched in the blood of a victim, what he would give could the memory of his crime be blotted from his spirit, could his dreams and musings be void of spectres, and he be enabled to look back upon an injury *forgiven*, not revenged; ask the gambler, even the old, successful, wealthy gambler, — if such a one was ever known, — how much of his treasures of hell he would pay for a past life ennobled by honor and useful industry, and the annihilation of a retrospect from which he cannot fly ; ask the undetected knave what he would give for an unpolluted heart, an unflawed conscience, the sweet sleep of innocence, and the rich glow of satisfaction, which a sense of steady integrity sheds over the retreating landscape of our earthly life, — and they will tell you with passionate tears, if you unlock their deepest confidence, " We would give all else we have." They would exclaim in words, as they often exclaim in spirit, Oh, come back to us, sunlit, quiet days of innocence, that lie in such serene beauty in the far-distant depths of memory; extend like a line of rich hills and checkered vales along the burning wastes of years, on which our eyes now fall; let our past be dotted with objects that may charm our backward vision, and gratify our self-respect, and win the approbation of conscience and God, and not mock us, as now, with such a spectacle of moral desolation; let us but be able to look with unshamed spirits and inward satisfaction on the past, and we will abandon, willingly and forever, all the pleasures, gains, and honors of iniquity. Remorse is a guilt-laden memory, pressing heavily on an awakened conscience that teaches us too late the folly of sin. It is from memory that the fiends arise which haunt and lash the guilty breast. It is from memory that the angels of light are born which gladden with their society and companionship the faithful soul.

And the good man has also resources of *hope.* It is the tendency of goodness to inspire and foster hope, founded on confidence in man and trust in God. To the intellectual sensualist and cold-hearted scoffer, the world presents a sad, cheerless problem. Such natures see only the sin, wrong, error, selfishness of men. They have no generous aspirations, no enlivening anticipations, no cheering prophecies of good. Theirs is the philosophy of indifference or despair. But among the treasures of a religious heart is a buoyant, animating confidence in truth and right, and the better part of human nature. A good man feels that goodness is the

great fact in the universe rather than evil; that
providence is more powerful than the finite obstructions and disturbances which it encounters; that
divine law is mightier than the anomalies which the
feeble senses see; that wrong and evil waste themselves, and that the deepest instincts and undying
sympathies of man seek and desire the holy and
the true.   And so the clouds are tipped and tinged
with a golden richness, from the bright light behind,
and the harmonies of providence and eternity absorb
the discords of the moment and of earth.   The
philanthropist who is brought in constant contact
with vice and degradation never loses his confidence
in man; the martyr never doubts God's goodness;
the reformer enjoys a premonition of the triumph
of his cause.   Out of the good treasure of their
hearts — hearts in sympathy with holiness and providence — come prophecies of the triumphs of holiness and heaven.

XI.

NATURAL AND SPIRITUAL PROVIDENCE.

I AM amazed, often, in reflecting upon the apparent listlessness with which most of us entertain the testimony of the visible universe for God's providence over men. Is not the argument unanswerable and irresistible? We cannot find a single object in the physical world which is not encircled by laws that are sleepless and perfect. The orbit of every asteroid is defended against dangerous intrusion by an art from which no resource is absent. The path of every filmy comet is so appointed that it shall not be dissipated by the sun which it brushes with vapor, nor lost in the cold depths of the outer darkness which it stains. The line of order is stretched from firmament to firmament. The harness of mathematics is laid upon every sun that draws his mighty load through the spaces of the sky. The invisible animalcule has a function and a sphere which cannot be invaded. Thousands of explorers — the most gifted of the earth's intellects — are ever studying, and are printing in countless volumes reports and demonstrations of the skill and wisdom which is subtile enough to enfold the mote kindly in its coil, and which plays with Sirius as

with a toy.   Nature is order.   There is no chance.
There is no finger-breadth of chaos in the whole cir-
cumference, sprinkled with star-dust, which the
telescope has swept.

And why, as a mere matter of science, will you
isolate humanity from this web of wisdom?   Science discovers that every arrangement of the physical realm, from the anatomy of a beetle to the
jagged oscillations of a planet in its orbit, and the
curve in which a constellation drifts, is the *best possible* arrangement which the human intellect can
conceive.   What right have we, as cool mental explorers, to suppose that man is overlooked, or un-
cared for, in this domain of which every atom rises
to attest not only a providence, but a perfect providence?   If we apply the induction of nature to
man, the highest fact of nature, we shall believe at
once in a spiritual providence; and I see not how
we can reject that conclusion unless we give up the
hypothesis of God.

But to come down from the general argument to
a particular instance of it, and the particular conclusions it suggests.   If it seems strong in the broad
presentation of it, it is more so in a more minute
inspection.   Christ himself has called us to consider
the lilies of the field; and let us do so.   He, himself has put the argument in this form: "If God
so clothe the grass of the field, which to-day is and
to-morrow is cast into the oven, shall he not much
more clothe you?"   Under the light of modern
science it is still more impressive.

If you should fix your eye upon a wild violet, which the return of this creative season has evoked into life, or upon any common vegetable of the forest, and could comprehend at once all the mechanism and all the foresight that are implied in its growth, you would be overwhelmed with wonder. Indeed, scarcely any intellect would be equal to the task. It grows there in the field, seemingly as a matter of course;—a chance seed, dropped by the winds, found lodging in the soil, and the mystery, we think, is solved. But stop. That seed was swollen in the ground by the warm moisture, and the first effort of vital force began. As soon as that began, however, the rest of the seed, by a subtile chemical process, changed into sugar, to nourish the infant life, too delicate as yet to grapple with the coarse ground. This, of course, was provided for. The tender root strikes down and finds the soil pliant to its first feeble energies; a delicate blade starts up and finds the sun ready to tinge it with a tint of green. The little fibres beneath the soil begin to draw chemical drops from the ground, and the blade inspires gases from the air, which they send up and down through tiny cells, until, by various processes of combination, a stem, a twig, a leaf are formed.

But the wonder is, that, as each new necessity appears, the new provision is at hand. The soil is friendly to the plant at every stage. It has just the elements that are necessary for its growing needs, not too abundant, not too scanty. The air,

too, has just materials enough in its treasury, and
yields them with just the requisite freedom to
the feeble stranger.   The attraction of the earth
is necessary to hold its minute fibres, and strength-
en its stalk.   But its attraction is not strong enough
to prevent the juices from rising through its cells
to carry life to its leaves, so that the all-pervading
law of gravitation, which is at once the floor and
the pillars of the universe, was appointed so as to
befriend the meek violet of the meadow.   The air
needs to be freshened in order to furnish pure material for its leaves to inspire, — and so there must
be winds and lightnings ; but how seldom is there a
tempest that destroys the life of the wild-flower !
There must be rains to nourish it.   But the ocean
does not evaporate moisture fast enough to flood it,
nor slowly enough to leave it long without its
draught of life.   It must have dews ; and the night-
skies weep upon it with a pity just equivalent to its
want of sympathy.   It needs so many hours of light
and so many of gloom ; and the huge earth spins
just fast enough to alternate fitly its seasons of work
and rest.   It requires a certain change of seasons ;
and the globe beats about its vast orbit to afford it,
in right proportions, the spring-time, the summer,
the autumn, and winter.   It needs not only light,
but heat, and not only heat, but also a certain principle of vitality which is neither one nor the other ;
and lo ! the sun-ray holds all three ; and in the
spring-time sheds one most freely, in the summer
the second, and in the autumn the third ; and sel-

dom does it shine so powerfully as to scorch it or
so faintly as to blight.

St. Augustine, fifteen centuries ago, reasoned
against the polytheism of his time by showing that
if one deity (as was said) presided over every function of nature, it would take a hundred goddesses
to weave a flower, — so complicated was its structure. What would he say if all the mysteries of
modern science that cluster around a single plant
were opened to him? The adaptations are so various, so subtile, so complicated; the relations of all
other forces and elements are so nicely balanced and
adjusted to its welfare, that one might almost suppose, looking at it alone, that the sun, the air, the
ocean, the globe with its inclined axis and annual
revolution, were created and set to work as God's
immense factory for the weaving of a flower.

The growth and protection of a violet or a tuft
of grass could not have been better provided for, if
it alone had been the object of the Almighty in the
creation; if the sun had been placed at the exact
distance, and the air so mixed, and the globe so
weighed, and the ocean so measured, and the clouds
so marshalled, and the storms so tempered, and the
seasons so graduated, as best to evoke it into life,
and tint its clothing, and sustain its existence. This
is one leaf of the gospel of science. This is the
result of its obedience to the Saviour's bidding, —
"Consider the lilies how they grow." And must
not the practical result be equally forcible, as science
looks up from a flower to a man? " If God so clothe

the grass of the field, shall he not much more clothe
you ? "

" *Much more !* "   " Much more clothe *you.*"
What a lamentable scepticism in the soul is that
which allows a man to think that the wisdom which
does so much for a plant, has no solicitude for that
which can think and love and serve the right! The
plant exists for a year. Its highest function is to
drink the dew and adorn the landscape with its hues
and sprinkle the breeze with fragrance.   But here is
that which studies this wisdom which the lily
preaches, and apprehends the beauty which it
wears,—yes, and comprehends the order of the sky ;
here is that which globe and firmament cannot
satisfy ; which sends its aspiration beyond them, and
cries, " Where art thou, that didst make these wonders, and canst not be bounded by thy creation ? " —
here is a being capable of feeding its faculties on the
glories of the infinite Creator, — feeling so akin to
him, that, at times, it pants for a fuller knowledge
of his spirit, " as the hart panteth for the water-
brooks ; " — and yet it stands in doubt before this
wild-flower, which lives by the love of God ;-stands
in doubt, amid this universe, — to all of which he
is infinitely superior, whether God really cares for
him, and oversees with wise and tender interest the
current of his experience ! The mere statement
of such an anomaly should be enough to blast the
doubt. The amazement we should feel at hearing
the difficulty uttered is the only logic that is worthy
to scatter it.

Do you look into the night-sky, my brother, as an atheist, or as a believer in God? Do you view the returning spring-time as a doubter in God's existence, or as convinced of his presence? If as an atheist, you are absolved from the dignity and comfort of faith in providence; if as a believer of God, for the credit of your mind, as well as for the peace of your bosom, be ready to see and to accept *all* that nature teaches, and to say, as the sufficient and final proof of providence, If God so clothe the grass of the field, which to-day is and to-morrow is cast into the oven, shall he not much more clothe us, the highest creatures of his power?

I remember once reading a most impressive practical commentary upon the words we are considering. The celebrated traveller, Mungo Park, relates that, in his first remarkable visit to interior Africa, to trace back the river Niger to its source, after unparalleled fatigues, trials, and reverses, he was one day robbed in the forest by some black banditti. His compass was taken from him, and with only a few coarse clothes he was left *alone*, — alone in unexplored and savage Africa, — five hundred miles from any settlement, amid wild beasts, and men as pitiless. Seeing no prospect but to lie down and perish, his mind became unnerved and despondent. As he threw himself upon the ground, a small and peculiar moss met his eye, whose root, leaves, and capsule were so curious as to excite his attention. He examined it carefully, and forgot his forlorn condition for a moment in his admiration of it. As he gazed upon it, the thought arose in his mind, he tells us, " Can that Being who planted, watered, and brought to perfection, in this obscure region of the world, a thing which appears of so small importance, look with unconcern upon the situation and sufferings of his spiritual offspring?" This thought cheered him, rekindled his courage, and through the efforts it inspired, he was saved, and enabled to publish the fact as a lesson to the world.

Well may we say, then, to the doubters of a spiritual providence, as an exclamation of wonder, almost of reproach, "O ye of little faith!" And yet, this objection, no doubt, will arise in some minds, "Why urge men to such a passive trust in providence, when it can do no good and may do harm? Say what you may, God does not and will not clothe men as he does the flowers of the field. We must work and do things for ourselves, and the statement of the text is false."

Of course, Jesus did not mean that God would *literally* clothe men, if they trust in him. Neither is that the kind of providence which he teaches us to believe in; for God does not clothe the lilies in *that* way. They *work* for their existence and their beauty. They toil not and spin not in human ways; but God does not paint them as a man paints wood. They are active; they absorb; they put forth all their inward energies; and it is when they do that, and on condition that they do thus much, that the other forces of nature become friendly, and the dew, the globe, the air, and sunshine, protect and nourish and paint them. The providence that maintains the flower is shown in the disposition of all the other forces of the universe, so that the flower can have its place, and will not be crushed. When the flower works, uses all the force God has given it, a path is open for it; everything works in harmony with it, and gives it a welcome and a joyous existence in the world of matter. God feeds the ravens only as they are obedient to their instinct, and *seek* their food. The doctrine of the Saviour's illustration is that God cares more deeply and tenderly for the spiritual creation that bears his image than for the material creation that is a trophy of his art. It does not urge us, or encourage us, to rely passively on God's goodness, and expect special material blessings from it, — food, wealth, and clothing; but incites us to work, to put forth all the spiritual force that is in us, assuring us that then he will work in harmony with us, as in the lower sphere he works in unison with the faithfulness of the flower, that all his laws will be friendly to us, and that existence, whatever its fortunes, will afford us inward peace.

XII.

PHILOSOPHY AND THEOLOGY.

DURING the last few years, our community has manifested a lively interest in philosóphical pursuits. We can trace very plainly the effects of that taste which the importation of French and German literature, a few years ago, has served to awaken. Besides her historians, her poets, and her artists, New England has now, at least, one philosopher. Journals, devoted to philosophy and kindred pursuits, are conducted by men of different schools, and find a fair support among us. American translations and reprints of the works of distinguished philosophical writers in Europe, meet with a ready sale; and in our universities the study of speculative philosophy has been entrusted to the direction of our soundest thinkers. The habits of thought, formed by a study of some philosophical system, may be detected in every department of the literature of the country, — the elements of Kantianism in history, transcendentalism in poetry, eclecticism in religious literature and reviews. It is not difficult even to interest "a popular audience" in the discussion of tenets belonging to speculative philosophy. Some of our readers perhaps may remember the crowded

assemblies that listened to the lectures of a celebrated professor, a few winters since, before a literary institution of this city.

This tendency is not surprising. We have arrived at a point in our intellectual culture which
must come to every.nation. Philosophy is a natural
want of the human mind. Without it, the cycle of
its development is not complete. It has sprung
from the intellectual soil of every people. There is
implanted in human nature a tendency which cannot be satisfied without speculative coherence in its
views of the universe. The mysteries which the
contemplation of nature perpetually presents to us
possess a charm that has always allured the keenest
intellects, and brought into action the noblest powers
of the soul. If we would seek the commencement
of the history of philosophy, we must go back to the
early twilight of civilization. The priests of Egypt
had their esoteric doctrines ; the Persians, their solution of the origin of evil; while in India the
judgment of immobility, which seems to have arrested the development of all the active powers of
the soul, could not hold back the tendency to speculation. Almost all the phases of modern philosophy were represented there under Indian forms, and
from an Indian point of view. The restless activity
of the Grecian mind was not more strongly manifested in its various governments, and its thirst for
conquest, than in its wealth of philosophical theories,
and in the rapid development of schools which exhausted the capacity of progress, in that line, for a

thousand years. The national life was equally in-
carnated in Plato and Pericles, in Aristotle and
Alexander. Even in the middle ages, under the
jealous eye of the church, heresies springing from
opposition to the dominant philosophy continually
needed to be checked. With regard to the present
rank of philosophy in the republic of letters, we
need hardly speak. It is placed at the summit of
mental cultivation. The importance which, since
the Reformation, it has attained, among the cultivated nations of Europe, seems to justify the remark
of a German writer, that "In the new hierarchy of
the understanding, the philosophical is the apostolic
chair, and philosophers are the cardinals."

It becomes an interesting and important question,
then, What is the effect of this tendency to philosophy upon religious truth? or, in other words, What
is the connection between philosophy and religion?
We cannot expect, within the limits of one article,
to do anything more than to point out the general
features of this relation, without stopping to examine the question in all its details. In the first
place, then, we may remark that whatever increases
the general cultivation of the mind improves our
sensibility to religious impressions, and enlarges our
capacity for religious ideas. None of our readers,
probably, will dispute this proposition with us, and
it hardly needs illustration. The progress of science has always added strength to the religious convictions of the devout spirit, and developed, in a
clearer light, the characteristics which reason and

revelation ascribe to the Deity. We have, for instance, an idea of the infinite. It is a necessary judgment of the intellect, is implied in our reasonings, and is indispensable to our conception of God. It is not, however, an idea which we can completely comprehend. It exists as a mere sign, a barren affirmation, until it is brought out clearly into consciousness, and strengthened by the aid of some positive conceptions of the finite, with which it may be contrasted. How powerfully has astronomy done this! It is when the magnificent conception of the immensity and grandeur of the material universe is awakened in us; when we become acquainted with the vast scale upon which this system of nature is constructed; when thought endeavors to seize the boundaries of that expanse in which the solar system is but a speck, which no figures can express, and beyond which no instruments can reach: it is then, and by contrast with this finite which science has explored, and at the grandeur of whose discoveries the imagination is overpowered, that the intellect feels oppressed, and bows with religious awe before the idea of the infinite. So, also, with our conception of the omnipotence of God. Every one feels conscious of such an idea. It is from a necessity of our intellectual nature that we ascribe it to the Deity. Without it, he would not be God. Yet who comprehends the significance of the term till he has formed some conception of the stupendous force that has disposed worlds into systems, and that moves and guides and governs all the complicated

machinery of the universe! Again; how has our
idea of the wisdom of the Deity been extended and
enlarged by an acquaintance with the simplicity of
arrangement exhibited by the geometry of the
heavens, and the nice adjustment between the forces
that sustain the universe, or by the innumerable instances of skill and adaptation, furnished by physiology and natural history? Whatever has increased
our knowledge of the works of the Creator has
deepened and added strength to our conceptions of
his nature and his attributes. Such is the intimate
and beneficial relation which science sustains to religion. But the same reasons that we have urged
to prove this position may we think, with equal
force, be urged in behalf of the claims of philosophy.

First, however, to guard against misapprehension,
let us define what we mean by speculative philosophy. Many, we are persuaded, look upon it as
merely a dry system of metaphysics, a mass of baseless speculations, concerned with inquiries, for instance, as to the nature of spirit, the cause of motion, or the medium of connection between the soul
and the outward world. So far, however, is this
from being the case, nothing has tended more to
banish such questions from the learned world than
the progress of philosophy. We define philosophy,
the complete science of human nature, the resolution of all human experience to order. Its ultimate
aim is to explain the human mind, to define its
powers, determine its tendencies, and unfold its
laws. This is no barren study. It demands, not

only an examination of consciousness, but also an acquaintance with the whole circle of science. We cannot completely know the powers of the mind till we have some definite conception of the products of its energy. In fact, a complete criticism of the laws of thought, itself, cannot be reached by a pure psychological analysis, by an examination of the thinking subject alone. Our theories, to be entitled to the claim of scientific accuracy, must be framed with reference to the developments of thought in some department of knowledge. No dispute, for instance, has more deeply agitated the philosophical world than the question as to the origin of many of our ideas. We have no intention of raising that question here, but only wish to remark, that a complete discussion of it is possible, only on condition of carefully examining the characteristics of those ideas, as they form part of the structure of many of the sciences. It is clearly in this way alone, that those peculiarities, which are the subjects of discussion, can be fully brought to view.

But a complete science of human nature must develop something more than a theory of ideas. All the phases of social, moral, and political life, are the outward expression of some tendency of the soul, and of course furnish materials for philosophical science. The ultimate aim of philosophy, then, is to elevate the science of human nature into universal science. The field of its research includes the whole domain of history, poetry, and art. Philosophy, then, is not any particular science; it does not deal with that mass of details, a complete and searching study of which is indispensable to establish a separate science. It is only concerned with the laws of scientific progress, with those intellectual conceptions which may be detected in the fundamental propositions upon which science is founded, and that ideal element which, although necessary to the very structure of science itself, forms also a portion of the philosophy of the human mind. The relation of philosophy to religion is, in principle, similar to the relation it bears to science. We understand by it a full examination of the religious element in human nature, a complete exhibition of the laws of its development, and a view of the harmony of its doctrines, with the conclusions drawn from other provinces of scientific thought. The philosophy of religion, then, no less than the philosophy of science, is indispensable to a thorough acquaintance with the laws and capacities of our nature. The spheres of the philosopher and the theologian cannot be completely disjoined. The one, engaged in a profound study of thought and of the human faculties, cannot rest satisfied till he has attained an idea of the highest objects of thought to an idea of God and duty and eternal order, thus giving to philosophy a theological aim ; while the other cannot consider his science as completely established until he has discovered, in the very constitution of the human mind, a capacity for religious ideas and a necessity for religious cultivation, thus giving to theology a philosophical basis.

It will be our desire, in the remainder of this article, to exhibit those points where the convergent lines of philosophy and theology meet and blend ; and the influence which must be exerted by philosophical study upon theological speculations.

In the first place, we wish to speak of the influence of philosophy in reconciling faith and knowledge. Religion springs from a primary and indestructible want of human nature. In its original character it is, if we may so express it, a spiritual instinct in the soul. Its foundation is a sense of dependence on a higher power; its central principle is faith. Side by side with its spiritual want, exists another element, which gives the mind a reflective tendency, which impels it to know, or, in other words, to account to itself for its ideas and its faith. This latter tendency, felt in some degree by every man, can only be satisfied when religion is raised from its primitive state as an instinct, and established as an idea. Now, until the demands of both these indisputable tendencies of the soul are satisfied, the growth and development of the mind is not complete. Of what use could be a belief in God, if reason discovers it to be nothing but a phantasm raised by human weakness ? What support could be drawn from faith in Providence, if it be found to depend on a necessity of our *sensitive* nature ; or what efficacy would there be in prayer, if it be felt that the object of our supplications is not a real being, capable of understanding and satisfying our wants, but merely a law of the soul ?

" Rather, would not the world, with its thousand contradictions, strike us with astonishment, if we could not see the eternal light glimmer through all its phenomena, and feel, from all around, an intimation of the great, first, and enduring Cause ? " The repose of the soul upon its religious nature imperiously demands, then, not only that this universal tendency to worship shall be shown to be an innate element of its nature, but it requires also a demonstration of the reality of the object of worship. Not only must we be conscious of a sense of obligation imposed by a moral law, but reason must discover grounds for faith in that eternal order towards which all things tend, and from which the moral law derives its sanction. Besides that "longing after immortality," which we recognize as a primitive instinct in our constitution, we must feel that everything which we know of our capacities, everything which, by the light of nature, reason can discover as to our destiny, awakes in us an idea of eternal life, and confirms the spontaneous prophecy of the soul. Religion grounded in mere feeling may, in periods of excitement, when under the influence of a luxuriant flow of spirits, and when the voice of the intellect is still, be completely satisfactory to us. But a religion upon which we may rely, in every state of mind, which can cheer us in despondency, and console us in seasons of gloom, must be ever before us a firmly-founded law, resting not merely on the uncertain basis of sensibility, but established on a foundation as immovable as

our surest ideas. Let us not be understood by
these remarks to undervalue the argument for religion drawn from its satisfying the instinctive wants
of our constitution. A religion purely rational,
which should aim to reach the heart only through
the head, would fail of accomplishing the end for
which it is designed. What we contend for, is,
that religion should satisfy all the cravings of our
nature; that it must be able to subdue the intellect,
as well as engage the heart, that it must be shown
to have, so to speak, its objective as well as subjective side. Now to do this is, in part at least, the
work of philosophy.

Perhaps, however, we shall be able to see more
clearly into the subject, by attending to the influence which must be exerted upon theology by our
theory concerning the origin of knowledge. This
is, in every system of philosophy, the all-important
point. D'Alembert called it the " terrible question
of metaphysics." No problem which we can raise,
in the whole circle of science, has such important
corollaries depending upon its solution. Among
other consequences, it involves the question as to
the capacity of the mind for religious ideas. If we
look back through the whole history of philosophical
speculation, we shall find that its direction towards
spiritualism, or materialism, has been determined
according to its account of the foundation and origin of knowledge. The solution that has been uni-
formly offered by one party among philosophers, is,
that all our ideas are resolvable into sensations.

According to them the mind is purely passive in the acquisition of knowledge. It is a mere susceptibility to impressions from without, destitute of any inherent tendencies, without primarily any distinctive nature. According to this view, it could scarcely be said that there is any principle belonging to our nature that can combine the scattered impressions of sense into a harmonious whole, and thus give unity to our consciousness. All our ideas are transformed sensations; the very capacities of mind itself, but internal modifications of our sensitive nature. Reflection, attention, memory, the power of generalization, are not faculties of the intellect, existing independent of experience, and employed by the mind as instruments in the formation of new ideas; but these faculties are themselves the result of sensations; they are more refined internal affections of the sensibility; the recurrence, in a more sublimated state, of some former impressions upon the organs of sense. This is not too strong a statement. We have before us, at this moment, the original statement of these principles, in terms as strong as we have used. Now, it needs no very severe logic to draw, from these premises, the conclusions which they contain as to the sphere and limits of knowledge. If "every idea is chimerical that cannot attach itself to its sensible archetype," if "every expression which cannot find an external and sensible object to which it can establish its affinity is destitute of signification " (we use the precise words of an exponent of this system), what foundation have we for the idea of God? The senses acquaint us only with finite existence; what room, then, is there in such a system for an idea of the infinite? By impressions upon our senses from the material world, we acquire a notion merely of appearances, of changes, of antecedents, and consequents; how then, in such a system, can we acquire the idea of a cause? we do not say of a first and eternal cause merely, but of any cause. How is the conception of a cause possible? If human nature be a mere blank capacity, and is, previous to education, as susceptible of one impression as another, what reason have we for the conception of a moral law, to which all intelligences are subject, that has a right to command our allegiance? There is no possible way, if we start from such a view of the origin of knowledge, to reconcile our logic with religion. No modification of this materialistic philosophy can harmonize with the faith which religion demands of us. Before we can admit any idea which belongs to the sphere of religion within the circle of knowledge, we must adopt some element into our reasoning which can be drawn from a spiritual philosophy alone. Take, for instance, the argument from design, to demonstrate the existence of God. The argument, as it has often been conducted, fails in an essential point. Leaving out of view the fact, that, upon the rigid principles of the philosophy of sensation, it is impossible to attain the abstract idea of *cause;* even granting that, from the various exhibitions of wisdom and intelligence in the construction of the universe, we may arrive at the conclusion that the designer of this admirable order must have pos-sessed intelligence; still we cannot prove his unity or infinity. The system of nature, so far as we are acquainted with it, is finite, and we cannot reason from a finite effect to an infinite cause. But any argument which fails in demonstrating the infinity of the cause of nature, must fail in demonstrating his self-existence; and, consequently, we cannot prove that there has not been a series of dependent causes, each in turn derived from a preceding cause. The only remedy for this radical defect in the proof from design, taken exclusively, is the introduction into the argument of an *à priori* principle, drawn from the laws and constitution of the intellect itself. A severe examination of the laws of thought discovers to us that the self-existence and infinity of the power that sustains the universe is a postulate reason. It is an idea of which the clear statement is sufficient, the truth of which is seen by intuition, and which cannot be strengthened by any ratiocination. It is, if we may so speak, a form of our thought, when applied to the argument as to the first cause.

Whatever hypothesis we adopt as to the origin or primal cause of the universe, we cannot rid ourselves of this necessary law of reason. We must predicate self-existence and infinity of something. If we take up the atheistic theory, and deny an intelligent cause, we must still admit that nature, the

material universe, is self-existent and infinite. Now
introduce this fundamental conception of reason
with the argument from design, and it becomes
complete and satisfactory. It will then rest on the
very nature of reason, as well as on the testimony
of experience. But this conception, so essential to
the validity of the proof, is at utter variance with
the whole fabric of the philosophy we are considering. In its vocabulary there is no meaning to the
term, *à priori* laws of reason ; for *prior* to experience, the intellect is a mere blank, a capacity alone
for receiving whatever may be conveyed through
the senses. There is no necessity of multiplying
instances to prove the weakness of its philosophy in
establishing the validity of our religious notions.
Religion deals entirely with questions beyond the
reach of the senses, and, consequently, before the
inexorable law of the philosophy of sensation, every
question with which religion is concerned must be
banished into the region of chimera and superstition. Let it not be said, however, that this point is
of no practical importance ; that it affects merely
the manner of stating the argument for religion,
but cannot weaken any person's religious convictions. There are many, no doubt, who do not need
the results of reflection to strengthen their faith.
"They never feel the burden of doubt, nor need
the aid of philosophy to explain the mysteries of
their being. On their virgin souls no blight can
fall, and they will pass upward unstained by the
breath of unbelief." The world, however, is not

made up of such as these. There are those of colder temperaments, who feel the spontaneous impulses of a common nature less, and distrust them more, and who, of course, can repose only on the conclusions of their intellect. And it is they who need to be preserved from the influence of a philosophy before which they will surely fall. We are at no loss for instances to establish this point. The theory of knowledge which Hume adopted, necessarily resulted in his scepticism. He applied, with unsparing rigor, the laws of evidence, with which his philosophy furnished him, to all the departments of thought; and of course concluded, to use his sarcasm, that "Our most holy religion is founded on faith, and not on reason." Had Gibbon been under the influence of a nobler philosophy, his pages would have been free from many of those sneers at virtue and disinterestedness, and that calm contempt of religion, with which they are now defiled. The whole literature of the age of Louis XIV. and XV. was poisoned by a false philosophy. The tone of thought among the higher orders may be gathered from a remark of Madame Du Deffand, in a letter to Voltaire, upon learning that he was engaged in a discussion on the existence of God: "Do not weary yourself, my dear Voltaire, with metaphysical reasonings upon unintelligible matters. Can we communicate or can we entertain any ideas which we do not receive through our senses?"

At whatever period of the world we find this sys-

tem obtaining sway, the evidences of its blighting
influences may be discovered in every department
of literature.   Under its domination, art can only
attain a stunted growth, and poetry is deprived of
its sweet and mysterious faith.   Its religion may be
seen in the " System of Nature ; " its morality in
the Maxims of Rochefoucauld, and in Helvetius's
"Sur l'Esprit."   The dignity of human nature is
sacrificed before it.   When Helvetius contended that
pleasure was the sole motive of all actions, and
that the sense of touch was so necessary to the
education of the human faculties that the species
would have been still wandering in the forest had
man been created with hoofs instead of wrists, Voltaire declared that he told the secret of all the
world.   Cicero long ago remarked, that in the
schools of Epicurus, in his day, the names of Ly-
curgus and Solon, of Miltiades and Epaminondas,
were never mentioned ; so terrible a fact is heroism
and disinterestedness for the contemplation of sensualism.[1]   And nothing, perhaps, illustrates better
the utter degradation of morals that characterized
the period preceding the downfall of the Roman
republic, than the general deification of Epicurus,
whose image, according to Cicero, was preserved not
only in pictures, but engraven on the cups and rings
of the household servants.[2]   A very just comparison between the moral tone of this philosophy and
that of some of the ancient pagans has been drawn
by Addison.   " It is impossible," says he, " to read

1 De Fin. lib. i.   2 De Fin lib. v.; see also Niebuhr, iv. p. 201.

a passage in Plato, or Tully, and a thousand other ancient moralists, without being a greater and a better man. On the contrary, I could never read any of our modish French authors, or those of our own country who are the imitators and admirers of that nation, without being for some time out of humor with myself and at everything about me. Their business is to depreciate human nature, and to consider it under. the worst appearances; they give mean interpretations and base motives to the worthiest actions. In short, they endeavor to make no distinction between man and man, or between the species of man, and that of brutes."[1] We do not say, that all who have adopted the ultra premises to which we have alluded are atheists, or indifferent to religion; such, at least, have not been their professions, and we know that many of the warmest partisans of this philosophy have been dignitaries of the church. But, in many cases, it is to be feared that the palpable inconsistency has been relieved by a belief that the essence of religion consists in mystery, and is therefore incomprehensible by human faculties. The only reconciliation that can be effected between such a man and his religion, must be obtained by some such position as this; for it is useless to talk of a man's holding one truth in philosophy on grounds which his reason approves, and assenting to an entirely different one in religion. The spheres of philosophy and religion are so intimately connected that false

---

[1] Tatler, 108. Stewart, vi. 108.

premises in the one must produce false conclusions in the other; and the manner in which the principles we adopt in either department must affect our conclusions in the other province, furnishes a criterion by which we may judge of the truth or soundness of those principles themselves.

We have seen to what result the theory of knowledge, which has been supported by a large class of philosophers, must inevitably tend. A sensual and materialistic system of philosophy, selfishness, and utilitarianism in morals, and, if the principles be rigidly adhered to, scepticism in religion, are the logical development of the position that the senses are the only source of knowledge. Change that proposition, and the whole complexion of the theories of morals and philosophy and religion, will be changed also. If, after a cautious and profound analysis of our ideas, we assume, as the starting-point, that experience is the occasion, instead of the cause, of all of our knowledge, that the mind itself has faculties the operation of which is implied in our fundamental ideas, that sensible impressions are only the exciting causes which call these faculties into action, the prospect of the whole field of knowledge will be changed as if the wand of a spiritual magician had been waved over it. The whole tendency of thought is directed to spiritualism. The icy grasp of materialism, which freezes all the pulses of feeling, yields to a genial warmth. A system of philosophy may, then, be logically raised, in which man may be viewed as superior to nature; the inspirations of poetry and art, as something more than impressions upon the outward sense; and religion, instead of being considered a mere chimera unworthy a place in the domain of science, be looked upon as a development of the highest faculties of the soul. The recognition of the double origin of knowledge as the fundamental truth in philosophy affords the only basis sufficiently broad for the harmonious development of every principle of our nature. A man may then be master of all his ideas. His logic will not be the implacable foe of his faith. He may face his convictions with a calm eye, and feel assured that they rest upon a foundation as immovable as the very laws of his being. Under the direction of those laws of thought which materialism presents, reason may demand of religion its passport to belief, may desire to know the *sense* to which its evidence is addressed; but a philosophy founded on a correct theory of knowledge, reverses this unnatural order. It shows that religion resides in us, not only as an ineradicable feeling, but that the great ideas which it supposes, are implied in every exercise of thought; that all around us is the infinite; that we cannot think, without an implied recognition, of something absolute, some independent law on which the exercise of intellect depends; that every question we raise, every thought we create, leads at last to the great mystery of the universe, before which it is the highest office of reason to bow and adore. Under such a system, religion may become rational, because reason itself may become religious. No attempts are needed to bridge the chasm between what we know, and what we feel. Religious ideas have their root in reason, and religious feeling in the nature of the soul; and they can be displaced only by that " consistent scepticism " which strikes at the root of all certainty and all knowledge.

But, it may be urged that the importance of correct opinions in philosophy may be necessary where the light of nature is our only guide, but that the question becomes unimportant when revelation is taken into the account. We need not speculate upon religion; we know; truth is revealed to us. We do not want philosophy; we have Christianity. This of course, opens the question as to the relation between philosophy and revealed religion. We might reply, in the first place, that the possibility of any religion at all is a question preliminary to the consideration of revelation. And this, as we have shown, is a problem which is intimately affected by our philosophical views. The man who, on philosophical grounds, denies that religious ideas can form a portion of knowledge, cannot be reached with arguments drawn from the sublimity of the truths which revelation exhibits, nor from their harmony with the wants of his nature. He admits no such principle of reasoning. You might as well talk to him of the objects of a sixth sense. His intellect, encased in the armor of sensualism, is impervious to such weapons. He can only be convinced of the truths of revelation by the historical evidence of

its founder; the truth of his miracles, and the probability that his doctrines have been transmitted to
us in their original purity; a mode of defending the
gospel in which, when addressed to such minds, we
have little confidence. Hume has shown that, in
such cases, it is much easier to attack the credibility
of miracles than to yield conclusions drawn from a
study of the human mind. At least then, so far as
scepticism is concerned, a false philosophy must be
disarmed with its own weapons before the claims of
Christianity can be successfully advanced. But we
think we can show that, besides being necessary for
the defence of revelation, philosophy has an important connection with our views of revelation
itself. There are some points, of course, where the
teachings of revelation are ultimate. We cannot
go beyond them. The great truth, for instance, of
the paternal character of God, is an idea which the
unassisted reason could never have attained. No
induction, from any facts within our knowledge,
could have reached it. The strong light of revelation must first be thrown upon nature, before natural facts can be seen to bear the impress of divine
love. Philosophy, before the Saviour, had attained
a dim and unsteady conception of the goodness of
God. Plato exhausted all the richness of his fancy
and the loftiness of his diction to prove that God
was the *Supreme Good.* But between this conception and the truth that God is the universal Father there is all the difference that exists between
Plato and Jesus, between the loftiest philosophy and

the purest religion. We admit, then, that in revelation philosophy has been helped over problems
which, by its own strength, it could not solve ; but
what we contend for is the conception we form of
the meaning of the truths of revelation, depends in
a great measure on our cultivation of mind, or, in
other words, on our peculiar philosophical views.
The doctrines of Christianity are stated in words ;
but the mere reading of those words does not give
a man clear conceptions of the depth and meaning
of the truths themselves, any more than the mere
reading of the words of Newton's Principia, or Laplace's Mecanique Celeste, would give him correct
conceptions of the magnitude and importance of
the mathematical propositions demonstrated there.
Why is it that we believe that Christianity, as a religion, can never be superseded ? Because we believe that the system of morality it teaches, and the
worship it demands, are the ideas of worship and
morality for all ages. To whatever degree of intellectual or spiritual advancement we may attain, we
can never exhaust, and never get beyond, the sublime and simple truths revealed by the Saviour. His
religion was a system of principles capable of the
widest application, and of indefinite expansion. It
assists the growth of the mind, — grows with it.
At the very time that it furnishes the elements of
human progress, we distinctly see that with all the
increased capacities resulting from progress, we can
never exhaust the materials contained in Christianity. A thorough conviction of this truth is of infi-

nite importance in strengthening our religious convictions, and our faith in revelation. And the discovery of this very truth is the work of philosophy,
It is not a doctrine of revelation itself, but is drawn
from an acquaintance with the laws of progress. It
is the humble confession of reason to revelation,
that the highest office of philosophy is to increase
our susceptibility to religion, and that its loftiest
ambition is satisfied with bringing the light of its
researches to bear upon the interpretation of that
truth, of which the Son was the appointed messen-
ger.

Our philosophy then will be, to a great extent,
the interpreter of Christianity. It will translate the
words of revelation in harmony with the conclusions which we may form of the human mind, its
wants, and its capacities. Whether, in the first instance, we derive the foundation of our philosophical views from Christianity, or from reason, still the
same tendency exists in the mind to reconcile the
teachings of revelation with the developments of
this philosophical creed. Take the doctrine of salvation, for instance. Christianity, one would think,
is explicit upon this point. And yet, about no
question in theology, is the church more divided
than about the teaching of Scripture in relation
to it. There is every modification of opinion as to
its meaning, extent, and mode. And every one of
the various hues and shades of the belief, respecting it, is dependent upon, or connected with, some
system of philosophy, of which this view forms a

component part. Let a man, through the prejudices of education, derive from Scripture the notion
of original sin, with its satellites, a corrupted nature, a vicarious atonement, and an angry God, and
he cannot adopt, in perfect good faith, a spiritual
philosophy in its full extent. He cannot believe in
the freedom of the will ; he cannot conceive the
possibility of drawing a system of ethics from the
study of a sinful consciousness ; he cannot consistently see, in a depraved nature, the germs of worship and faith in God. On the other hand, no man
who, from the study of the will, of consciousness,
and of the original instincts of human nature, has
arrived at a faith in freedom, at a conception of
moral obligation, and a belief that religion is founded on a law of the soul, can see in revelation a doctrine which sets at naught all the conclusions of his
intellect, to say nothing of the sensibilities of his
heart. Men are never wilfully illogical or inconsistent in their opinions ; and surely no man in his
senses would attempt to reconcile propositions so
fundamentally incongruous. Before Pelagius and
Augustine can agree, Pelagius must abandon his
philosophy, or Augustine must give up his faith.
But this fundamental difference as to the nature of
salvation affects also the question as to the mode.
And here again, the influence of philosophy is involved. The corollary of the first view we have
mentioned, is, that salvation is instantaneous and
supernatural, affected upon man, not in him, and by
himself ; a work in which he is an instrument not

an agent; in which he is passive, not active. If
salvation is thus instantaneous and final, where is
the room for progress? Where is that intimate harmony between virtue and religion which philosophy
sees intuitively, and which Christianity implies on
every page? If the essence of salvation does not
consist in being formed in the image of Jesus, that
is, in the practice of the loftiest virtue, where is the
incentive to take him as our pattern? and what
hope may we indulge of ever attaining to his perfection, if we must view him as the Infinite Father?
The philosophy which the spirit of Christianity in
the world has helped to form, and the conclusions
to which the study of man, as he has been affected
by Christianity, has led, rise in rebellion against
such a construction of the words of revelation.
They cannot harmonize. Between them there is a
great gulf fixed.

If we reflect, too, upon our conception of the Deity
himself, we shall find that our interpretation of the
Scripture teachings as to his character and attributes
is greatly modified by the tone of our philosophy.
Much of the purity of thought upon the other essential points of Christian doctrine depends upon our
fundamental conceptions of God himself. We are
taught in the New Testament that " God is a spirit; "
but how few are there whose views of the nature of
the Divine Being are not formed after the idea of
the Old Testament, whose conceptions attach themselves to the qualities of gross power and material
force; and who consequently never pass through

the Jewish, and attain a Christian idea of God. One
of the most difficult things which the mind has to
contend against, in forming a definite notion of the
nature of the Deity, is the conflict between the
senses and the reason. The senses always tend to
anthropomorphism, to some limitation of form, and
some precise idea of place ; views which the cultivated
reason, of course, rejects with abhorrence. The
root of this difficulty lies in the constant association
of the philosophical ideas of substance and being,
with matter and organization, and can be eradicated
only by such a discipline of mind as will enable us
to entertain these ideas wholly separate from each
other. The noble conception which Plato developed
of the nature of God, necessarily sprang from
philosophical habits of thought. He could not have
held an anthropomorphic notion of the Supreme
Good, till he had reconstructed his theory of virtue
and the powers of the soul. They were inseparably
intertwined. On the other hand, the phantom gods
of Epicurus differed from the ardent fire which the
stoics conceived to be the vesture of the Deity, precisely because the whole tone of the philosophy of the
former was grovelling and mean, and of the latter
lofty and ennobling. Gassendi, who, although a
Catholic priest, was a very strong advocate of the
doctrine that all our ideas originate exclusively in
sensible impressions, and who may be considered the
founder of that school in modern times, maintained
that " we must conceive God under the image of a
venerable old man," — that being the noblest form

under which a sensible conception could be entertained by the imagination. And are there not now large bodies of Christians whose ideas of God are drawn from the imagery of Daniel and the Apocalypse, — the great white throne, and garments of snow, and the chariot of fire, rather than from a full realization of the meaning of those sublime words of the Saviour, " God is a spirit, and they that worship him must worship him in spirit and in truth " ? Let it not be said that this point is of little importance. Connected with our views of the nature of God as our ideas of his providence and omnipresence must necessarily be, we cannot err in the one and be sound in the other. And here, of course, the question becomes vitally practical. Faith in the Christian doctrine of universal providence of course demands a belief in the intimate and abiding presence of God in his works. He must be viewed as the life of the universe, the present cause of all things, the all-pervading essence which supports and maintains and directs the phenomena of nature. Without this constant recognition of the omnipresence of God in its strictest sense, nature to us is a machine whose movements are governed by a pre-established harmony, not a manifestation of the constant presence and prevading activity of an all-wise agent. God is separate from his works, providence is the law of fate, prayer a foreordained and component element in the working of a vast spiritual mechanism.

We are taught in Scripture that the hairs of our

heads are numbered, and that not a sparrow falls to
the ground without the notice of the Almighty. But
the theory of providence we see revealed in these
words must form a component part of our rational
views of the nature of God, and of his relation to
the moral world. It is in the light of these conceptions that we interpret the meaning of the verbal
relation itself. The signification of the terms expands with the breadth and extent of our spiritual
ideas. Certainly, when science has unveiled to us
its exalted view of God's omnipresence, and revealed
his intimate nearness in the action of every natural
force, the Christian view of providence may be
accepted in its most literal sense, and partakes of the
precision and extent and certainty of our scientific
conceptions. The very simplicity of the gospel is
linked with the discoveries of science and the depth
of our philosophical ideas. But there is another
point where our independent speculative views exercise an important influence on the interpretation of
revealed religion ; I mean in the connection we
establish between the finite and the infinite, between
God and his works. The immense diversity of
opinion that has been entertained by Christians upon
this question proves that revelation lacks sufficient
precision to preclude the necessity of personal reflection. And here the danger to be apprehended does
not consist solely nor chiefly in the adoption of a
narrow and gross system of philosophy, as in many
of the cases we have named, but in most cases
springs from an opposite tendency, from spiritualism

itself become ultra and exclusive. Men, starting from a conception of the infinity, omnipresence, and spirituality of the Deity, have seen only him in the universe; fixing their view exclusively on the eternal substance, they have looked upon man merely as an accident, or mode of that substance; accustomed to direct their thoughts to the efficacy of the Infinite Agency alone, they have seen in man no central and self-determining power, no inherent and personal force. A spirit completely saturated with such a view may be religious, but its religion is diseased. Religion, to be healthy and strong, must include a view of human liberty, as well as of Divine power; it must see that we have nobler relations to the Deity than that of absolute dependence. The piety which Christian Pantheism inspires in man is a dreamy quiescence, a losing of self in contemplation of the Infinite. All the powers of the soul are absorbed in meditation upon the awful ideas in which the Deity is revealed to us, till an unnatural humility ends by sacrificing the noblest elements of human nature upon the altar of faith. The fundamental vice of this view of the relation of the Creator and his creature may be, and has been, manifested in a variety of forms, and has tainted almost every doctrine of Christianity.

Revelation warns us of the influence of sense and passion; and mysticism, seizing upon this point of duty exclusively, has driven men to cloisters and solitudes, that they might yield themselves to the luxury of unobstructed meditation. We are com-

manded to recognize the claims of duty before those
of society and kindred ; and a rigid asceticism, trans-
lating this command into the language of its favorite
views, has condemned the exercise of every social
feeling as sinful, and placed the perfection of virtue
in the infliction of exquisite self-torture.

Christianity is replete with expressions of the
grandeur and holiness of the Deity ; and Calvinism,
from an exclusive view of the divine majesty, has
placed a false estimate upon human agency, and
resolved all morality into considerations for the glory
of God.   It was with a view to these instances of
the corruptions of Christianity, that Channing profoundly remarked, "It is a fact worthy of serious
thought, and full of solemn instruction, that many
of the worst errors have grown out of the religious
tendencies of the mind.   So necessary is it to keep
watch over our whole nature, to subject the highest
sentiments to the calm conscientious reason." Although the spirit of quietism of which we have
spoken is foreign to the tone of modern civilization,
still, under its practical influence, we may trace the
working of the same views with a different form. A
false transcendentalism has seduced some of the
noblest minds in our very midst. We open their
works, and read of the ideal in religion, of the
manifestation of God in the instincts of the soul,
and of uniting our life with the universe in the perception of eternal beauty.   Such theories are pretty ;
that, however, is not our objection to them ; they are
enervating.   There is nothing in them to stimulate

that substantial virtue which is the morality of Christianity. We do not object to art; we object to the theory of the identity of art and religion; to that philosophy which would substitute poetic reverie for the practical duties which Christianity enjoins as the exhibition and proof of sound religious life. The existence of Christ in human form, by giving us at once a definite conception of the perfection of humanity, and a full revelation of the nature and will of God, is a perpetual rebuke to that dissipation of the human faculties and that sickly hue of thought which is the inevitable result of every modification of Pantheism.

The most remarkable instance, however, of the effect of philosophical systems in modifying the doctrines of revelation, may be detected in the structure of the theology of the Catholic Church. It is developed there on a colossal scale. In the Middle Ages two great and rival schools contended for the empire of the intellectual world — Realism and Nominalism. The seal of authority was given to the former. The realists contended that all knowledge was deducible from abstract ideas of the mind; the testimony of experience was distrusted as unworthy the confidence of a philosopher, and reality was attributed only to the general notions of the intellect. Their system was a compound of Platonism and Aristotelianism, of Platonic ideas under an Aristotelian form. Its great maxim was, "Invisibilia non decipiunt;" *things invisible never deceive.* Nominalism, on the contrary, denied the validity of general notions unless verified by the testimony of experience; and thus in a dark age was the prophet of the modern scientific method. It is curious to observe the facility with which a false philosophy lent itself to the service of the Catholic faith. All the theories of the Church were cast in the mould of the dominant philosophical system. The doctrines of the eucharist and the Trinity, of predestination and grace, bristled with philosophic formulæ. As early as the ninth century, the testimony of the senses was officially impeached to obviate objections to the doctrine of the real presence. Heresies were met with more subtile distinctions, and a finer analysis of the subject and predicate of Scripture propositions. It was as if a solemn incantation had shrouded nature and revelation in an obscurity which Aristotle's system alone had power to dispel. The schoolmen saw everywhere, and in everything, but the outward symbol of an Aristotelian truth. The doctrine of the Trinity was a scientific view of the principle of causation. The dignity of Aristotle was blended with that of Jesus in the papal chair. The Son was the principle of intelligence, and was generated from the Father, as thought is generated from mind. The Spirit is the love of God to his creation, and proceeded merely from the Father. The terms diversity, difference, separation, distinction, disparity, division, applied to God, became heresy, as they were inconsistent with the great Stagirite's view of substance, according to which God must exist as a Unity of essence under a Trinity of forms. The prevalent theories of justification, of original sin, and of free-agency, were all explained by the physical and moral speculations of Aristotle upon creation, and the relation of the Deity to his works. But the points in which the Church received the most efficient aid from philosophy, may be found in the defence of the Catholic view of the Sacrament and Transubstantiation. The problem was to satisfy reason, and reconcile the theory with common sense. According to the physical theory of the schoolmen, nature was conceived to be a vast system of powers secretly directed by the sovereign will. All the forms of existence could be analyzed into substance and accidents; substance being the last point to which analysis can attain, the secret ground and support of all appearances, and accidents including everything which does not enter into a rational conception of the being or nature of the thing defined. Of course, in accordance with the fundamental doctrine of Realism, substance and accident being clear and distinct ideas of the mind, must have distinct and separate existence in nature, and therefore may not always be conjoined in the actual world. Now, in the mystical consecration of the elements in the eucharist, the form of the sacrament, that is, the official ceremony conducted by the priest, partaking of the creative energy of the Divine word, changes the distinctive substance of the elements, and infuses the Divine substance of Christ himself. The accidents, such as the form, the taste, the color, and dimensions of the elements,

18

still remain, not existing in Christ as their substance, but as simple phenomena divorced from all ground of support. The vicious character or forgetfulness of the priest, at the moment of consecration, could not affect the efficacy of the form, as the priest represented no individual authority, his personality being resolved into the abstract individuality of the Church; and it was the general intention of the Church that was manifested in the sacramental ceremony. Realism here became an effectual means of power. " It was an admirable expedient of ecclesiastical policy thus to rest the power of the church on the purity and indefectibility of an abstraction. Religious imagination was sustained on the picture of the church as the great mother of the faithful, cherishing her beloved children in her pure bosom ; whilst her many-handed agents in the world were securing their hold on the consciences of men by that prerogative of veneration which they enjoyed in her person." [1] This connection between the logical philosophy of the schoolmen and the Catholic religion were not accidental., It is upon the principles of that philosophy alone that the theology of Rome can be defended now.   Luther, who was, according to Melancthon, a strenuous partisan of the sect of Nominalists, declared that a reform of the church would be impossible until the whole scholastic philosophy, theology, and logic should be eradicated.   The study of physics cured Bayle of Catholicism ; and Gibbon has left a record of the

<hr>

[1] Hampden's Bampton Lectures, p. 324.

raptures he experienced when the important and recondite truth flashed upon his mind that the doctrine of the real presence is attested only by the sense of sight, which receives the impressions of Scripture texts, while it is disproved by three senses, — the sight, the touch, and the taste. Catholicism has always opposed philosophical innovation. When Descartes, with his principle of universal doubt, and his distinction of substances into material and thinking, broke the spell of the Middle Ages, an angry controversy was at once excited upon the doctrine of Transubstantiation, which drove the partisans of the new system to the most subtile artifices in order to maintain the show of congruity between their views and the dominant theology. The revival of an ideal philosophy in France in modern times, occasioned an outbreak of jesuitical bigotry, owing to fear for the doctrines of the church; and, in our own country, we have lately seen a distinguished theorist, remarkable for severity of his logic and the consistency, for the time being, of his opinions, after having been led, by a metaphysical formula, into the bosom of the Catholic Church, turn and decry the whole tendency of modern thought and cultivation, and speak in the most exalted terms of the wisdom and depth of the philosophy of the Middle Ages.

In the history of modern philosophy, too, the reaction of the opinions of every school upon theology, admonishes us of the inseparable connection between these separate pursuits. The peculiar views of Kant, as to the powers of the mind and the laws of science, necessarily led to a peculiar theory of revelation. He aspired· to show, *à priori*, what, from the nature of the human mind, revelation must contain, and the evidence it must adduce in support of its authority. Soon, the influence of his system called forth theologians like Paulus, and Rohr, and Krug, and Wegscheider, and a host of others, who swell the ranks of German rationalism. The dreamy and poetic spirit of Schelling's philosophy of nature, added to the Catholic influence some of the most celebrated names which German literature in the nineteenth century can boast. Hegelianism embodied its religious results in Strauss's life of Jesus, and the theological opinions and spirit of Schleiermacher and De Wette were allied with a criticism of the human faculties and a theory of knowledge, which found a scientific form in the philosophy of Fries. And in our midst it is easy to trace the influence which the general philosophical spirit, the belief in the *absolute* agency of man, and the dignity of human nature, among the Unitarians, has had in moulding the form of their theology, and in determining their views of revelation. A full discussion of the points of difference between them and their opponents involves at the outset the justness of their conception of human power.

Among us, it is evident that the topic of which we have been treating is a new one. Obliged as our denomination has been to maintain an antagonistic position, in order· to support its existence, it is

no wonder that it has not meddled with questions
which demand more leisure, a higher cultivation,
and different habits of thought. Perhaps, too, it is
to this polemic tendency that we must ascribe a certain distrust of such pursuits as visionary and uncertain, too often built on abstractions that are the
dreams of a distempered imagination, or the creations of a disordered brain. Many of our reasoners,
so long accustomed to decide all questions by an appeal to Scripture, seem to have become unfitted for
the discussion of questions where the subject is the
human mind, and the requisites a delicate analysis
and subtile discrimination. They want the positive-
ness of authority, and suspect the soundness of conclusions drawn by unassisted reason. They are
fearful, moreover, that the simplicity of the gospel
may be corrupted ; forgetting that mysticism may
revel in fanciful constructions of the sacred writings,
and sophistry lurk under a rigid collation of Scripture texts. But, be this as it may, the wants of a
higher cultivation are beginning to be seriously felt
among us, and, as a help to attain this cultivation,
a philosophical training is not only desirable, but
necessary. The laws of the human mind are not
suspended nor reversed in behalf of religious science. It requires training and discipline and severe
reflection, to reach the highest walks in theology, as
much as it requires them to reach the highest walks
in any intellectual pursuit. There are questions at
this moment pressing upon the attention of the
American theologian, to which he must bring a mind

versed in history and science, and trained to habits
of patient and untiring thought. Disputes as to
the authenticity of the Scriptures, the reality of
miracles, and the nature of inspiration, however
we may regret that they have been raised, cannot
be settled by the dogmatism of common sense, or
charmed away by the contempt of indifference.
Neither, of course, can they be laid by appeals
to Scripture. Philosophy, by examining into the
grounds upon which faith is built, has raised them;
and it is to enlightened philosophy alone that we
must look for those principles of historical criticism
which can conduct to a satisfactory solution.

This relation of religion to philosophy, let it here
be observed, is not peculiar. A man who is not
penetrated with a philosophic spirit cannot attain
to eminence in any intellectual pursuit. All the
provinces of thought are under the dominion of
philosophy. It is the air from which they draw the
sustenance of a lofty or a stunted growth. The
study of history has been revolutionized by modern
philosophy; its aim has been changed, its sphere
enlarged. Underneath minute events it looks for
the spirit of the people, the manners and life which
determine national character, and searches for facts
in order to attain the ideas by which they may be
interpreted. Beyond history now lies the philosophy of history, which is the creation of the modern
intellect, and the noblest product of modern cultivation. Science, too, has received its laws from
philosophy; and, like a dutiful child, returns to its

parent the fruit of its researches, to be used as the material of still wider progress. Literature and art spring from the inner life of the times, and always exhibit, in a form a little obscure, the tone and direction of thought and cultivation. Philosophy, then, is indispensable to critical and exact scholarship, and is at once the basis and summit of a thorough education.

Before closing this article, however, we wish to say a few words upon the objections which have been brought against modern philosophy. With some, the terms in which it deals afford an insuperable obstacle. They are so uncouth, nonsensical, and absurd, as to provoke laughter and disgust. But distinct and different ideas require peculiar forms of expression, and, in fact, one of the great obstacles which has obstructed the progress of the science of the human mind, has been the employment of terms borrowed from material operations, and suggesting material analogies. We do not admire the euphony, nor defend, in all cases, the propriety, of the philosophical nomenclature; but we cannot see the justice of condemning a pursuit for the precision of its terminology, any more than of condemning a mechanic for the sharpness of his tools. When such criticisms shall be applied to botany or chemistry or physiology, they will at least acquire the merit of consistency. Again; the variety of philosophical opinions and schools, has been considered a weighty objection to the usefulness and value of the pursuit itself. But religion

exhibits the same variety of opinion, and the same
diversity of sects.　In fact, the apparent multiplicity
of philosophical schools is delusive, and does not
really exist.　The great central ideas which are the
nucleus around which philosophical systems are
formed, will be found to be very few and simple.
They may, without any violence to facts, be reduced
to four; and we think a rigid analysis might resolve
these into two : Sensualism and Idealism.　The
most comprehensive and minute survey of the history of philosophy cannot find, we will venture to
say, another idea as the basis of an additional classification ; and certainly this is as near an approach
to unity as theology can boast.　But this objection,
like the last, proceeds, in too many instances, from
a weakness of mind or a narrowness of spirit that
pretends to decide upon what it does not know, and
cannot comprehend, and only proves the necessity
of the very cultivation it decries.　Some, however,
object to speculative philosophy, that it is visionary
and unscientific, its method too rash, and its results
not valid.　To a certain extent this objection may
be well founded, and it leads us naturally to consider some of the faults of modern speculation.
The great errors of modern philosophy have been
a hasty generalization, and too great confidence in
the power of the human intellect.　The limits of
knowledge have not been clearly defined.　Philosophers have forgotten the rules of philosophy, and
have endeavored to pluck from the universe the
" heart of its mystery."　Speculation has attempted

to reach, without patient toil, results which patient induction alone could promise; it has desired to wear, without winning, the crown of science. Such attempts, of course, must fail. When men attempt to express in one formula the secret laws of the universe, and the reason of all things, they may expect to see their splendid generalizations turn to "splendid follies." Every endeavor to penetrate beyond the power of the mind to know, has overthrown the system it was intended to adorn, and men are beginning to see that the perfection of reason consists in the recognition of mystery that underlies the whole. This tendency of modern philosophy may be easily explained; it is a reaction against the laws by which, in the eighteenth century, it was confined. Reason, set free from its narrow limits, would tolerate nothing but itself, and consequently has overlooked the importance of the affections and feelings, and aimed too much after a colder, lifeless, and purely rational view of nature. These are faults of philosophers, not of philosophy; and the remedy must be sought in a rigid adherence to true philosophic method. All the great discoveries in mental science, like the discoveries in the material sciences, have resulted from a patient and exhaustive analysis of the facts of consciousness and history, in order to attain a thorough classification, and to construct a legitimate and valid theory. The method of the student of philosophical history is not different from that of the astronomer; the same speculative laws which the botanist observes are equally applicable to the pursuits of the philologist.

Finally the great argument, with some, against philosophical pursuits, is that of irreligious tendency. That some philosophers have been sceptics cannot be denied. But Laplace was a sceptic; and is astronomy injurious? Shelley was an atheist; do we estimate the moral tendency of poetry by his belief? Paine was an infidel; but are the principles of common sense to be distrusted, because he professed to be governed by them? Moreover, a thorough theologian would desire to understand the nature of the attacks against his system; and if they come in a philosophical form, how shall he refute them? Must he abandon the ground to atheists, and thus tacitly admit that the advancing cultivation of the age has outrun theology? Old Jerome applied himself to study, in order to improve the tone of sacred literature, and that Christians might be able to reply to heathens, who despised them as infants in learning and ineloquent in style. And Tholuck, recently, after avowing his belief that theology and speculative philosophy cannot be separated, declared, with reference to the present tendency of philosophy in Germany, that he should not feel that he was discharging his duty as an academical teacher, did he not struggle to become master of a system which is striking its roots so deep into the spirit of the age. Those are the most dangerous sceptics, who are continually fearing the effect of intellectual progress upon religion. What would have been the influence if, a few years since, geology had been abandoned to the opponents of religion, and the whole array of theological force and skill, clinging to a rigidly literal interpretation of Scripture, had set against it? Would the progress of science have been impeded? Or rather, would not religion have lost a most useful ally and defender? But it is for others to make this plea of irreligious tendency against philosophy. If we will not give it our countenance, still let us not be plaintiffs. Modern philosophy and modern cultivation, in every department, are leagued with liberal Christianity. This is a sign of hope. The dogmas of a narrow theology cannot breathe the air of philosophy or science; it is too pure. Who can rise from a study of the exquisitely perfect and simple mechanism which every branch of science unfolds, in every corner of the universe, and assent to the theological doctrine of the Trinity? The ethical system of Stewart or Jouffroy is not the ethical system which flows from the doctrines of total depravity and predestination; neither can the works of Combe find fellowship in the theory of vicarious sacrifice and atonement. All those arts which spring from the finer feelings of the soul condemn them. What music would satisfy the genius of Calvinism? what would be its ideal of art, but the "writhing agonies of Laocoon?" Shall we, then, be behind the partisans of these very systems in cultivating the sources of sound literature? Orthodox theologians are daily making themselves familiar with German Bib-

lical critics and German literature, and, consequently, with German philosophy. If the experi-
ment will level their theology to the level of German orthodoxy, the friends of religion will have
cause to rejoice. Everything in the tendencies of
the age is favorable to the progress of liberal Christianity. Moral and intellectual philosophy, science,
literature, and art, are in harmony with it and are
moved by its spirit. The implements are prepared,
if theologians will use them. We have nothing, of
course, to fear from atheism, and, least of all, from
the progress of knowledge. The great question
which, from recent developments, bids fair to agi-
tate the higher circle of theologians, is a question
between rationalism and supernaturalism. In the
discussion of this point, a thorough examination of .
the grounds of religion will of course be involved.
The spiritual and elevated character of modern
speculation is a pledge for a satisfactory solution.
Any apparent hostility between religion and philosophy will be reconciled by a simple decision. Philosophy does not want supernaturalism as the starting-point; religion does not want rationalism as a
goal. Both will be satisfied with supernaturalism
grounded in rationalism, with Christian faith as the
crown of human reason.

XIII.

NATURAL AND REVEALED RELIGION.

THE object proposed in the present article is this: to point out the relations and the reciprocal influence between natural and revealed religious truth; between those ideas of God, the spiritual relations of men, and human destiny, which inquiry, research, and reflection have attained, and those ideas which are unfolded with authoritative clearness in the Bible. It does not come within the scope of our plan to refer at all to the preliminary question, so widely agitated in our time, whether the Bible itself contains a revelation, in our common understanding of that term, or whether its truths are merely the highest discoveries as yet attained by the religious nature in its natural and ordinary development. Standing on the commonly recognized Christian ground, without reference to that point, we wish to trace the connection between the religious truths of the Bible, as they are clearly unfolded, whether supernaturally revealed or not, and the development of philosophical and scientific researches in the same field.

And, in the first place, we must remark that the distinction between the two provinces of natural

and revealed religion is founded, not in a difference between *things*, but in the relation which certain truths bear to the laws and limits of human
knowledge.   By the terms "natural" and "revealed," we do not distinguish different *kinds* of
religion, separate fields of investigation essentially
distinct; we do not intend an intellectual partition
such as, in the realm of science, is conveyed by
the terms astronomy and geology, chemistry and
mathematics.   Evidently, there can be but one
religion, one absolute system of spiritual truth, as
there can be but one science of geometry, or one
theory of light and of mechanic forces.   And this
absolute religion remains true, independent of human thought and culture, entirely unaffected by
the faith or the ignorance of men.   The difference
marked and conveyed in common speech by the
terms we have used, is a difference of relations
solely; it implies, not a generic separation, but refers to a diversity in the methods of attainment, and
the character of the evidence adduced.   To the domain of natural religion belong all the features of
this universal truth which human reason in its
highest elevation can attain.   It includes all those
discoveries which, in accordance with the natural
adaptation between our finite intellect and the laws
of mental light, flow in upon us from the infinite
depths of being; while revealed religion, supply-
ing a higher instrument, and collecting and concen-
trating the rays into a powerful focus, *intensifies* —
to use that word — our natural knowledge, at the

same time that it extends the range of our acquaintance with the universe, and brings within the circle of our vision vast relations, which must forever have been denied to the most ardent researches of the unaided eye.   The distinction in the terms reposes, then, not on *objective* peculiarities in *truths*, but on *subjective* powers of *discovery*.

Reasoning *à priori*, we cannot discover that, independent of the pleasure of the Deity, there need be, to us, any natural connection between the evidences for these two divisions.   The infinite cannot exhaust itself by any revelations, and there would seem to be no necessary relationship between the actual manifestations of the Deity in the mechanical arrrangements of nature and the powers of the mind, and any further communications which he might choose to make directly through an accredited agent, and by super-ordinary means.   It was within the option of the Deity to rest revelation on independent evidence entirely overwhelming; to introduce it into the world like light borne suddenly into the midst of total darkness; to strengthen it with evidence that should command the belief of all times, not at all by the harmony of its truths with known or observed or supposed principles of divine agency and action, but by the crushing exhibitions of supernatural interference which establish, beyond all cavil, the communicated facts. Nature might have been constructed so meaningless, or the intuitive energies of the mind might have been so dull, that, for any practical knowledge of the char-

acter and will of the Almighty, we should be obliged
to rely entirely on definite statements, indorsed by
evidence addressed to the senses, — evidence which
should always consist of historical and material
proof.   Beyond any attainable depths "a lower
deep" still opens in the infinite ; and, as the scale
of revelation, through common or uncommon means,
is solely the arbitrary pleasure of the Deity, we can
discover no necessary tie, which, in the nature of
things, binds the truths of the two departments into
mutual relationship and dependency.

But this, although it might have been the order
of providence, is not the order of fact.   It will not
be pretended by any — we think not by the blindest
zealots against human reason — that there is no
connection subsisting between these separate ranges.
It is the plan of the Infinite Wisdom not to over-
power the mind by certainty, but to lead it along
the path of analogies and correspondences and probabilities, to faith.   Nature is neither so empty of
moral significance, nor the mind so devoid of heavenly attractions and spiritual instincts, nor is the
dogmatic and extraordinary evidence of revelation
so irresistible, when examined by itself, as to require,
on the one hand, or to permit on the other, the introduction of a set of truths claiming to be a revelation, and yet entirely beyond the range, and independent of the confirmation and support which
are given by the dim testimony of the outward universe and the soul of man.   And thus, while we
affirm a radical distinction between natural and re-

vealed religion, relatively to the powers of the mind, which must not be confounded, neither the actual weakness of the one nor the admitted strength of the other will allow us to deny that they do, in some way, mutually imply and sustain each other.

If the supernatural proofs of revelation be not assumed to be in themselves entirely overwhelming, so as to repel the possibility of collateral aid, we may state, in the first place, that the truths of revelation must be connected with natural religion, at least to this extent; they must be in harmony with it; they must not contradict it. For, with the present constitution of human reason, it can hardly be entertained as possible that any pretended revelation could win a general belief, even though seemingly indorsed by miraculous aid, if it contained a theory of God and Nature entirely opposed to the researches of science, and if it unfolded a system of morals from which the finest sensibilities of conscience spontaneously recoiled. Reason will not entertain the question of supernatural testimony, if it be vitiated by an association with absurdities. Men could easily evade any testimony to a miracle; they would distrust their senses if they saw a miracle wrought in support of a revolting scheme. Such a system, besides miraculous testimony, would find it necessary to induce a miraculous change on human reason, and as an indispensable preliminary reverse the laws of the intellect. And thus, with the present structure of the human mind, the possibility, not indeed of a revelation's

19

being given, but of its gaining credence, involves
the necessity of its being in harmony with the general laws, and what we believe to be the *possibilities*
of nature.

Farther than this, moreover, we may assert that
natural religion is so far the basis of revelation that
it supplies the antecedent probability that further
and higher communications from the Deity will be
made. The argument for a system of revealed truth
is essentially weakened when no hints and no probabilities can be detected in the world and in the
wants of man, which that system meets and confirms. The defences of revelation are left open to
the inroads of scepticism when the outposts of natural analogies and confirmed anticipations have
been stormed and beaten down. Before the full
weight of miraculous evidence even can be appreciated, a certain prior purity in our conceptions of
the unity and goodness of the Almighty is almost
indispensable. Although we cannot excuse the wil-
ful enmity of the Pharisees to Jesus, still, had the
Jewish notions of God's unity been sufficiently precise to have excluded their belief in the power of
demons and the hostile agency of Beelzebub, the
miracles of Christ would have exercised a greater
power over their unbelief. Wherever miraculous
proof is obliged to meet this faith in the duality of
agencies which control the powers of nature, there
must be some circumstances connected with the
miracle or its author or its purpose, which determine the mind from its prior natural associations,

to ascribe to it either to the one or the other of its preconceived deities. And accordingly as these circumstances harmonize with the supposed proper agency of the benevolent or malignant power, will the revelation be accepted. And it was, perhaps, to the purity of the Jewish notions of the power and goodness of the Deity, and to the harmony of his own works and words with those higher views, that Christ appealed as an argument for the validity of his claims in that language, "Ye believe in God, believe also in me."

If we extend our inquiries beyond the field we have already occupied, into the connection between the doctrines of Christianity and natural religion, we find ourselves perplexed with many embarrassing problems. The truths of the Christian revelation were above the attainments and capacity of the age in which they were given. There was nothing in the history or the tendencies of religious and philosophical speculations that seemed to point to or promise them. Besides, they came with authority in a different way and with higher sanctions than truths attained by unassisted human culture. And thus they are forever separated from the same facts if they should be developed by moral evidence alone. This cordially granted and firmly believed, the question of the exact relation between the doctrines of the gospel and of natural religion is still a question of speculative, if not of practical interest, but one which, from the difficulties which attend it is, in our opinion, almost if not entirely insoluble. To receive a satisfactory answer, evidently we should first understand the limits of intellectual power in the domain of religion. We must go back to the time when revelation was given, and comprehend not only what men had learned of God and nature, and not only what they seemed likely to learn, but also what, by the sole aid of thought and culture, they could *ever* learn. We must see not merely the relation of the new doctrines to human attainment thus far, but also to the possible capacity of reason. We must understand the extent to which human reason uninfluenced by the Bible, *can go* in the construction of a religious creed, and then look into the schedule of revelation and note the difference. No other method can be effectual. The mind of Christ was above his time; but we have no authority for asserting that, in the course of centuries, some spirit could not naturally arise who should discover and reveal by the power of spiritual intuition and in a philosophical form many of the truths which Christ revealed by authority and as a religion. We can never prophesy the exact limits of intellectual power. History warns us against doing so. The genius of Plato was naturally evolved from the capacities of the Pelasgic race. But who, in Homer's time, could have conceived the possibility of Platonism! It would have been a revelation — strange enough — in the heroic age. Cultivation prepares the way for him, however, and Plato comes, the perfection of Grecian genius, and by a singular law, at the declining moment of Gre-

cian inspiration. It would have been unwarranta-
ble presumption in the time of Copernicus, or even
of Hipparchus, to have denied the possibility of an
intellect like Newton's. Every genius is an impossibility till he appears. There are never facts
enough in human experience to serve as a basis for
safe induction as to the mental capacity of men.
We cannot reach the law that governs the development of genius. Two centuries before his time
Shakspeare was a poetic miracle; he is a poetic
wonder still. From the average powers of boys at
ten, it would seem monstrous that there should be
heads like those of Zera Colburn and young Saf-
ford. They appear like new planets taking a wider
sweep in the universe of mind; and the limits of
human nature are carried out. And so it is now
impossible to determine how far the *doctrines* alone,
of Christianity, separate from their *proofs* and the
circumstances of the teacher, were merely anticipations of possible discoveries.

It may be urged, however, that the results of inquiry, the developments of research, *since* the introduction of Christianity, have extended the range of
natural religion; and, therefore, a comparison of
the results of the two systems *now* may aid us in
settling the question of mutual influence. But
here we are met by another difficulty. In order
that this method should be effective, it would be
necessary to assume that revelation has had no influence in aiding this culture and unfolding these
results. If Christianity has not been entirely inop-

erative as an intellectual aid, we can no more conclude from the after tendencies and triumphs of
thought what the real extent of natural religion *is*,
than from the former weakness and failures of
thought we could properly have concluded what its
limits *must be*.

We cannot stop to discuss the question, whether
revelation has aided the *discoveries* of science; but
we think it is evident on philosophical grounds, that
the *religious value* of those discoveries has been
powerfully affected by the truths of the gospel.
And now, if this be so, instead of possessing the
pure results of natural religion on the one side, and
of revelation on the other, we have both blended.
The union is so intimate that no analysis can separate and hold the elements apart, even as an exper-
iment.   We have no moral prism to divide the rays.
Like a current formed by the junction of two
streams, the waters have mixed until it is a hopeless task to distinguish the drops, and refer each
one accurately to its original source.

Physiology, for instance, and an acquaintance with
the mutual dependence of physical laws throughout
the universe, have unfolded and confirmed the idea
of God's goodness, and have transferred it to natural religion.   But unless that conception had been
supplied beforehand so purely by the gospel, the conclusion could not be reached with so much ease, nor
would it lie in the mind with so much certainty.
The notion itself was ready, deeply impressed upon
the faith of men, and applied *to* the facts to be tried,

not reached from the facts alone as a purely inductive result.   The force of the gospel was in it as a
Christian conception when given : it lies in it after
it is established seemingly on scientific grounds
alone.   The idea of God's spirituality and omnipresence has been immensely supported by inquiries
into the essence of the laws of nature, and by the
revelations of chemistry and astronomy.   But they
were pure ideas, present at hand to be interpreted by
science, offered as hypotheses immediately to natural
religion ; they were not really the suggested notions
after the facts were all revealed, the key proposed
by the guess of some shrewd thinker to explain the
scientific phenomena.   We must constantly remember that the Christian mould is ever ready to give
the facts their form.   Modern philosophy has drawn,
from a profound investigation of the phenomena of
evil, a beautiful, and it should seem impregnable
argument, in confirmation of the unity and the
goodness of the Creator.   In this respect the natural
religion of our times is incomparably higher than
the general spirit of the speculations in the ancient
classic world.   For, however our faith may still be
disturbed at times by the sudden and violent irrup-
tion of the thoughts of evil upon the mind, the question of a duality of agencies, or any pure malignity
in nature, is finally set at rest by the discovery that
seeming evil grows out of the same root with good,
is always the incidental, never the necessary development of the same law, and that it thus points to the
intentional agency of One who has included it in

the plan of human discipline, and inwoven it in the
web of being for some design, inexplicable as yet
it may be, of ultimate perfection.   Who can doubt
that this discovery has resulted naturally from the
pressure upon the mind of the sublime doctrine
of Christianity, that God is the Father, — a doctrine
which has become so intimately a part of our religious
cultivation, and which lies in the soul with such
authoritative power, that the mind has felt impelled
to probe the secrets of nature to their last hiding-
places, in order to reconcile its cheering faith with
the gloomy show of facts ?   The pure, unceremonial
theory of worship too, in Christianity, — its ritual of
deeds, — is powerfully supported by the unfolded
grandeur of the universe ; that is, all which we have
learned of nature is in harmony with such a view
of God and piety.   But we cannot know that the
piety required by St. John — the law of love as the
highest worship — would have been *evolved* from
the facts which now give to it additional force.
Christian cultivation and Christian views of the
world have infused themselves into the whole frame-
work of education.   Under Christian civilization,
natural science, instead of being obliged to encounter
the hostile influence of a degraded and impure
system of religion, instead of being fettered by
anthropomorphic and physical notions of the Deity,
established by a theological training from which it
must work itself free, is aided by ideas so lofty and
spiritual that they cannot be surpassed.   And it is
these ideas, commented on and unfolded by science,

of which, for the most part, natural theology now consists. For, strictly speaking, induction cannot reach to the attributes of God and the elements of a religion. These can be known only from a complete survey of nature, from a knowledge of all the evidence furnished in her realm. But induction can never deal with more than a partial, limited range of facts. And thus, what is claimed in modern times to be natural religion exclusively, is merely a portion of Christianity given as hypotheses, and then translated into the language of nature, and interpreted by the facts of natural research.

We would insist upon this point as one of vital importance in the discussion of our present question. Every student of philosophy, and of the laws of scientific discoveries, knows that a vital portion of the process of discovery consists in the *à priori* application of the idea which is appropriate to the facts under investigation. The mind does not work mechanically, even in observing the rigorous rules of induction. With Columbus, the causal step was taken in his prophetic and firmly held conception of the roundness of the globe. The failures of Aristotle, and the fundamental error of all Greek physical speculation, consisted not solely, we cannot say *chiefly*, in a false scientific method, in a lack of sufficient observation and patient classification, but rather in the reference of facts to inappropriate ideas. In mechanical science, the fundamental idea upon which all discoveries rest is the conception of force as the cause of motion ; but Aristotle, in attempting

the solution of mechanical problems, refers to
geometrical instead of mechanical ideas.   Hence
his whole system is confused, and even his correct
conclusions unscientific and accidental.   Had Kepler
distinctly conceived the mechanical character of
the problem to be resolved, he would perhaps have
worn Newton's laurels as the first discoverer of
universal gravitation.   The great obstruction in the
way of the further progress of the sciences of biol-
ogy is, as scientific men inform us, the confusion of
ideas relative to the principle of life, and a lack of
clearness in the conceptions of assimilation, secretion,
and voluntary motion.   The possibility of any theology depends on the despotic demands of the idea
of cause, which will not suffer the mind to rest till
it has solved the question of creation.   And any
one can see that an essential alteration, or a lack of
clearness in the idea of *skill*, would disturb mate-
rially the domain and alter the value of natural
theology.   Seeing that every science is constructed
of intellectual and *à priori* elements, as well as of
materials given by experience, a modern philosopher,
Mr. Whewell, has proved at length, in his "Philosophy of the Inductive Sciences," that the advance of
knowledge depends as much on the clear "explica-
tion of conceptions," as on the proper "collegation
of facts."

And thus, on rigid principles of science, we see
the aid which Christianity has extended to Natural
Religion.   It has furnished to it those pure conceptions which have thrown light *on* nature, while in

turn they have been strengthened by the evidence *from* nature. In no case can it be claimed that the evidence of science has gone one jot beyond the proper interpretation of gospel theology. Strike out the doctrine of universal moral providence from the record of Christ's teachings, and, destitute of the prior, unconscious aid of that conception; modern research would find it hard to restore it. The revelations of science, by showing us God's action to be seemingly omnipresent in outward nature, give to it the strong support of analogy, and help us to conceive it in its simple beauty. But they go no farther; and they go thus far by the aid of the idea of universal providence, supplied in advance from the Bible itself. And even here, we may say that the essence of the argument was anticipated by Christ's figure of the lilies, and in his allusions to the esoteric theology of the sunshine and rain.

At all points, in the development of what is called natural religion, the truths of Christianity have served as categories of our spiritual nature, which, by their positive influence, have assisted in the *creation* of natural religion. As, in intellectual philosophy, the ideas of cause and substance and relation are furnished from the mind as part of the structure of knowledge, so the doctrines of providence and immortality and omnipresence have been furnished from the gospel as the cement of rational theology. They are the unconscious forms, the divine die, impressed upon the facts offered by science, and imparting to them a significance which they might never have acquired. Thus we see the utter impossibility of following the two provinces into any parallel developments for the purpose of comparing their value and unfolding their relations. The demand upon natural religion should be to furnish her positive and independent doctrines as to God, providence, and destiny ; when, in reality, the conclusions of another system have been interwoven and used as aids in unfolding the testimony of her facts. The two systems, to-day, are inextricably involved. And so long as we have no moral calculus through which we can reason mechanically, by signs, upon questions which baffle the analysis of simple thought, we cannot hope to answer the question of their relation with much precision.

Of course, we must not forget that, so far as evidence for the truth of the gospel is concerned, this concurrent and corroborative testimony of science is of great importance. It should be a matter of the deepest joy to every Christian believer. It furnishes a powerful weapon against scepticism, and valuable assistance to a failing faith. The significance of revelation itself, doubtless, expands in proportion to our acquaintance with the mysteries of the world. So that, other things being equal, the best Christian may be he who has drunk deepest at the fountain of wisdom, and who has seen the harmony between God's works and word. Science, also, may be valuable to correct errors which had arisen from a misconstruction of revelation. And, as we said before, if the results of science positively contradicted the statements of revelation, it would be impossible to preserve our faith. All this does not affect our position. We are seeking to determine, not precisely the religious value of the discoveries of science, nor what might have occurred had they been different, but how far they may claim to be the trophies of unaided reason. And so long as the truths of natural religion do coincide, so far as they go, with the truths of Christianity, it is improper, seeing the influence of revelation in disclosing them, that they be attributed to the original creative power of the mind.

Setting aside, then, the endeavor to determine the exact relations between Christianity and natural religion as hopeless, we would define the general relations thus: that it is one office of revelation to aid human reason, and assist it to see for itself. It does not follow, because the Almighty communicates a set of truths by supernatural means, at a time when the world is waiting for a new impulse in its march, that it was his intention those truths should always remain above the capacity and beyond the reach of reason. It does not follow that reason, once quickened and assisted, may not think *up to* them, at least, so far as to see their natural harmony. Revelation we believe to be a benevolent condescension of the Deity to the weakness of the race. It is intended not only to relieve a present darkness of mind, but also, in that process, to infuse greater strength of mind for the future. It is spiritual food to the famishing soul, appeasing want, and also strengthening the fibres for a greater vigor. Thus many of the truths supernaturally revealed to the Jews are perfectly simple to us. To them, Christ's theory of spiritual worship, his doctrines that the Sabbath was made for man, and that all men are brethren, were new and startling. They were not only above their reason, but they shook their reason. They were blasphemous, for they contradicted the laws of Moses. To our cultivated minds they seem plain and natural: the influence of the truths has purified and refined our spiritual nature until, to a Christian of to-day, these propositions seem religious axioms, hardly demanding the support of any proof. One great office of a revelation, one law of its coming, seems answered and fulfilled when the faculties which it has awakened by their expanding growth embrace its leading truths, and make them part of the constitution of natural theology. A constant accommodation of the teachings of the Deity to the demands and capacities of the race is one of the plainest lessons unfolded in the Scriptures. Revelation is for human assistance, as well as for human satisfaction. Men thought up to the patriarchal dispensation; it assisted the piety of the aged patriarchs, but, as a whole, failed to satisfy the demands of reason and the necessities of a denser population; and the patriarchal dispensation melted into the dawning light of the Mosaic economy. Men *thought up* to Judaism; its spiritual nutriment became absorbed until, in a large party, the advanced spiritualists of the Saviour's time, the

Simeons and Annaus of Israel, a want was created which Judaism, with its spiritual commentary, the prophetic dispensation, could not satisfy; and although it had been given from God's own hand to Moses, Judaism was withdrawn with a signal manifestation of the sanction of the Deity. It was withdrawn, not in the sense of being overthrown, but by being *fulfilled*, carried up to a higher law. Christianity we believe to be a final religious dispensation, not because it is a *Revelation*, but because it contains within itself an expansive power as a revelation, able to quicken the capacities of the humblest mind, to satisfy the deepest spiritual desires which it calls forth, to aid the energies of the intellect, itself expanding with the discoveries of science, keeping ever in advance of the soul, and filling the loftiest mind with its ideal of-excellence and its views of God. Making allowance for the necessary difference in the nature of the case, we should say that revelation has done for theology what Newton did for science. It has introduced and established principles which were, and perhaps would always have remained, above the capacity of the intellect, but which, once developed, may aid the mind, at last, to see and comprehend their reasonableness and force. Strike the Bible from the hearts of men, erase the memory of it forever from their minds, leave them the cultivation it has infused, and though on far less satisfactory evidence, many of the tenets of Christian theology would be reconstructed. The light which the gospel has. kindled in the mind would reveal a vast significance in nature and in man.

Not comprehending this one office of revelation as the *educator* of the race, many in our time use the fact of the *education* as an argument against the necessity of supernatural aid from God. They cannot see its value, and deny the fact. But they stand in the unfortunate position of denying it, by virtue of the very assistance which from it they have insensibly received. To their enlarged capacity of mind the speech of nature is sufficient. Her language is articulate to them, and they can understand it. But their enlarged capacity of mind forgets to recognize the *cause* of its enlargement. They inherit the power by which they see. It is an endowment of the very revelation whose value they decry. They transfer their own capacity of comprehension back to the time when revelation was given, and imagine that men could easily have *originated* what they now so clearly comprehend. Because revelation has, for them, fulfilled a portion of its office by aiding them to see the reasonableness and simplicity of all its doctrines, they talk of the intuitions of the soul, and wonder that men can be so credulous as to admit the former need of any revelation. By a too frequent ingratitude they forget, in their pride of power and place, the friend to whom they owe their elevation. While light is reflected back to them in some one of its varied hues from every object in the universe, while the whole air is inundated by a general flood of brilliancy, they calmly turn to their less philosophic neighbors, and, brandishing their torches, themselves kindled from the bounty of a Divine Prometheus, cry, "Foolish men, to think that, amidst this all-embracing splendor, the radiance of our rush-lights, we need that distant sun!" Is it not as if school-boys, because, with their limited faculties and untrained thought, they can understand something of the symmetry, and take in the vast proportions of the universe, should, *therefore*, while they stand upon their shoulders, decry the value and revile the useless labors of Newton and La Place!

Since our last article was written we have met with such a calm and vigorous statement from the pen of Dr. Neander, of the truth which, in the last few pages, we have endeavored to present, that we cannot resist the temptation to transcibe it here. "Although Christianity can be understood only as something which is above nature and reason, something communicated to them from a higher source, yet it stands in necessary connection with the essence of these powers and with their mode of development; otherwise, indeed, it could not be fitted to elevate them to any higher stage; otherwise it would not operate on them at all. And accordingly, we see the evidence of this connection whenever we observe how human nature and reason do, by virtue of their original capacity, actually strive in their historical development towards this higher principle which needs to be communicated to them in order to their own completion; and how, by the same

20

capacity, they are made receptive of this principle, and conducted onward till they yield to it, and become moulded by its influence. It is simply because such a connection exists, because in all cases where, through the historic preparation, the soil has been rendered suitable for its reception, Christianity enters readily into all that is human, striving to assimilate it to its own nature, and to interpenetrate it with its own power, that on a superficial view it appears as if Christianity itself were only a product resulting from a combination of the different spiritual elements it had drawn together; and the *opinion* has found advocates, that it could *thus* be explained." [1]

We return, then, to the idea that there is but one religion, by whatever means its truths be attained. So far as they are developed by the natural operation of the mind, it is natural religion; so far as they are supplied by a higher power in advance of the capacity of the soul, it is revealed; while so far as the elements of it are established or strengthened by physical and natural evidence, after the truths have been supernaturally communicated, it is the common product of revelation and reason, and cannot be considered to be exclusively either.

From what has now been said, it will be seen that an exact determination of the extent of natural religion, compared with Christian theology, cannot be attained. We cannot know how far the mind

---

[1] Neander's History of the Christian Religion and Church, recent Boston edition, page 2 of the Introduction.

of Christ, in its authoritative disclosures, merely anticipated the future power of speculative reason, and thus foreclosed the possibility of their original and natural development. We cannot say in what degree the religious results of science have been produced by the influence of Christian perceptions, applied to and aiding the discoveries of the mind. What might have been had Christianity been withheld, precisely what has been done because it was given, we are equally unable to unfold. Enough, however, can be seen not only in the apparent influence which the gospel has exerted on the world, but also in the effect and the fortunes of former religious communications, to confirm the belief that it is one great office of Christianity to quicken reason and assist its growth, to aid it in seeing for itself the natural grounds on which its doctrines rest. And thus it seems to be the mission of Christianity to efface the distinctive line which separates natural religion, as an independent system, from its own revelations. The gospel is continually absorbing it into its own sphere. What is called natural religion to-day, whether founded on scientific or moral research, on inquiries into the world of nature or the world of man, is but the demonstration, on other grounds, of Christian truths,—the commentary and exposition of the spiritual aphorisms of the Saviour.

We talk of the moral evidence afforded by the satisfaction which the gospel gives to the deepest wants of the soul. One of the strongest natural arguments for Christianity is, that in proportion as

we rise in spiritual excellence, and live in a higher
sphere, a stronger sense of certainty in regard to its
foundation takes possession of the heart. This is
right. But we must remember, also, that the gospel
has created many of those wants.; it refines the spiritual capacities of the mind, and then satisfies them
by its purity; it elevates us into the very sphere
from which we derive this influx and inspiration of
spiritual peace. Christianity is "a well of water,
springing up into everlasting life." Although it be
true as an evidence, "If ye do his will ye shall know
of the doctrine whether it be of God," it is the *Revelation* of the nature of the will which is the real
condition of the promised proof. To the piety of
Fenelon no doubts may come; but it is Christian
education which nourishes and refines that piety.
The overflowing compassion, the boundless love of
the gospel, may be satisfactory proof of its Divinity
to the benevolent soul of Howard; but Christian
culture had much to do with preparing in his heart
the capacity for that satisfaction. The mind of
Newton, filled with the simplicity and grandeur of
Creative Wisdom, may be sustained and strengthened greatly in its faith by the purity of the Christian ritual; but it was partly owing to the prior and
elevating effects of that purity upon his religious
nature that he was enabled to see its harmony with
the universe. And thus in the moral, as in the
material world, Christianity has supplied the very
means, which in their operation, have returned so
many proofs; it has planted the seeds which have

rewarded the sower with such an abundant harvest.

It is a sign of hope, for the permanence of the gospel, that it sustains this relation to what is termed natural religion. For it is owing alone to the complete harmony between the statements of revelation and the discovered testimony of nature that it becomes so difficult to analyze and separate them. Christianity furnishes the key by which to read the cipher of the world. The solution is fitted to all the difficulties of the enigma, else the elements would not yield so consistently to the interpretation. From the domain of natural religion is echoed back the voice of revelation;—an echo so distinct that it has been taken for an original tone. Were there a dissonance, not only should we hear it, but it would disturb the security of our firmly-rooted faith.

And it is not to be forgotten, besides, that this sympathy between the doctrines of science and Christianity, although complete in many instances, does not at all lessen the value and the continual need of the assurances of the gospel. Let Christianity quicken the faculties and exalt the energies of our nature as it may, it cannot discharge itself completely into the reason of man. At every stage, in the great academy, the authority of the teacher is needed still. On many points, and those too of the deepest interest, it is and must always be our only available instructor. Nature gives no definite proof that God is the Father, and so far as mere science is concerned, it removes objections to rather

than furnishes arguments for a future life. By the
strong confirmation it lends to other points of Christian theology, it strengthens our confidence in 'the
truth of these, and thus leads the mind so far on
the way of analogy as to give foundation for a faith
that, could more be known of nature, they might
easily be discovered there. It prepares us, in a word,
to listen with deeper reverence to the prayer of
Jesus, and to hear with greater joy the language,
"*I am* the resurrection and the life."

And if, as the teacher of much of the natural religion we have, we discover the superiority of Chris-
tiauity to the whole scheme, we must also add, that
the evidence which the gospel brings removes it yet
farther and higher. However we may legitimate the
miraculous proof, when once heartily received, it
gives us a repose different from the common results
of moral probability. Let us feel that a truth is
spoken from God, by his special sanction, and, although that sauction does not make the truth truer,
it gives it greater intensity and force with our own
minds. Men will not worship mathematics, and
whatever religious ideas stand entirely upon the
skill and logic of the intellect, are so vitiated by an
association with the weaknesses of our nature as
to stand as a system of philosophy alone. So that,
whether it be honorable or derogatory to men, it is
a principle of our constitution, dispute about it as
we may, that when we have satisfactorily established
the fact by reason, that an idea comes *from God*,
we have given it greater force than when, by simple

demonstration, we end with the discovery that it is *true*. In some way the mystery of the Infinite hallows it, while science and logic give to it only a clear, cold, icy lustre. This sanction which lends such a religious authority to truths, which quickens and impels the conscience to fulfil the moral obligations which they imply, natural religion cannot be expected ever to acquire. The halo which encircles the head of Jesus will never radiate, in the imagination of the world, from the sharp outlines of a metaphysician's face. The force, too, which the life of Christ has exercised over men as a revelation of duty, and of the beauty of Christian life, must forever remain a distinct peculiarity of the gospel. And thus, in many ways, the revelation in Christianity, from its peculiar nature and evidence, is placed above and beyond the reach of natural religion. Received in faith, it is the key published with authority, containing the answers to the problems of creation, duty, and destiny. And though science and philosophy may go on, furnishing their demonstrations and their solutions on natural grounds, it cannot fail to give their answers additional weight, when we may look into the key, and find that they coincide with the solutions offered there.

XIV.

THE IDEA OF GOD AND THE TRUTHS OF CHRISTIANITY.

THERE are two roads to a satisfactory faith in Christianity, — cultivation of the higher feelings, and education of the mind. Men belong in different classes, and arrive at truth in different ways, according as spiritual sympathies or a critical understanding gives the tone or temper to their nature. Some become conscious of faith by what is called *intuition*, — the quick and uncomprehended response of their souls to a given doctrine or principle ; others are led to faith by the gradual perception of its logical legitimacy. A weight may be attracted and held up by a loadstone, or it can be suspended on a hook ; and we may say that one class of minds are brought in contact with truth in a manner analogous to the first of these methods, another class in a manner analogous to the last. In the souls of one class truth exists rather as a deep sympathy ; they feel it more warmly, and utter it with greater force ; in the minds of another class, it dwells rather as a clear idea ; having attained it by clear reflection, they see it more distinctly, and present it more methodically to others.

What is stated thus as a general principle is peculiarly applicable to the evidences of Christianity. The *heart* may become so pure and all the moral affections so refined that Christian principles shall be acknowledged intuitively to be the natural laws of the soul, and the character of Christ shall be accepted spontaneously as the model of our nature; and, on the other hand, the *intellect* may be so trained and applied that the proofs for the truth and claims of Christianity will exercise an overwhelming force. To minds of a certain order, the natural door to Christian faith is through the head; Christianity as a whole is set before them as a problem for solution, and their reason is determined toward assent or scepticism by the historical or philosophical arguments which can be adduced in its behalf. And there are other minds that never think to inquire into the scientific claims of the gospel as a system, who yet rely with undisturbed assurance on the satisfaction and peace which faithfulness to Christian laws infuses into the soul. The former examine Christianity, and find that all the conditions of belief are fulfilled in the evidences which may be presented, and therefore they cannot doubt; the latter are not prompted to examine, and never doubt, because they naturally believe.

We may assume, I think, that among the disciples of the Saviour, John was a type of the last-named order of natures, and Thomas of the first. In the language of Jesus, too, we find allusions to this difference in the structure of men's souls. To one class of Jews he said, "Ye believe not, *because* ye are not of my sheep;" their natures had seemingly no affinities with his doctrines and demands; while he affirmed the same principle in a positive form in the passage, "all that *are of the truth* hear my voice." Upon another class he urged the propriety of believing "for the very work's sake," because the *argument* for his supernatural mission was too strong to be resisted. And in all ages of the church has this distinction been apparent. The faith of Fenelon, and the faith of Chillingworth, when analyzed, reveal the power of different methods to induce conviction. Refined sentiment, through the spiritual insight which it quickens, and the attractions which it brings into play, and rigorous logic, the power of persuasion which it may exert upon the reason, will equally generate a healthy confidence in the truth of the great features of the gospel. The soul may be lifted into an instinctive assurance; the mind may be coerced into a lagging assent.

The proofs of Christianity which may be brought to satisfy reason are of two kinds. We may present the historical argument which establishes the facts of the gospel narratives, or we may urge the harmony which the truths of Christianity manifest with the religion of nature, and trace the probabilities that follow from an adequate idea of God.

Of the two departments of evidence for the divine authority of the gospel, the first or practical argument is undoubtedly the highest, and induces in sensitive and cultivated hearts the most secure and cheerful faith.   It cannot be questioned, either, that the historical evidences may be so arrayed that a sceptical mind cannot evade, and must acknowledge their strength.   It is the design of this article, however, to consider particularly the last division of the logical defences of Christianity, — to show by a rapid survey, and such suggestions as our restricted limits will enable us to present, how naturally the principles of the New Testament theology evolve themselves from the conception which we are obliged to form of God.   Such an argument should be often urged in this day, we believe, since it is calculated to meet the state of mind of many in our time who give little attention to the historical proofs of Christianity, and who are afflicted with a lurking scepticism.

When we talk with intelligent persons on religious topics, such as piety, providence, prayer, a future life, etc., we are often met by the remark: "I believe in a Supreme Being, an overruling agency, but farther than that I am very ignorant, it is all uncertain and dark."   This is either the polite way in which many persons intimate their scepticism to clergymen, or the natural mode in which it unconsciously breaks out.   Every minister knows that there is a large class of men who will readily confess, when their intimate confidence is secured, that they have no staunch, firm faith in the teachings of the gospel, that they cannot pretend to that serene conviction which induces general equanimity of soul. And yet they are very earnest in asserting unwavering belief in God. They are perfectly confident of his existence, but their creed contains no other article of faith, and here their confession ends.

Now this is the state of mind for which there is the least possible excuse. Setting aside the historical and practical evidences of the gospel, a Christian can easily show the folly of this narrow, barren deism which contents itself with a confession of the existence of a Deity, and declares its ignorance of all other elements of religion. If a man does not believe more ; if his religious faith does not extend a good deal farther than the proposition there is a God, — the trouble is that he does not firmly believe *that*, or does not have a worthy conception of the God of nature. For no person with a healthy mind, it seems to us, can have an enlightened faith in God, without seeing that the main elements of Christian theology are involved in that belief, and must be accepted with it. The alternative for every fair logical mind is, atheism or a broad Christian theory of life. There is no middle ground on which the intellect can stand. It is a characteristic of every system of simple truth that the whole scheme is implied in each position, as the whole structure of an animal or fish may be constructed from a fossil tooth or scale. And Christianity has the unanswerable argument in its favor, that all its doctrines seem to be the natural evolution of our highest conception of God. The pure deist is the most illogical of all men ; and the language of Jesus to his disciples states with fine simplicity the force of the natural argument for his religion : " Let not your heart be troubled ; you believe in God, believe also in me."

Let us see how natural it is for an unprejudiced mind to hold a simple, abstract, fruitless faith in a mere existence of Deity.

Of course, if one believes in an overruling power, that power must be intelligent.   The ultimate ground and cause of all things, too, must be infinite and eternal, and therefore the Creative Spirit, which is the object of faith, must be an infinite, self-existent Intelligence.   So far the first step in reasoning carries us, or rather, so much the very conditions of reason necessitate.

Now if the universe be the work of an Infinite Creative Spirit, whatever characteristics and qualities are found clearly impressed upon. and exhibited in the world, must be supposed to exist fully and perfectly as attributes and characteristics of the Deity.   The appearance of any intelligent trait in the structure of nature is the hint that such a trait exists in perfection as a feature of the Creative Spirit.   We discover in nature, in the widest and most contracted sphere, numberless, overwhelming traces of a foresight and adaptation fertile in resources, simple in plan ; and from these the mind irresistibly ascribes to the Creator a *wisdom* that is perfect, and an exquisite *skill*.   We see, too, that all the arrangements of this natural mechanism point to and promise good, so that, when they are not thwarted by wilfulness and vice, happiness, enjoyment will prevail in the world; and of course, since the natural action of things would produce good alone, *benevolence*, goodness, must be a distinctive feature of the creative mind.

Neither can our conception of the qualities of the Deity stop here. The principles which we have laid down develop further results. Looking into the intelligent creation, we discover a law of duty which reigns supreme over the souls of men; we find in every breast a *conscience* which conveys the warning of a mysterious power, and which no one can with impunity, reject. All the ranks of conscious spirits feel naturally the despotic claims of truth, holiness, and virtue, as a myriad of needles point, with regular convergence and tremulous accuracy, to a common pole. Whence is the origin of this dread law? what the sanction of this authoritative principle which dignifies the most ignorant and the meanest, which abases the most powerful and cultivated of our race? Our religious instincts answer and logic confirms the reply: Its home is the nature of the Deity; its sanction is the character and pleasure of the Most High. It can be nowhere else. As skill in nature proves a wise, designing mind; as pleasure points to goodness in the creative Spirit, so the instructive voice of morality and conscience in the human heart points to a nature infinitely holy, a God all pure.

And now we are urged another step onward in the path we have taken. When we reflect that space is boundless and time is infinite, and when we consider that science reveals no limits to the physical creation, but shows us every spot of nature which the eye can penetrate and all the regions which telescopic power has explored, alive with the energy of forces that sustain the present order of the universe ; and since from what we know of our own souls, we are compelled to believe that spirit is a subtile, impalpable, formless essence ; reason can rest in no other view of the Deity but the belief that he is an Omnipresent, all-pervading principle of life and order, vivifying and encircling the world. He is not only the Creator, but the supporter of all things ; " in him we live and move and have our being."

If a man *believes* in a God, if his recognition of a higher power be not merely the instinctive, untrained feeling of dependence which moves alike the savage and philosopher, if reason clearly conceives the idea of God as an item of faith, it must hold it in some *form*, with certain definitions ; and in the light of modern thought and culture, we are obliged, by the very considerations that lead us to a belief in a Supreme Being, and through the very process which establishes it as a certainty, to believe also that the Deity is good, wise, and holy, and that he exercises an omnipresent providence over the whole creation. If we do not believe that these qualities form part of the Deity, it is because we do not reason on the question at all, it is because we do not have a *conviction*, but only a dim *instinct* that there is a God; for these qualities — goodness, wisdom, holiness, omnipresence — necessarily flow from, or rather they must go to make up, the idea of God which the mind acquires. And these are precisely the attributes which distinguish Christian theology, which underlie and vivify the religion of the New Testament. So far the deist must recognize the same elements of faith with the Christian, and to this extent the injunction of the Saviour is enforced, — "Ye believe in God, believe also in me."

There is no point of religion, probably, about which there is more concealed or practical scepticism than the idea of immortality. This is always supposed to be a distinctive tenet of Christianity, and to be so connected with the New Testament theology that it falls to the ground when once the gospel is denied. And yet enlightened faith in Deity necessitates this point. On natural, independent grounds, the idea of God suggests and establishes the belief that the human soul has a higher destiny than *is* attained, or than *can be* attained on earth. If we attempt to interpret life in the full blaze of the truth that it is ruled by a wise, holy, omnipresent will, we are impelled to the hypothesis that the present is the initiatory stage of a nobler scene. No man who has an *adequate* conception of the Deity can disbelieve his immortality; and the widespread practical scepticism on this point only reveals the faintness and *haziness* of our faith in a Supreme Intelligence. A wise, benevolent, and holy governor must have a *purpose* in the creation of intelligent and moral beings ; if he be perfect and infinite, that purpose must be the noblest and most benevolent we can conceive, which is spiritual development, education, progress. Now this is precisely what man, when we study the structure and laws of his nature, seems to be created for ; and this goal cannot be reached in the present life, for two reasons : 1st. There are obstructions, trials, and mysteries here which must often impede our progress and even degrade our aims, if this life be all our destiny. There is not area or time enough for the plan of spiritual culture to vindicate itself in this finite state. And, 2d. Spiritual excellence is of such a nature that the more one acquires the more capacity is generated to acquire ; it is the only work in which the soul cannot get exhausted, and where the field widens as the feet press on ; attainments expand the *power* to go on ; " it is a well of water " within him, and therefore, the very statement— " We are made for spiritual excellence " — implies and includes the tenet that we are to be immortal, since immortality is the indispensable condition of reaching the goal or of unfolding the expansive energies enveloped in our nature. Independently then of the Christian revelation, the skill, holiness, and providence of God — all the qualities that make up our conception of the Deity — are pledged to the truth of our eternal being ; human immortality is a necessary sequence from such premises ; if such be not our destiny, the idea of God

21

which all other departments of nature suggest to us, is overthrown by the phenomena of the intelligent universe ; and the alternative is presented to accept the tenet of immortality or to throw away the attributes which all nature ascribes to the Most High.

Thus far, we have spoken only of the abstract principles of theology. We see that mere belief in a God, under the light of modern culture, forces upon the mind a *system* of *religion*, a system corresponding to the essential principles of Christianity, and that no man can say, " I believe in a great first cause, but farther than that I cannot go." *In believing* that he must, to be consistent, go a great deal farther. He must believe in *some kind* of a Divinity, and the only conception of the Infinite which reason in our time is able to approve, necessitates a train of conclusions parallel with the revealed theology of the gospel.

And not only does the idea of God include these speculative tenets which form a religious creed, but *duties* grow out of faith in a supreme intelligence. No man who firmly believes in a Deity can excuse himself from cherishing and manifesting a class of religious emotions or sentiments similar to those enjoined and educated by Christianity. Is not gratitude a natural sentiment, obligatory in appropriate circumstances upon all men by the laws of our nature ? Nay, do we not brand him who is habitually and coolly faithless in this respect, as unworthy the name of man ? What claims for gratitude can be so great as that which grows out of our existence, the benevolent laws that surround us here, and the countless means of enjoyment supplied so liberally at every hand? Can the fact that the Giver works unseen cancel the demand, if we firmly believe that the Giver exists? Is not reverence, too — the blending of awe and love — an instinctive affection of the soul, whenever it meets or contemplates a union in some man of the highest mental and moral qualities — justice, purity, mercy, and wisdom? And shall not faith in a Being perfectly pure, holy, and wise, of whom conscience is a feeble representative in our own bosoms, excite and sustain the feeling of reverence as a deep, vivifying, consecrating affection of the heart?

And we maintain that trust too, the highest of the pietistic sentiments, is a natural disposition of the soul, and is aroused and sanctioned by a worthy conception of a God. The very intellectual perception of an omnipresent essence of skill, holiness, and love, from which we were born and by which we are upheld, — and this is the form in which, as we have seen, we are forced to conceive the Almighty, — invites the heart to *trust*, suggests the propriety, even the necessity of such a feeling; and where the proposition is believed and the affection is not exhibited, there is an inconsistency between the mental and moral life. Thus there is a piety appropriate to natural religion growing out of, and enforced by, the idea of God. If a person's reason be healthy, and be applied to the subject, he cannot escape the obligations which belief in a Deity imposes on his heart; and the theory of worship which Christianity enjoins — humility, reverence, love, and prayer — is equally approved by a scientific faith in a Supreme Intelligence.

There are other considerations, also, flowing from a sufficient and exhaustive idea of God, which are fatal to a barren deism, and which invite the mind to confidence in Christianity. The qualities which study of the universe leads us to ascribe to the Almighty, naturally suggests the probability of a clearer moral revelation of himself. Can we conceive it possible that a Being perfectly wise and good, will refuse to communicate with his creatures, or can refrain from such a communion? It is the tendency of complete goodness and wisdom to publish, to manifest itself as widely and clearly as possible. No person, even though he be indifferent in practice to the truths of religion, will deny that the knowledge of a benevolent, infinite protector would be one of the greatest blessings for humanity. How then, if his mind believes in a wise and merciful divinity, can he, *on natural grounds*, resist the probability that he would, or has, declared his character and the more secret counsels of his providence to his children? To believe that revelation would be a most valuable blessing, and to believe in a perfectly wise and merciful Deity who has not revealed himself, is practically to say that our own minds can conceive a good which we do not believe Infinite benevolence is prompted to bestow. The tendency to reveal himself seems, therefore, to be part of the conception of a perfect Deity. The mind, too, feels deeply the need of revelation. It needs it to enlighten conscience, to educate piety, to inspire strength, assurance, and serenity in affliction, adversity, and gloom. Now the wisdom of the Creator has been so provident and watchful, that not a single native, healthy want of our structure, bodily, mental, or affectional, has been left unsupplied. We feel hunger and there is food; thirst, and there is drink; taste, and there is beauty; desire for knowledge, and there is truth; sympathies, and there is society; love, and there are objects for love. This wide-spread, exquisite adaptation, never failing in any instance of deep native need, indicates the truth that the Governor of nature is perfectly wise and good. How then, with the whole mechanism of the universe to support and urge the argument, in the light of such continual divine interference for our benefit, can the deist resist the conclusion that perfect wisdom has considered this abiding moral want of the soul, and has answered it, as it only can be answered, by an authoritative voice, conveyed through some agent to the waiting world? Can reason believe that God would create intelligent creatures for development and spiritual excellence, — as he evidently has done, — and then leave them destitute of the highest means of education, means which only could be supplied by a disclosure of his nature to meet and satisfy, and to inspire and quicken them? This is equally inconsistent with divine skill and divine benevolence, and, as at other points we saw that the idea of God suggested doctrines analogous to those of revelation, so on this point we find that the idea of God prompts the expectancy of revelation itself. Therefore, since on every hand the tenets of natural religion and Christianity harmonize, and confirm each other, fresh meaning breaks from the Saviour's language, and we feel from another side the force of the principle — "Let not your heart be troubled; you believe in God, believe also in me."

It seems to us, also, that the obstacles which in our time often lie in the way of a grounded and secure faith in Christianity, will easily be removed by a clear and adequate conception of the Deity. Many persons, whose minds assent to the native probability of a revelation, and who are attracted to the doctrines and spirit of the gospel, feel repelled by the miraculous agency connected with it, and cannot reconcile their intellects to the occurrence of such violations of natural law. They confess the propriety and spiritual beauty of the Christian miracles, allow that they are worthy of God, and if once confirmed, furnish solid and consoling evidence of the gospel's authoritative character, but they are unable to conceive how they were possible, being contrary to the custom of the universe. Now a pure and firmly-grasped conception of a God does away this reluctance, by dissipating the prejudice on which it rests. When we realize that God must be omnipresent, the sustaining power of the world, and

immediate cause of every event, as the soul sustains
the body and directs its motion, we see that nature
is only the manifestation of the successive volitions
of a hidden spirit in its frame, we discover that
there are no laws of matter established for independent action, and thus are led to perceive that a
seeming miracle is as natural and credible as any
other occurrence, if the Creator but *pleases* that it
should be wrought. Nothing is more needed to inspire a correct understanding of the kind of universe we live in, than a constant recognition that
God is omnipresent in it, as the source of life and
action. All mechanical theories fade before this
view, and miracles, which to thousands are the only
stumbling-blocks in the path of Christian faith,
seem in themselves no more marvellous than the
rising of the sun, or bodily death. And thus, if we
can perceive the fitness, force, and need of the wonderful agencies recorded in the gospel, as proofs in
a sensual age of the divine mission of Jesus, all
natural objection to them, all prejudice against
them, is dissipated by the spiritual view under
which God must be recognized as the sole source
of power.

We have endeavored thus to intimate the vital
connection between a firm belief in God and the
truths of the Christian religion. The idea of a supreme intelligence naturally expands into the principal tenets of theology, while it leads us to antici-
pate a clearer revelation, indorses the doctrines of

the gospel and dispels the only antecedent hindrances to its acceptance by the mind.

It is not very marvellous that there should be sceptical tendencies generated from the feverish materialism of modern life. Opportunities for special culture or religious meditation are either too rare, or are too steadily slighted, to allow the purity, grandeur, and harmony of the gospel to attract, vivify, and uplift the heart into an appreciation of its symmetrical, inspiring truth. From all the sources of evidence which spring up in a serene and mellow heart, — the very highest and most satisfactory of all proofs of its divinity, — by the fretful, seething sensualism of modern life we have been almost entirely debarred. Amid the roar of the machinery of our artificial, unhealthy, contentious existence, the charming influence of Christianity which falls upon the ear in gentle tones and invitations, sweet as the voice of birds or the melodies of reviving nature, can hardly, by any possible means, be felt. To acquire the saintly assurance — the point where belief rises into insight — we must reach the saintly excellence, the rest and calm of more natural and simple experience. Hence the greater necessity of maintaining firm the bulwark against scepticism on the side of *thought*. If faith may not yet be established beyond the possibility of question, by means of sentiments Christianized and refined, it is a more binding duty to take care that unbelief makes no irruptions into the enclosure of the intellect, and that we preserve the reason untainted by a doubt.

This may easily be done. We may be Christian philosophers if we may not, because of the poverty of our hearts, attain the Christ-like conviction which only rewards a consecrated life. And so long as a man holds to and confesses faith in God it can only be weakness of logic or intellectual disease that can excuse any insecurity or hesitation with regard to the primary principles of Jesus' theology. Atheism is more consistent than a cold, unchristian, naked deism. Let any man who has any tendency to scepticism upon the great themes of human interest, and who would discipline his mind to repel its ingress and refute its force, fall back upon the idea of God; let him reflect upon all that is implied in that belief, and he shall find that it is the basis and buttress of a vast system of theology which enlightens the mysteries of the world, hallows the most soaring hopes, and imposes the most solemn obligations on the heart and will. Though we slight the historical claims of Christianity to our regard, it has still an ally in reason and the teachings of nature, which we cannot silence by contemptuous unconcern. With calm assurance the gospel addresses the intellect of the world in the language, " You believe in God: believe also in me." Its logical foundations are secure so long as faith in an overruling power shall endure, and that can only fail when the structure of the human reason shall be radically changed.

XV.

HARMONY OF OPPOSITE QUALITIES IN THE SAVIOUR'S CHARACTER AND TEACHINGS.

THERE are great differences among men, in respect of comprehensiveness of character. We often see a person who appears to be the embodiment of one thought or one passion. So narrow and intense is his life that you can readily tell what he will do, and almost prophesy what he will say, in any circumstances, even in a peculiar emergency. There is only one side to his soul; it can show but one phase, and take but one attitude; and any fair description of him will seem to be a caricature. One person of this class may be ruled by the passion for money getting, and never can be betrayed into momentary generosity of hand or lip; another is incarnate pride; another is concentrated foppishness; another is organized gossip; another is the slave of some special study or profession.

And, on the other hand, there are some persons whose *characteristic* quality it would be hard to tell. They are many-sided men. Their resources are rich and deep; they have great practical wisdom; and when they pronounce a judgment, it is from

thorough insight, and when they act, they do not
reveal any chronic peculiarity, but suit their action
to the circumstances which called it forth.   All great
genius, such as Shakspeare's and Homer's, has this
many-sidedness.   The best judges can never agree
whether they excel in pathos or humor or sublimity or description; nor can they determine what
kind of characters they draw most powerfully.   It
would give any man fame if he could excel in any
one line of literary excellence as they easily excel
in all.

The greatest practical men, such as Cæsar and
Washington, are equally comprehensive.   Who can
tell the distinguishing trait of Washington's character?   His virtue is the poise of many qualities; he turns
a new phase as we view him from different points;
and all we can say is, that many moral elements, by
their marriage, make up the pure patriot, the wise
statesman, the courageous, humane, disinterested
and unstained soldier.

And, in the Saviour's nature we discover a most
wonderful breadth and complexity.   The narratives
of his life embrace but a small portion of his deeds
and conversations; but they show plainly that all
forms and phases of virtue blended in his character.
Indeed, the richness of his nature shows itself in
seemingly opposite qualities, jarring opinions, and
discordant acts; so that, if many of Jesus' sayings,
deeds, and characteristics should be put abstractedly
before us, we should be apt to say that they could
not be harmoniously united, so as to compose a sim-

ple and symmetrical life. And yet this union shows the fulness and power of the Saviour's nature. In his short career he swept the whole orbit of duty, and shed light along every segment of its curve.

In the first place, we may notice the two-sidedness of which we speak, if we study the relations of Christ with respect to formalism and spiritualism. The New Testament teaches us that piety is a spirit, is of the heart, that it must not be confounded with formal rites of devotion, that " the true worshippers worship the Father in *spirit* and in *truth*." Ultra spiritualists, antagonists of all forms, anti-sabbath men, come-outers, all shelter themselves behind the words and examples of Jesus. And to this extent — that a mere form of devotion is not necessarily worship, and that a person can possibly be pious without joining in the consecrated and customary rites by which men seek to foster and express their piety — the language and spirit of Jesus will permit any one to go. But these protests against the excesses of formalism do not fully portray the Saviour's position. They give us only half the truth. The Saviour's example, when we see the whole of it, is against these ultraists. We find that he was baptized, that he had such respect for the solemnity and propriety of that rite as to insist on receiving it from an humbler hand. He observed the ritual of the passover, and engrafted upon it another form which he perpetuated by an affectionate command among his first followers. And notwithstanding his insight into the spirituality of devotion, it is written that, "as his custom was, he went into the synagogue on the Sabbath-day." Superior as he was to any preacher he could hear, we must believe that the chants and psalms and spirit of the place were delightful, beneficial, and almost necessary to his nature.

So, too, Jesus taught that it is the inward light which illumines us, and that he who believeth "hath the witness in himself." Yet he frequently appealed to his miracles as convincing and authoritative proofs of his Messiahship, and bowed with deep reverence before the written Scripture ; for he supported his own threatened virtue, and silenced Satan, with "*It is written*, thou shall not tempt the Lord thy God."

Christ, too, went through cornfields on the Sabbath day, and took occasion to perform many merciful miracles on that day, when he knew that the sensibilities of the ritual Jews would be shocked by his freedom. See, therefore, it is said, how Jesus walked rough-shod over the superstitions of his age ; and a class of men now find warrant in this phase of his ministry for the most rabid hostility to Sunday-laws, and the most freely-uttered contempt for the notion that one day should be accounted more sacred than another. But look at the reverse side of the picture. Christ was *a formalist.* As if with the intention to balance his character upon this point, his biographers have recorded his driving the money-changers out of the court of the temple. Gentiles, we know, were permitted to worship in the outer court of the temple, and the Jews had no objection to the traders occupying those spaces, and selling articles that were required for offerings or incense. But Jesus saw that the place where Gentiles or partial proselytes regularly worshipped was a holy place, and he could not bear that it should be polluted by any secular uses; and he banished the brokers with the rebuke, "Make not my Father's house a house of merchandise."

There is a great difference between spiritualism and anti-formalism. Jesus was *a spiritualist*, and because he was a wise and thorough spiritualist he was, of necessity, a wise and strenuous formalist. Whoever sees that religion is a vital and glowing principle or spirit will see clearly the use and power and indispensableness of forms; for wherever in nature or society a vital principle, a quickening spirit appears, it clothes itself instantly with, and manifests itself through, a form. God's wisdom is announced to human senses through forms, and a fixed and stable ceremonial.

The sky enfolds a magnificent revelation of arrested order and materialized geometry. That old celestial institution stands; our souls are educated by it; and the Almighty is not too spiritual to suffer his thought and feeling to take substance, and be bound to the observance of despotic rules. For ages, in the great cathedral of the universe, roofed with hazy firmaments, and lighted with brilliant constellations, planets have swung before him like censers of incense, and worship is offered before him in the obedient sweep, and constant harmony of suns, satellites, and systems. Every flower, too, is a *form* of God's art, a tiny ritual of beauty, conducted by stem and leaves and petals and hues. And all the great institutions of the world, — the senate, the throne, the court, the asylum, the school, — and every poem, and every painting and statue and treatise and machine, are forms of human thought, justice, art, and love. Paul has said, " There is one spirit *and one body*," and wherever there is a spirit there will be a fitting body. A body without the spirit is dead ; and a spirit without a body, *a form*, is a ghost, and cannot live in the busy daylight of the world. Wherever a person is found so spiritual as to despise all forms and never to use any, it is a pretty sure sign that his spiritualism is ghostly, ghastly, and nebulous ; not too pure to pollute itself by a ritual, but too shadowy to be able to find a body, too feeble to condense itself into fact.

Christ saw that the forms of worship were a mockery, if a living spirit in the heart did not fill them with meaning, and therefore he revealed and attacked the mockery. And he saw, too, that a living spirit of devotion in the heart needs, and must find, some form of revealing itself, and some forms that will educate it when it flags, and therefore he used, recommended, and established forms. He saw that his religion required a new and different ceremonial, as the planted acorn unfolds into a different form from that which a planted plum assumes. And so he said, No man putteth new wine into old bottles, lest the bottles burst and the wine be spilled ;

but new wine must be put into new bottles. That is, we must have the bottles — or the forms — that we may save the wine, or the spirit.

With respect to the question of conservatism and reform, and the relative value of the past and the present, we notice a similar two-sidedness. How radical his thoughts and speech in the Sermon on the Mount, when he says, " Ye have heard that it hath been said by them of old time . . . an eye for an eye, . . . but I say unto you that ye resist not evil ; " thus announcing the principle of progress in revelation, introducing a deeper and more searching spiritual law in the place of the Mosaic morality. Yet, at another time, we hear him saying, " Think not that I am come to destroy the law or the prophets ; I am not come to destroy but to fulfil." " Not one jot or tittle shall pass from the law till all be fulfilled." How can these things be reconciled ? How can one mind stand in these two attitudes ? The reason is, that Jesus' mind reposed at the centre of truth where conservatism and radicalism run together, and are reconciled. He was a wise conservative, *because* he was a wise reformer. He read the law by which truth expands in the world, — that it spreads, not by conquest, but by development.

God never snaps and hacks away the live cords and arteries of society, never creates a wholly new moral world in which truth shall find institutions perfectly adapted to it ; but ordains that truth shall swell and develop gradually and easily from one

set of institutions to another, so that society shall
be jarred as little as possible. The Saviour saw
that there is an organic life in the race, flowing
down from Adam through history into every man ;
he saw that the conquests of truth were like the
growth of a tree, and that there must be new
boughs, and leaves, and twigs, and wider circles
forming in the trunk, — in a word, that the tree
must change, season by season, and become different, because it is the same living tree. In accordance with this principle, he put away Judaism by
ripening it, by quickening the germ of truth that
lay in it, so that its imperfect form might be thrown
off, and a perfect one be gained. All Judaism was
in Christianity, as the life of the caterpillar is in
the butterfly ; its coarse skin was shed, and it was
taken up into a new and winged life. Christ's
truth was inconsistent with Moses' teaching and
destroyed it, just as the apple destroys the apple-
blossom, and as the sunrise destroys the morning
twilight. It was a destruction in which Moses'
system was more honored than if it had been let
alone ; for if it had been let alone it would have
died ; but in Christ's thought it found its resurrection into a celestial body, and put on immortality
in a glorious and perfect form.

We know how sharp is the dispute at the present
day between the partisans of natural religion and
of revealed religion, — the naturalists and the su-
pernaturalists. One party contends that the teachings of nature and the intimations of the soul are

22

sufficient to instruct us in the truths of religion, of our duty and destiny. The other party contends that nature and the soul give us very little light, and that we owe all our stable knowledge, all our possible peace of mind and heart, and all redeeming influences, to a supernatural grace, granted in a special communication of truth, which we call Christianity. But, strangely enough, both these parties appeal to Christ; each maintains that it alone conceives his history most accurately, and interprets him most fairly. And certainly, if we look through the Gospels, we shall see that Jesus honored nature, and trusted deeply in the affections and instincts of the soul. He tried to lead his disciples to deeper sympathy with nature; he enforced many of his distinctive and most important doctrines by the testimony of nature; he evidently had the keenest sympathy with the material universe, and delighted to interpret the special meaning it enclosed. He also said, "the pure in heart see God." He made the human affections the interpreters of God's love, and the parental relation suggest the nature of the Divine Paternity, and showed that love is the fulfilling of the law.

Christ was a naturalist, the priest and apostle of natural religion. And yet he affirmed revelation, the absolute necessity of supernatural instruction and aid. He said, "Without me ye can do nothing." "I am the way," "I am the vine," "I am the door," "I am the bread of life;" "no man cometh to the Father but by me." These apparent contradictions are both true. Christ was the supernatural interpreter of nature. What he read in nature, he read by reason of his extraordinary faculties. It was one of his offices, as a supernatural and miraculous teacher, to tell us what nature means, and pour light upon us from that quarter. It was one prominent office of revelation to restate and reinforce *simple* truths, — what seem to be the simplest of all truths. Thus we owe what we call the teachings of nature and the human heart, to Christ, as much as we owe the teaching of the resurrection and the confirmation of immortality, to Christ. And we owe other blessings, besides these interpretations of nature, to Jesus, — influences and attractions to goodness, declarations of God's pardoning mercy, and his own spotless character, which lift the race out of bondage to evil, and are the redeeming influences of society; and these, so great is our indebtedness to them, more than justify the other class of passages, that declare his supernatural relations to the soul. We have only to look deep enough, and we see these surface contradictions reconciled, and discover that they bear testimony to the breadth and comprehensiveness of the Saviour's thought and mission.

Again, we find both sides of the perplexing controversy about foreordination and free-will, God's sovereignty and man's moral freedom, recognized by the Saviour. The fatalists and their opponents can both appeal to him. He was continually striving to impress men with a sense of their sinfulness, and presenting motives to make them seek a nobler life; thus assuming man's freedom and responsibility. And yet he said, "Not a sparrow falleth to the ground without your Father;" "the very hairs of your head are all numbered;" "no man can come unto me, except the Father which hath sent me draw him." Jesus never attempted to reconcile these seeming contradictions, and it is a revelation of his greatness and wisdom that he did not. For no human intellect can bring them together and marry them. To our minds they seem *hostile* truths, but both are truths. They blend somehow to the eye of God, as the centripetal and centrifugal forces of nature blend; but the process we cannot fathom. So long as man has a conscience, he will feel his spiritual responsibility, will know that he is free, and in his highest moods will say, "Lord, be merciful to me a sinner!" So long as he has an intellect, he will see that God "ruleth in the armies of heaven and among the inhabitants of the earth;" and so long as he has a heart, he will trust in Providence, feeling that it is wiser than our reason, and in seasons of sorrow will say, "Father, thou dost appoint our discipline; we have faith that thou doest all things in mercy and love; and that goodness and order will one day triumph in thy realm."

With respect to the value of good emotions and good works, we find the same two-sidedness. Throughout the gospel of John, religion is recognized, chiefly, as indwelling spiritual life, a sense of union with God, a feeling that naturally expresses itself in prayer, meditation, inward discipline, and retired exercises of mystical pietism. But Christ had no sympathy with a weak, pale, sickly, hothouse piety. He wanted it to be robust and practical. He insisted that it should be rich in outward fruits of beneficence and moral faithfulness. The parable of the talents tells us this ; and in his terrible picture of coming to judge the world, the accepted are those who have done something, even trivial acts of mercy in his name. His mind held both facts, saw their equal necessity, and was able to poise them. In his own experience he blended perfectly the active and the mystic virtues. " Behold a friend of publicans and sinners," said his foes ; while Matthew tells us that, " when he had sent the multitudes away, he retired into the mountain apart, to pray, and when the evening was come, he was there alone."

At times, also, we find the Saviour recognizing the law of expediency, and extricating himself from dilemmas by the exercise of a keen prudence and sagacity. What a fine worldly wisdom is revealed in his reply to the Pharisees, when they asked him if it was lawful to pay tribute to Cæsar ! How skilfully he confounded the crafty malice of his foes, and taught them a religious lesson, too, by his evasion of the point where they hoped to entrap him ! And he who accepted calmly the lot of crucifixion, and refused to call angels to his aid, often requested those whom he healed to refrain from telling the

priests and elders; and when John the Baptist was
beheaded, consulted his personal safety by leaving
Judea, and dwelling in Galilee. What gentleness
and meekness of spirit distinguished him in his intercourse with the world; what warm sympathy
with the penitent; what tenderness towards the
guilty; what forgiving love to his most cruel foes!
Yet it was he of whom it is written that, " when he
was reviled he reviled not again," who showed by
the most scathing denunciation, which the literature
of rebuke cannot surpass, the rottenness of heart
in the Pharisees, and called them hypocrites and
vipers and whited sepulchres.

We can readily see, moreover, that dignity and
grandeur of presence were united strangely in his
character with familiarity, ease, and condescension.
He " came eating and drinking;" he was the friend
of publicans and sinners; he passed most of his
life in constant and social contact with the vile and
the outcasts; yet the record always implies that his
companions were awed by his very mercy; and he
lost nothing of that personal sway and imposing
mien which commanded the veneration of Nicode-
mus and the ruler Simon, and overawed the soldiers
who came to lead him to his death. So, too, we
find in Jesus great calmness and great enthusiasm;
an enthusiasm that manifested itself in intense
calmness, as the spinning-top whirls swifter when it
is motionless and sleeps. " He was a man of sorrows and acquainted with grief;" " he was made
perfect through suffering;" yet he speaks of his joy

being full; and truly we may believe that, under all
the hardships of his discipline, his breast was open
to currents of bliss, which the prosperous worldling
cannot conceive. He had friends, and yet was
alone; he loved the world, and yet he overcame the
world; he was the opposite of an ascetic, and yet he
was the only perfect saint.

This same contradictoriness, enclosing both poles
of truth, attaches even to his words. He, who said,
"The Son of man is not come to destroy men's lives,
but to save them," said also, "I came not to bring
peace, but a sword." At one time, he instructed
his disciples not to take weapons with them on their
missionary tour; at another, he told them to sell
their scrip and buy a sword. Once, he said, "I
and my Father are one," "He who hath seen me,
hath seen the Father;" and again, "My Father is
greater than I;" "No man hath seen God at any
time."

We have called attention to these peculiarities of
the Saviour's nature, because by insight into the
structure of his character, we gain new light upon
the glory and fulness of his system. Christ and
Christianity, in a certain sense, are one. "The
Word was made flesh, and dwelt among us," that
the grandeur of God's truth might be commended
to the eyes and hearts of men. And, moreover,
every instance of greatness, every intricate manifestation of breadth and harmony in the nature and
office of Jesus, which can be pointed out, confirms
the proof of the reality of his mission, and increases

the impossibility of believing that we owe the records of him to the tricks of deceivers, or the accidental symmetry of myths.

We are also taught by the theme we have considered that truth always presents two aspects. It is an honest double-dealer. Duty branches out into seemingly opposing forms. The most contradictory qualities run together, and come to identity in living principle. At bottom, there is no difference between true formalism and spiritualism, between proper self-reliance and dependence on God, between healthy trust in the inward light and trust in a written revelation, between necessity and free-will, between the doctrine of faith and the doctrine of works. Narrow minds take in one phase, and are fierce partisans, always logical and consistent with their premises, and always false, because their premises are too narrow; great minds see both phases, and are calm and catholic, and their speech is often charged with inconsistency. But their inconsistency is only consistency with both hemispheres of truth. Christ saw deep enough to be a reconciler, to hold both poles of nature in his mind, to be inconsistent as life and the thought of God.

And, at bottom, too, there is no difference between justice and love, humility and strength, gentleness and dignity, true expediency and principle, complete self-sacrifice and the sweetest self-indulgence. Christ's soul was so faithful, and so permeated with spiritual life, that all these qualities were united in him; and the manifestations of his virtue, when we study them separately, seem inconsistent, because his character, when we look at its essence, was so harmonious and so rich, that it could not be confined to one form of life, but must flower out into every possible element of spiritual power and grace.

As we stand before the massive structure of the Saviour's character, so complex, yet so simple, pervaded by a great law of unity and harmony, that reconciles all its parts, it is like standing before some gothic minster where each niche and turret and pointed window conspire to the simplicity of impression, and its grandeur results from its myriad details of grace. It is like listening to a symphony by some great master, in which various movements, and a thousand melodies, and occasional discords even, contribute to the sublime and inspiring effect. That life is God's greatest gift to us; it enfolds the fulness of truth.

XVI.

THE CHIEF APPEAL OF RELIGION.

THE points which have generally interested people most in relation to religious things are, What shall we have, if we take up the denials and burdens of a Christian life? or, what shall we lose, if we remain as we are, and do not take them up? Take Christendom through, and we think it will be found that a true life, harmonious in its spirit with that Jesus led, is presented to men in the light, and urged by the motives of a low and earthly interest. The animus of Peter's question is still dominant in countless hearts, "Behold, we have forsaken all and followed thee; what shall we have, therefore?"

We do not propose to spend much time in criticising this method of presenting religion, and in showing the folly of it. It has its root in truth. We all know how frequent is the appeal to the terrors of perdition, and, on the other hand, to the glories of the saintly world, as influences to keep men from sin, and to bind them to God's service. These appeals have their root in truth. There is terrible reality at the foundation of the coarsest denunciations of fire and wrath; for the evil effects of sin, however inaccurate may be the forms of our conception of them, can never be too powerfully impressed. And the joys of heaven cannot be more attractively depicted than the reality deserves.

But still we-have no right to use these, or to feel these, as motives to reverent and righteous living, until we have a proper sense of a motive that is higher and nobler than both ; and cannot really see and appreciate the dangers of sin and the rewards of duty, until we have a central sense of something which makes a religious life *more binding* than either those terrors or those rewards. For, if we look at it close enough, we shall see that there is nothing in the idea of hell alone, or of heaven alone which makes a religious call appeal to the spiritual and infinite part of our nature. An angel may come down and tell me that if I do not live in a certain way henceforth, I shall burn for it here-after, and that if I do, I shall be lifted to everlasting joys ; but if he does not tell me something more, although this may be all true, he has not said any-thing which makes that life *binding* on my soul ; he has not touched the *immortal* core of my being ; he has not made me look up and revere law, and aspire to goodness, and adore God. If I walk in the way he marks out, for the reasons he prescribes, I walk as an earthly being, from dictates of interest, and without the nobility of any spiritual motive behind my action.

There is, then, a preliminary question to the inquiry, " What shall we have, or what shall we lose, as the consequence of our faith or our worldli-

ness ? " - The strong motive, the steady impulse to
a Christian life should flow from that feature of it
which makes it *binding* upon men ; that view of
it which makes it a disgrace and a shame for a man
to be indifferent to it ; that view of it which makes
one less a man when he does not possess it, and
truly and only a man when he is crowned by it.

Religion, when truly conceived, has vital analogies
with all other vital relations which the human soul
sustains, and may perhaps be most powerfully presented in the dress of those analogies. Let us use
therefore, for a few moments, this form of unfolding
the thought we desire to impress.

Imagine the case of a man afflicted with some disorder that drains his vitality, allows his best organs but
a feeble play, and so imposes on him a languid and
miserable life. A person skilled in the treatment
of such a disorder goes to him, and lays before him
a course of treatment for his consideration, which
will restore him to health. But it will require
great care, strict and long-continued obedience to
the bodily laws, exercise that may be painful, reso-
lute resistance of the temptations to sloth and sleep.
And, often, medicines must be taken that are repulsive to the taste. What, now, if the man believing
what the physician says, believing that he can be
cured by such means, should fix his attention on
the hardships and the long, painful discipline connected with the remedy, and should ask, "What
shall I have if I submit to this process ? what recompense can you promise for these sufferings ? "

Would not such a question be an indication that the malady had affected his mind, as well as his body ? that it had withered his *manliness* as well as his muscles ?

The physician, it is true, might eloquently portray to him the sadness of his sickly state, and point out the evils to which he will be surely doomed in future, if his disorder is not rooted out ; but, would not anybody expect that the *great* motive which would strive with the sick man, and lead him to adopt such a treatment, would be the desire *to be well ?* And if any argument was needed, if any address or stimulus was required to arouse him, should we not suppose that enough would be found in that one word, *health ?* Should we not think that the most joyful speech the man could listen to would be, " You can have health again ; your blood may flow with pleasure, and your step be strong ; you shall be able to enjoy the fresh air and delight in the glories of nature ; you shall be able to do your work as a man, and as a member of society, and the food earned by toil shall be nutritious, and the sleep that refreshes your limbs for duty shall be sweet ? " Should we not suppose that any drugs, any regimen, any hardships, that should bid fair to bring a man to such a state, would be welcome, *because* of that state ? Should we not be amazed, if the man required any other impulse, any bribe, any promise of a good unconnected with such a return of health, to bring him to the adoption of those means ?

This analogy is important, and the truth it points to more important. Let us take another instance that the force of the principle may be more clearly seen. What if one should go to a *blind* man with the news that, at the price of certain unpleasant conditions, his lost faculty could be regained! Would any other inducement be necessary to insure an eager attention? Would he not say, "Fix any conditions, within the limits of honor, and they will be a trifle to the joy of having my eyes again? Let me undergo anything, if only this thick darkness — this unnatural night — can be broken, so that the sun shall shine for me again, and the faces of my friends be visible, and the world be painted with the glory of the rising and setting sun." Would you think it anything less than insanity if the man should ask for any other inducement to the adoption of the proposed cure — even though that cure might require the most painful surgical operation — than the thought that his eyes could be restored to him?

Or, again, suppose the case of an ignorant man, who has a strong mind and a capacity of being eminent as a student; — perhaps a capacity to rank as high in the realm of acquired truth as Newton. You offer him all the means of instruction. But he sees that the path of study is laborious; that the acquisition of principles and the steps of advance are toilsome; that the price to be paid is consecration and systematic drilling and patient application and contentment with slow progress. Suppose, therefore, he should ask you, "What shall I *have*, if I continue in the line marked out? What recompense shall I find if, at all this expense of discipline I attain a cultured intellect, and rise to be fellow with Newton, Herschel, and Humboldt?" Could you present anything that would be a more stimulating motive than the prospect of arriving at such a state? Would you not strive to make him see that such a hope could *not* be abased to a secondary place? You might talk of the *power* which knowledge gives; of the station, dignity, wealth, enjoyments that often follow in its train; but you would tell him that all these are of less account than the possession of knowledge and wise faculties; that the supreme thing is to know the treasures of God's wisdom and the riches of human nature, and that the glorious reward of culture is to be wise and wealthy in the mind.

It is a great pity that the analogy of religion with other subjects belonging to human life and human interests is not more clearly seen. We should be saved from a world of follies, and should feel the appeal and the authority of religion more intensely, if we felt that there are these analogies, and if they always shed their light upon what we call the interests of the soul. Just as the highest thing which you can propose to a sick man is health, just as the most excellent boon which you can offer to a blind man is his eyesight, just as the most desirable thing which you can propose to the mind of the untutored man is knowledge, — so the most precious thing which can be set before the aspirations of a spiritual being is goodness, holiness, a Christ-like life. The great motive that should stimulate our affections and brace our will must flow down to us from the objects themselves that are offered to the ambition of our heavenly nature.

But we need not say that this is not the way in which men generally regard the subject, or have it set before them. The absorbing question with a great many people seems to be, not whether the law of Christ is true, not whether the claim of conscience and the call of God are right, but *what if we don't follow them?* And the most fervent Christian eloquence seems to flow in showing that God has infinite power to enforce his laws, and an eternity to do it in. So that the costs, risks, and sacrifices of a Christian life are commended on the ground of the loss that attends the failure to make them. Let us not object that the penalties of wrong living should be set before men; the more vividly the better, if truthfully done. But should not the first question of every fair mind be this: "Is a law *true;* is the Christian life the highest life for a being that has a soul?" Independently of the question of penalties or hardships, of what it will cost if we neglect, or of what it will come to if we honor religious principles, is not the *first* question — the question which should decide a man's course — simply this, "Is a religious career the right career? And should not that preaching be called the most wholesome, searching, powerful, and evangelical,

which scatters and burns up all mists that lie between the soul and the truth of things, so that a
hearer must go away from it speared through the
brain and conscience with the conviction that an
unconsecrated life is falsehood and moral idiocy?
Countless subsidiary and additional appeals and influences of course, in all great preaching, will be
brought to bear to invest this truth with charm,
with pathos, with sweetness, to kindle the emotions of penitence, and to nourish the seeds of
grace; but this must be the granite basis of any
healthy dealing with human nature in respect of
religion.

If some one should come to you with a proposition which he wished you to believe, and which it
was important that you should believe, would you
think of asking him first, "What shall I *gain* by
attending to it, or what shall I lose by disbelieving
it?" Would you think of looking to any other
sources than *the evidence* he could bring for the
proposition? Would you imagine that any bribe
or any threat could effect the real merits of the
subject a hair, or deserve to be thought of a moment by an honest mind? Can you conceive such
a thing as refusing to believe it if the evidence is
sufficient to establish it? Now a question of action, set before the moral nature, is precisely analogous to a question for belief set before the mind.
The all-important thing is, whether it is *right* or
not. To refuse to do it, if it is right, because it
runs counter to some of our pleasures, is as mon-

23

strous a thing as to refuse assent to a demonstrated doctrine, because it runs counter to some of our prejudices. The idea of gilding a moral truth or a Christian call with anything different from it-self, as a temptation, is like the idea of bribing a judge to bend his opinion. Just think of setting up a Christian virtue with a necklace around it or any ornament upon it to make the soul aspire toward it, and choose it. It is true, as the hymn says, —

> " Wisdom has treasures greater far
> Than east or west unfold,
> And her rewards more precious are
> Than all their gems of gold."

But spiritual wisdom has no treasure and no reward so precious as *itself*. The moment we bring something foreign from Christian goodness, as a controlling motive to the choice of goodness, even though it may be a joy or an honor that naturally results from being good, we practically set something above a true life ; we practically say that there is something in the universe of greater worth than holiness, to which a true life is the path. This is a profanation of Christianity ; however serious the preaching sounds that deals with such implements, it commends worldliness in spiritual guise. The Saviour, in the beatitudes, promised certain rewards to certain dispositions, — the inheritance of the earth to the meek, and the kingdom of heaven to the persecuted ; but the preciousness of the highest states of mind he placed in those states themselves.

He said, "Blessed are the merciful, for they shall obtain mercy; blessed are they which hunger and thirst after righteousness, for they shall be filled; blessed are the pure in heart, for they shall see God."

If a man asks, therefore, "What will be the consequences to me if I remain in sin?" we may answer, "The very worst possible consequence will surely be your doom,—the possession of a sinful love, contentment in sin; and the more placidly look around you for *extraneous* consequences to warn you from such a state, the more deep is the judgment of that state now upon you. Extraneous consequences, and bitter enough, will doubtless coil around you, as the years roll off, but in the sight of God, the direst punishment that besets you is the state that you are in. The feeling that rules you is the architect of the hell you suffer; every fiery wave that will ever roll in upon you will be the infernal creation of that temper,—a terrible parody, by the spirit of evil, of the first creative fiat of divine goodness saying, 'Let there be darkness and torment,' as the holy word first said, 'Let there be light.' And the spirit that rules you will be as much more dreadful than the consequences of it as the black, billowy turmoil in the breast of Satan, when he tumbled from heaven into the pit, was more awful than the sullen heat of the burning marl that awaited his frame."

If a man asks, "What shall I *have*, if, in obedience to the calls of religious truth, I conquer difficulties, and walk in ways that the worldly nature does not love?" We may answer, "You will have the divine quality, the inward nobleness, the conscious fellowship of God's spirit, which such a walk brings. Other things you will have, — peace, satisfaction, heaven, as the consequence, but nothing so valuable or so glorious as *the thing itself*, which generates every consequence." Would you think of expecting anybody to reward you in external ways for being just, or for loving your child? Would you think of carrying any account to the eternal bar setting forth, "So much is due me for helping a sufferer with a coin that might have purchased pleasure for me at the theatre?" The just and lovely disposition is its own recompense. God does not and cannot pay for it in guineas and soft climates, any more than you can sell your attachment and respect to another for gold. If the pulpit could make men see the intrinsic excellence of goodness as a Christian state of heart! God would have us see that, and feel the impulsive motive that comes from seeing it. It was for this that the Christ was clothed in flesh, and made our humanity translucent with the divinest charm.

We all of us have souls, we all of us have infinite natures, and they cannot find their objects their food, their exercise, except in the sphere of things with which religion invests us. The worth of piety to the spirit is like the worth of health to the body; the importance of religious truths to the best part of us is like the value of light, and the colored glories of nature to the eye. If we do not have a

pious spirit within us, we are diseased; and nothing
can express the dreadfulness of our state more than
the simple declaration that we are in that state.   If
we do not live amid those objects we are blind; and
nothing further that can be said can add anything
to the description of the misery of our condition.
The buildings in which people gather to listen to
pulpit words are not more firmly founded on their
corner-stones than the church and its doctrines are
based on the needs of human nature and the truth
of things.   ,

The most solemn and efficient sanction of the
gospel is this, that we are absent from truth in our
falsehood to religious law and claims; that we scorn
things which are in themselves the highest and most
valuable things, — as health is the best thing for the
body, sight for the eye, and science for the mind.
And here the subject becomes impressively practical.
It springs of itself from an essay into a sermon.
What person will not say, what person *does* not often
say, that a Christian life is better than a selfish one,
— the highest condition of the soul?   What person
will not say that humble dependence upon God is
not a higher state than proud self-reliance, that a
sincere, filial prayer, every morning, is not a better
way to begin the day than thoughtlessness or ingratitude?   Who does not believe that doing good to
others is a better work than bending every hour to
his own enjoyment? that practical faith in God is
a higher spirit than practical unbelief? that a
sweet, forgiving, charitable disposition is more de-

sirable than a harsh and coarse and self-seeking spirit?
Who will not say that a man of probity and holiness
and deep usefulness is not infinitely more worthy
than a man of mere wealth and avarice? Bring
together all the typical characters of history — the
warrior, the statesman, the artist, the monarch, the
pleasure-seeker, the man of money, and who is there
that will not deliberately place such a character as
Jesus above them all, as alone worthy the heart's
deepest reverence and love, and as showing more
gloriously the worth of man? Who is there that
does not pay this homage of his judgment and
approval to religious principles and a Christian
character?

What more powerful call, what more urgent
motive, can appeal to any person, to go higher up
the Christian life, or to begin a Christian life, than
this worship of it by every inmost soul? We have
heard something of the eloquence of revivalists in
their calls to men to forsake sin and serve God, but
we know nothing in their most gorgeous pictures of
hell, or their most fascinating fancies of heaven, that
has a tithe of the weight, as a motive, which the
fact ought to bring with it, that a religious life is
indorsed as the best possession, in the centre of every
heart. "This is the condemnation," said Jesus, in
a passage whose meaning will never be exhausted
while a sinner lives in the universe, "that light is
come into the world, and men love darkness rather
than light because their deeds are evil." Yes, dam-
nation is the choice of that which we know is not

worthy of choice. Hell is a life in that which is not true, and which our own souls condemn. The devil is the father of lies, the arch-falsehood, and his chain is on all spirits, and his stamp seared into their forehead, who obey what they confess is not deserving obedience, who dream of finding good in what the heart refuses to revere as best. Deep down below all hells, the root of hell, is the feeling of satisfaction in what conscience condemns. High up above all heavens, the very sun-source of the radiance of heaven, is the splendor of holy virtue in itself; and the fountain of its power, and its most authoritative appeal to the human heart, lie in the fact that it is the highest truth and the highest good.